The Psychoanalytic Interpretation of History

the text of this book is printed on 100% recycled paper

The Psychoanalytic Interpretation of History

Edited by Benjamin B. Wolman

FOREWORD BY WILLIAM L. LANGER

HARPER TORCHBOOKS
Harper & Row, Publishers
New York, Evanston, San Francisco, London

This book was originally published in hardcover by Basic Books, Inc. It is here reprinted by arrangement.

THE PSYCHOANALYTIC INTERPRETATION OF HISTORY

First HARPER TORCHBOOK edition published 1973

STANDARD BOOK NUMBER: 06-131714-4

THE AUTHORS

GUSTAV BYCHOWSKI M.D. is Clinical Professor of Psychiatry at the Downstate Medical Center in New York City and is affiliated with the Institute of Psychiatry of Mount Sinai Medical School.

RONALD GRIMSLEY is Head of the Department of French at Bristol University, and has been a Visiting Professor at Yale and Harvard. He has published books on Existentialism, Kierkegaard, and Rousseau.

WILLIAM L. LANGER was formerly Coolidge Professor of History at Harvard. He is the author of numerous books and articles on the history of international relations and diplomacy.

ROBERT JAY LIFTON is currently Foundations' Fund Research Professor of Psychiatry at Yale. He has been active in the development of the new field of "psychohistory." His publications include *Death in Life: Survivors of Hiroshima,* which won the National Book Award in the Sciences for 1969.

PETER LOEWENBERG is Assistant Professor of History at the University of California, Los Angeles. He has held Fulbright, Ford, Social Science Research Council, and American Council of Learned Societies fellowships. He received the Franz Alexander Essay Prize in Psychoanalysis for 1970.

R. G. L. WAITE is the author of *Vanguard of Nazism: The German Free Corps Movement: 1918–1923.* He is currently Brown Professor of History and Chairman of the Department of History at Williams College.

BENJAMIN B. WOLMAN is Professor of Psychology, Doctoral Program in Clinical Psychology, Long Island University. He is editor-in-chief of the *International Journal of Group Tensions,* and is an associate editor of *The American Imago.*

ROBERT WAELDER was Professor of Psychoanalysis in the Department of Psychiatry at Jefferson Medical College. His publications include *The Psychological Aspects of War and Peace, Basic Theory of Psychoanalysis,* and *Progress and Revolution: A Study of the Issues of Our Age.*

THE AUTHORS

FOREWORD

William L. Langer

The present collection of essays is yet another manifestation of the interest in the relationship of psychoanalysis and history that has developed during the last dozen or fifteen years. In that interval there has been much discussion of the theoretical aspects of the problem, and increasing efforts have been made to translate the basic principles into practice.

In this age of rapidly mounting production in all fields of learning and, consequently, of an ever-growing trend toward specialization, conscious and concerted efforts are required to avoid fragmentation of knowledge to the point where general understanding becomes impossible. Within individual disciplines the proliferation of data and the multiplication of monographic studies have already made command of anything more than a segment of the subject impossible. Synthesis of the findings of specialized research has become a matter of the highest priority. Correspondingly, it has become imperative to study systematically the relationship among various disciplines, lest many of the valuable contributions to knowledge fail to have their proper impact.

In the relationship of modern psychology to history the current of influence is bound to flow more strongly in one direction than the other. That is to say, the analyst in his work can benefit from knowledge of history only in a broad cultural sense, just as he can benefit from conversance with literature, religion, or art. On the other hand, the historian will ignore or neglect the support to be derived from psychology only at his peril. Basically his mission is not only to establish the facts of the human past, but also to further understanding of human motives and human reactions in varying situations.

The value of psychoanalytic teaching in the writing of biography has long since been recognized, particularly in the fields of literary and artistic biography. It is now finding wider acceptance among historians. Their long struggle to expand the field of historical research beyond the confines of political and military affairs to include economic, intellectual, and social factors has been brought to a successful close. Many historians—notably younger scholars—now see the need to deepen their understanding of the past by far more rigorous analysis of individual and social action. For a time it was fashionable to disparage historical biography, on the ground that even outstanding personalities were but pawns of major forces beyond human control and defiant of human understanding. This position has been abandoned by an age that has seen its Lenins, Stalins, and Hitlers. If we are to understand the world-shaking and world-shaping events of either the past or the present, we historians need all the help that other disciplines can provide—not only economics, geography, demography, and so on, but also and especially psychoanalysis.

It stands to reason that psychoanalysis cannot solve or even enlighten all important biographical problems of the historian. One can probe the personality of men of the past only if they have left behind them a generous volume of correspondence, autobiographical material, and kindred records. Where such records exist, they are apt to be of special value because they were set down not with an eye to the analyst, but for very mundane, practical purposes. Erikson has shown how psychoanalytic knowledge can be brought to bear on a historic figure such as Luther, because the latter left an enormous corpus of writings and correspondence, much of it very outspoken and revealing. Similar studies could certainly be made of other major figures for whom voluminous records exist. Napoleon is an obvious example, but Marx, Mazzini, and many others come to mind. Indeed, analysis of some of these personalities might teach us much about the revolutionary mentality that developed during the nineteenth century and has in our own day become so important. In the case of Mazzini, one of the most active and influential of the nineteenth-century revolutionaries, there is now a national edition of his writings and correspondence which is in more than 100 substantial volumes.

The great hope of the historian, however, must be for help in understanding the group or mass actions of the past, which in a sense determine the course of human development. To those of us living in an uncertain period of amorphous unrest, violence, and destructiveness, it must be plain that tides of emotion can never be understood without full analysis of the psychological aspects. As yet social psychology has been able to contribute but little to the solution of such problems, but some progress is being made in the study of religious movements and also in the analysis of revolutionary mobs. One must hope that in the future more and greater efforts will be made in this direction.

It cannot be denied that attempts to integrate psychoanalysis and history are fraught with difficulty. Basically, they require a certain competence in more than one discipline, which in itself is a tall order. The analyst has less of a problem than the historian, for there is nothing esoteric about historical method and criticism and, besides, the historian has managed to fight shy of specialized terminology; he still writes English and is still comprehensible to the average man. Nonetheless, he has set himself high standards in the handling of evidence; failure to observe these standards will nullify any attempt to apply psychological knowledge. Analysts interested in extending the application of their professional competence beyond the sphere of individual therapy have not always recognized the exacting requirements of historical scholarship. Trained as they are to work with imaginative material, with bits and pieces of human recollection, they are apt to overlook the rigorous standards that historians have set themselves.

Historians, on the other hand, have been dubious about benefiting from the teachings of modern psychology. Those who have attempted to utilize such teachings have for the most part been those who have undergone analysis themselves and therefore have some comprehension of fundamental principles and procedures. Others, even when interested, are reluctant because they feel the need for more systematic knowledge than can be acquired by independent reading.

Ideally, provision should be made to facilitate the interchange between disciplines. Some psychoanalytic institutes already provide survey courses for the nonprofessional. These are all to the good. But it would be better yet if, at the major universities, basic courses in psychoanalysis could be offered, designed especially for students in various fields, such as literature, art, and history, where competence in the psychological field is essential or at least desirable. By the same token, analysts desiring to undertake historical studies might well enroll in some systematic course in historical method and criticism, so as to acquire greater familiarity and aptitude in the handling of evidence.

Meanwhile substantial progress has been and is being made. For one thing, the notion of bringing psychoanalysis to bear on historical problems is no longer so shocking as it once was. Furthermore, the flow of essays and studies by competent scholars is constantly increasing. Among recent contributions the present volume of essays, the work of qualified psychoanalysts and historians, is worthy of particular note. It is a sound and impressive addition to a fascinating, albeit difficult and thorny field of learning.

CONTENTS

Foreword
WILLIAM L. LANGER vii

PART I
Interpretations of History

1 Psychoanalysis and History: Application of Psychoanalysis to Historiography 3
ROBERT WAELDER

2 Protean Man 33
ROBERT JAY LIFTON

3 Psychoanalysis and Literary Criticism in Historical Perspective 50
RONALD GRIMSLEY

4 Sense and Nonsense in History 79
BENJAMIN B. WOLMAN

PART II
Biographical Studies

5 Joseph V. Stalin: Paranoia and the Dictatorship of the Proletariat 115
GUSTAV BYCHOWSKI

6 Theodore Herzl: A Psychoanalytic Study in Charismatic Political Leadership 150
PETER LOEWENBERG

7 Adolf Hitler's Anti-Semitism: A Study in History and Psychoanalysis 192
ROBERT G. L. WAITE

Index 231

PART I

Interpretations of History

1

PSYCHOANALYSIS AND HISTORY: APPLICATION OF PSYCHOANALYSIS TO HISTORIOGRAPHY

Robert Waelder

History is the story of human destiny. Psychoanalysis gives a new dimension to the understanding of human destiny through the discovery of the unconscious psychic life that powerfully influences man's conduct while being withheld from his self-awareness. Psychoanalysis, thus, seems to hold the promise of a deeper understanding of history.

Yet, after three-fourths of a century, the actual results of psychoanalytic study of history are disappointing. There is nowhere a new vista; the actual applications of psychoanalytic viewpoints to history are few and often speculative. Some have been products of the poetic imagination.

The reason for this disappointment seems to be obvious. In order to apply a set of principles of one field to the data of another, one must be in command of both fields. Those who apply genetics to cancer research must be well versed in genetics and in the biochemistry and pathology of neoplasms. Those who apply mathematics to physics must be abreast of both. It happens often that a theoretical physicist finds his own mathematical knowledge inadequate for dealing with the problem on hand and has either to do some ad hoc studying or call on mathematicians for help; but, at least, he must have a fundamental grasp of mathematics.

The full potential of the psychoanalytic approach in history could thus be realized only by those who are equally, or nearly equally, at home in both history and psychoanalysis. So far only Ernst Kris has fulfilled these requirements. But his historical training was in a somewhat peripheral field of history—the history of art—and he devoted most of his short life to problems other than the psychoanalytic approach to history. Even so, his are the best contributions to this subject. Most historians know nothing about psychoanalysis or, worse, have a warped image of it. A very few have a grasp of its main ideas. Most conspicuous among the latter was Lewis Namier, whose limited knowledge of psychoanalysis stood him in good stead. Psychoanalysts, on the other hand, have often approached history in complete innocence and have fallen into all possible traps.[1]

The Three Tasks of Historiography

The naïve applications proceed on the assumption that there is a solid body of historical fact—"what has happened in history"—either already known to historians and found in their books or available to them through research; to the interpretation of this body of established fact psychoanalytic principles can be applied. This naïve view has some backing in the famous, though rather vacuous, dictum by Ranke that history tells us, *wie es eigentlich gewesen ist,* what it really has been like.

But historical facts are not solid givens to be taken simply as bases of interpretation. They are themselves results of complex processes of reasoning. There are, actually, three problems of history of which the interpretation of behavior is but one; they are (1) the selection, from among the multitude of past events, of those events that are historically relevant, of the historical facts as opposed to mere private facts of little or no historical significance; (2) the determination of what, in this historically significant domain, has actually occurred; and (3) the interpretation of events—how they can be understood—in terms of environmental pressures and the nature of man in general and in particular.

1. There are historical facts and mere private facts. We may, perhaps, find in an old graveyard a tombstone and learn from the inscription that four children of a family died within a month. Our imagination can conjure up the anguish of the parents who had to bury four children in rapid succession. Perhaps we may be inclined to speculate about the probable causes of the disaster, and if other tombstones record other childhood deaths at the very same time, we will perhaps surmise that they have all been victims of an epidemic—an assumption that will gain in probability if a record of such an epidemic at that time and place exists. We are here dealing with traces of past human life and destiny, but what they reveal is not, as such, a historical fact, that is, not a fact likely to be recorded in a political, economic, or cultural history of the country or the age.

These traces at any time become historically relevant if we are interested, for instance, in a history of childhood epidemics or in some other problem for which this private event would be pertinent material. Which of the countless events of the past, reconstructed from available indicators, are historically relevant facts and which are mere private experiences thus depends on the nature of our questions. And what we ask about the past is determined by our interest, that is, by the interest of contemporary men.

2. We must determine what has actually happened, externally speaking. Have these children actually died at the indicated time? We can think of the possibility of fraudulent claims on a tombstone; perhaps parents pretended their children were dead to save them from murderous persecution, such as happened in Biblical Bethlehem, or from being taken as sacrifices, such as by a Carthaginian moloch. Perhaps there were other motives. These are remote possibilities, but they cannot be a priori ruled out. Then, there is the question of the causes of deaths. Was it the same for all the above-mentioned children? This seems likely in view of the coincidence in time, but it is not the only possibility. Even if there is independent evidence of an epidemic at the time, it is still possible that these four children perished, let us say, by being thrown out of a cart drawn by a runaway horse.

All these are questions of fact and we decide them, as far as we can decide them at all, on the basis of surviving traces. The academic professions make a sharp distinction as to whether the traces are written records; the "historical method," as the term is commonly understood, is largely a method of evaluating the authenticity and reliability of written records of the past. But this distinction is more practical than fundamental. It is not true that written records are always more reliable than other empirical evidence. Just as in criminal investigations circumstantial evidence—such as attribution of a bullet to a gun in the comparison microscope—may be more convincing than the testimony of a witness, so may the medical examination of a skeleton be more convincing with regard to the cause of death than a contemporary biographical record and a date derived at by the carbon-14 method be more convincing than the one found in the records. Ruins may sometimes tell a clearer or truer story than archives.

In reconstructing the facts we proceed according to the laws and regularities as we know them. Sometimes these are natural laws—

for example, the inference drawn from the medical examination of the physical remains of a body, or in the principles of carbon-14 dating. Sometimes these laws are of a psychological nature—for example, the evaluation of the credibility and the bias of a particular reporter or the plausibility of an action attributed to a particular person. On the assumptions of such laws or such probabilities of nature or of human affairs we base our reconstructions of the past.

3. We must interpret human actions or inaction in terms of the external situation, on the one hand, and of human nature or the characteristics of the people involved, on the other. Sometimes there is no clear boundary between this endeavor and the second, fact-finding, task; one gradually shades into the other. This will be the case when psychological considerations have already entered into the assessment of what, more likely than not, has happened.

Psychoanalysis—the doctrine about the newly discovered unconscious mind, its contents, and its ways of working—has a bearing on all these aspects of historiography, not only the third one. Psychoanalysis can pose new questions by raising previously private facts to the rank of historically relevant facts and can contribute to the assessment of how things have probably happened, and, of course, to the interpretation of human events in terms of human motives and operative procedures.

Not much has so far been done in reconstructing the past, a fact partly owing to the paucity of available material. Yet, it would be very interesting to know more about, for instance, the changes of sexual expressions throughout the ages or about changes in early child-rearing methods. An attempt in this direction was made thirty years ago by Norbert Elias in a piece of historical research that was probably undertaken under the influence of psychoanalysis; the book was hardly noticed when it came out, and it is probably difficult to locate today.[2] Elias studied what he called "the process of civilization" in the upper strata of the Occident, that is, the growing barriers to direct expression of sexual, particularly pregenital, urges in the upper layers of European society from the later Middle Ages into the twentieth century, and traced it many "trivial" attitudes of daily life. Were the book to be brought up to date today, a chapter would have to be added about modern developments in the opposite direction.

As far as the second question of history is concerned, it seems clear that inasmuch as everything we know, or think we know, about regularities of nature and social life contributes to our assessment of what is possible and what is probable, psychoanalytic (and, of course, general psychiatric) knowledge is bound to affect the assessments. This can be seen first in its negative role of undermining the enormous amount of popular psychology, or myth, which historians often take for fact and use uncritically in their reconstruction of the past. Two examples, taken from a famous work by a noted orientalist, may illustrate the point.

William Foxwell Albright discusses the origin of the monotheistic sun worship commonly attributed to Akhenaton, and states:

> His mummy . . . was examined by the famous anatomist and authority on Egyptian mummification, Elliot Smith. According to the latter's examination he was definitely pathological, with an abnormal pelvis and peculiarly shaped skull; he was between 25 and 28 years old when he died. These facts agree with the evidence of art, which exhibits him with distended skull, protruding abdomen, and almost feminine build. The fact that he was not over 28 when he died and that he reigned 17 years would make him not over 11 at his accession. In view of these circumstances of age and physical health, it is quite absurd to consider Akhenaton as the founder of the Aten cult.[3]

Albright takes for granted that a sickly adolescent, with abnormal pelvis and almost feminine build, could not possibly have originated a religious concept. Needless to say, his assumption rests on nothing but the folklore of an age of rationalism. Neither clinical experience nor a psychoanalytic view of the dynamics of adolescence makes it impossible, or even unlikely, for a religious innovation to be made by a sick and troubled adolescent.

In another passage of the same work, Albright deals with the time of Israelite servitude in Egypt. He refers to the report in Exodus 1 according to which Israelites worked on the Egyptian corvée in Ramese (Tanis), built by Rameses II during the early thirteenth century B.C., and states: "Since Tanis was called *Per Re emasese* (the house of Rameses) only for a couple of centuries (cir. 1300—1100), it is most improbable that the tradition could arise if it were spurious."[4] Here Albright seems to assume that it takes a very long time for a distortion, or myth, to emerge and take hold—a strange assumption indeed. It is remarkable how scholars who apply the most rigid standards of verification to any psychoanalytic hypothesis can themselves be so reckless in their assumptions, which are taken from popular psychology and on which they base their reasoning.

Psychological reasoning has regularly been applied by historians in their evaluation of the credibility of a source and their attempt to discover and undo distortions. Results of such historical criticism have sometimes been corroborated by independent evidence. This historical criticism operates on the assumption of conscious psychology, that is, it sees distortion as either a product of outright falsification or as a manifestation of bias, and finds in both cases interest in the ordinary sense of the word is the driving force (material gain, power, revenge, self-justification, and so on). Psychoanalysis should be able to enlarge the list by including unconscious motives and irrational solutions.

A psychologically most plausible reconstruction of an event need not be the correct one. We cannot rely on psychological plausibility and consistency alone in reconstructing the course of events; we should ask for independent evidence of at least some elements in the reconstruction. On the other hand, where material data leave room for more than one interpretation, all equally possible in terms of available evidence, we may wish to choose the most plausible psychological interpretation as the most likely one.

GENERAL CONSIDERATIONS

The Image of Man

History has been written on the basis of assumptions, explicit or implied, about the nature of man in general and the character of the players. These assumptions usually have been the general ideas prevailing at the time or the ideas of the particular historian. Psychoanalytic views are bound to alter these pictures—at any rate, to make them more complex. Historical personages have often been drawn in stark simplicity. Plutarch's characters are ideal types, as typified and simplified as the heads of classical Greek sculpture; a single motive seems to determine their actions. Close to our own time, Theodor Mommsen's Caesar understands everything, foresees everything, unhesitatingly subordinates minor issues to the grand design, and acts in every situation with resolution, speed, and unwavering courage. Bernard Shaw's and Thornton Wilder's fictional Caesar still bear these features of perfection. These are extreme examples, and other historical writers have seen man as a more complex creature. But they hardly approach the complexity of the picture that a psychoanalyst composes from the fragments of his observations.

A single-minded dedication to one goal, unwavering throughout the changes of fortune, is a relatively rare phenomenon, to be met with mainly among paranoid types and even there subject to the exacerbations and partial remissions that occur in this kind of personality structure. Far more common than the monolith is the person with permanent inner conflicts that have not gelled into a rigid style of action, the person who reaches decisions only after long wavering and whose decisions recall the five to four rulings of the Supreme Court: a slight change of circumstances or temper and they might have gone the other way.

President Kennedy decided to react forcefully to the installation of missiles in Cuba, a decision supposedly taken once evidence of the Russian foray had been received. But reports about suspicious activities in Cuba had been circulating for some time, and it seems that some members of the administration were willing to persuade themselves that there was, after all, no great difference between intercontinental missiles a few thousand miles away and intermediate-range missiles in close proximity. It may well be that Kennedy's mind was made up only after considerable wavering, and it is possible that he reached this resolve during his trip across the country in which he perceived the temper of the American people.

Moreover, attitudes may change not only with changing external conditions but also through internal changes in the course of life. We may do one thing in a particular situation for some time and then, suddenly, do a different thing; we may have become gradually disillusioned with the results of a policy, or have just grown tired of it, or have become more impatient, or the closeness of death in old age or cerebral changes may cause a different attitude. Emperor Francis Joseph of Austria was a peaceful ruler for sixty-five years, going to war only in self-defense and then ready to compromise for peace; but toward the end of the sixty-sixth year of his rule he decided to make war on Serbia, which started World War I.

Psychoanalysis has demonstrated time and again that there is, as a rule, no unified human will but that direction emerges from conflicting tendencies emanating from different layers of the personality. This fact is as important for the understanding of history as it is for the understanding of the individual personality. There are, for instance, numerous cases in which radical minorities have dominated, in varying degrees, an indifferent or moderate majority or have carried it along: the revolutionary wing in the France of 1789 and the Russia of 1917, and the radical wing within the revolutionary camp; the Irish Republicans of 1916; the Nazis in the Austria of the 1930's; the Algerian rebels of the 1950's; the Vietcong in Vietnam; the Black Power activists among American Negroes today. These cases differ from one another in many ways, but they have a basic pattern in common: the people did not approve, or did originally not approve, of the actions of the revolutionaries, or would in any case not have embarked on these activities on their own initiative, but they did not put up as determined a resistance as they might have, and many moderates were won over to the revolutionary cause in the course of events. In matters of lesser historical significance we find a similar relationship in countless professional and other organizations—practically all of them dominated by active minorities. To some degree this is owing to the single-mindedness and dedication of the few as against the inertia and absorption by private concerns of the many; but another factor must also be considered.

Though the majority did not favor the actions of the radicals, the latter's cause had yet a measure of appeal to their superego. This appeal paralyzed them and rendered their resistance half-hearted and ineffectual. Intimidation or terror, practiced by the radicals, has then its full impact because the others are paralyzed by inner inhibitions.[5]

Mixed Motivations

Human motives are almost always mixed; action is, as we say in psychoanalysis, overdetermined. Under such circumstances it is hardly possible to determine the relative weight that the various component motives contributed to the whole. A young man may marry a girl for a variety of reasons: perhaps she strongly attracts him sexually; she is pretty and it satisfies his pride to show her off among his friends; the young man and the girl are congenial in many ways; she comes from a good family; and she has an aunt who is reputed to be well-to-do and some day may leave her a sizable legacy. We do not know the relative weight of these various reasons. No experiment is possible; we cannot test under varied conditions what this young man would have done if one or the other of these advantages were lacking. We may estimate, or assess, the relative importance of these motives not on the basis of experiments actually carried out but of thought, or imaginary, experiments based on our impressions of the person. If we analyze this young man, our estimates can be further improved by various means. We can ask him, for instance, how he would have acted under changed circumstances; we may suggest our own view of what his main motives are and then observe his reaction and sift the emerging material for signs of corroboration or refutation; we can compare his behavior, and his self-interpretation of his behavior, with his behavior in other situations and confront him with these comparisons, and so on. We cannot experiment in the real sense of the word, but we have various ways of probing.

Simplified theories have gained wide acceptance in history and politics. There are, for instance, the debunkers who take it for granted that all respectable motivations are rationalizations to deceive others and, perhaps, oneself. They watch out for an ulterior motive, and once they have spotted one, they have the famous "aha" experience; everything clicks, and they are convinced they have found the real motive. In our example, the debunkers would take it for granted that the young man simply married for money.

Thus, when in the Suez campaign of 1956, the United States joined the Soviet Union and the Afro-Asian states in condemning her allies and friends, England, France, and Israel, and forcing them to withdraw, many people took it for granted that this policy was owing to the influence of the oil interests. It is quite likely that the oil companies did not want anything to be done that would jeopardize Arab good will, and they certainly had ways of making their views heard in high places. But other strong forces pointed in the same direction: America's old anticolonial tradition, based on the illusion that the United States was itself an anticolonial power, made the United States encourage emancipation movements in the colonies of European powers at the end of World War II and during the following years; the desire to court the Afro-Asians; the wish to strengthen the United Nations and the illusion that if America demonstrated her loyalty to the United Nations by sacrificing her friends, all other nations would follow her example; the desire to avoid a confrontation with the Soviet Union, who threatened Paris and London with missiles; the anger that London and Paris had acted against Washington's advice and had tried to force America's hand by a fait accompli; and, last but not least, the fact that President Eisenhower was in the last phase of an election campaign conducted under the slogan "Peace and Prosperity." Under these circumstances, one may wonder whether the outcome would have been any different if there had never been a barrel of oil drilled in Arab lands.

Psychoanalytic experience can here supply not the means of probing the merits of the alternate constructions available in the analysis of individuals but the general knowledge of the multiplicity of human motivation and the attitude of caution toward appealing formulas. It may even suggest the reasons for the appeal of the debunking theories for so many: these theories give believers a sense of superiority over the "dupes"—a spurious but nevertheless satisfying feeling.

Jacob Burckhardt said once that the study of history should make us not smarter for the next time but wiser forever. Perhaps one could say that familiarity with the "beautiful diversity of mental happenings"[6] should make men wiser in their approach to all things human.

Current Pressures and Personality Patterns

Men stand and act within a social reality and their actions are conditioned by the kinds of challenges they confront and the kinds of responses typical of the situations. They are, however, individuals, conditioned by genetic dispositions selectively activated by their personal life experiences, and they also bear the imprint of all their previous individual history, especially of the most sensitive times—childhood and adolescence. Men are thus operating within two overlapping power fields, and only by considering both can we hope to approach an understanding of their conduct.

It would be a fallacy to assume that human actions are determined exclusively by the pressures of their current situation (though this seems to be fashionable at the moment); their previous conditions largely determine the way they react to the external challenges, and inner compulsions may often, unconsciously, create the external situations they need. But it would be equally wrong to view men, particularly those in responsible positions, as merely acting out inner fantasies without regarding the current pressures.

The famous geographer, Sir Halford Mackinder, once formulated the relation between man and natural conditions in these words: "Man, and not nature, initiates; but nature in large measure controls." If we replace the word "nature" by the word "society," we have a fair description of the psychoanalytic view. The word "reality," preferred by Freud, covers both nature and society.

We have seen in recent years how France, defeated by her enemies—the Germans, the Vietminh, the Algerian nationalists—has been trying to restore her prestige by selling out her friends—the Americans, the British, the Algerians who had fought in the French army, the Canadians, and now apparently the Israelis. This is quite understandable as a rational, albeit Machiavellian, way of restoring one's sense of power; these friends could not retaliate—the Americans because they were too busy elsewhere, the loyal Algerians and the Israelis because they were too weak. But it would not be surprising if this pattern of political action were also a pattern of Charles de Gaulle's personal makeup, as his treatment of his benefactor, Petain, and his behavior to the French *colons* who brought him into power might suggest. Or, as Ricarda Huch, in her German history about a particular policy of Rudolph of Habsburg, said: "Circumstances were such that he had to do it; but it seems that his disposition was such that he could do it."[7]

Myth Formation

All events become subject to what in dream theory is called "secondary elaboration," that is, to distortions that make it more suitable to our sensual appetites, our hopes, our need for security, our amour propre, our self-esteem or self-torture. The cover memory, as Ernst Kris has once said, is not an exceptional case but the normal condition; memory *is* cover memory, and history is, to some degree at least, a myth. All history, universal or personal, is *Truth and Fiction*, as Goethe titled his autobiography. Freud gave to the original manuscript of his "Moses and Monotheism" the subtitle "A Historical Novel" in order to suggest that it should take its place somewhere in the spectrum of truth to fantasy in which all human memory—and history—dwells.[8]

Of course, historians as well as psychoanalysts, the historians of individual life who are mapping, in A. P. Thornton's words, a "historical geography of a personality,"[9] try to disentangle truth from fiction. But they can succeed only to a certain degree, for resistances operate in history as well as in individual psychoanalysis.

An example for myth formation in our days is the emergence of the Kennedy myth after his assassination. It is basically the myth of the gallant young hero who was slain by dark forces, but who some day will somehow be resurrected to lead his followers to victory. If reality does not fit in with the myth, it has to be distorted until it fits. For instance, the man who, according to available evidence killed John F. Kennedy seems hardly suitable as the embodiment of dark forces. He seems to have been one of a long list of individuals who felt himself called on by destiny to interfere with the course of history.[10] The wish to make reality fit the myth probably has its share in the passionate search for a conspiracy, masterminded by powerful forces, behind the Dallas murder; it would be a more plausible representative of the archetypical evil.

The passionate hatred the left intelligentsia in this country and abroad developed against Kennedy's successor, led them to look at Kennedy as the representative of an opposite policy; if Johnson was the man of war, Kennedy appeared to be the man of peace. Yet, President Kennedy said in his inaugural address: "Let every nation know, whether it wishes us well or ill, that we shall pay any price, bear any burden, meet any hardship, support any friend, oppose any foe, to assure the survival and success of liberty." And after his meeting with Mr. Khrushchev in Vienna, President Kennedy stated:

> The facts of the matter are that the Soviets and ourselves give wholly different meanings to the same words: war, peace, democracy and popular will. We have wholly different views of right and wrong and what is an internal affair and what is aggression. And above all, we have wholly different concepts of where the world is and where it is going.

President Johnson never described the gulf between the two powers as quite so wide; on the contrary, he tried to play it down. President

Kennedy authorized the Bay of Pigs invasion, which aimed at the overthrow of the Castro regime. He decided to defend the status quo in Berlin despite the fact the logistics of the situation were highly unfavorable for the United States and superiority in conventional warfare was on the other side; had Russia persevered, the United States might have been confronted with the alternative of defeat or recourse to nuclear weapons. He went to the brink in the Cuban missile crisis. All this does not sum to the foreign policy as advocated by the American left.

The strongest point in the bill of particulars against Johnson is the war in Vietnam; but if Johnson deserves to be censured on this account, the censure should extend to Kennedy as well because it was Kennedy who first committed American troops to battle and got American prestige deeply involved. It has been argued that, had Kennedy lived, he would have extricated the country from the involvement. That is possible, but it is merely a surmise; nobody can know what Kennedy would have done in 1965. Not even John F. Kennedy himself, were he able to watch events from another world, could be sure what he would have done had the responsibility been his.

Thus, the realities of Kennedy's brief tenure of office give scant support to the contention that his foreign policy was the foreign policy of the left, and they were not so considered by the left intelligentsia at that time. Though the Cuban missile crisis lasted only a few days, opposition sentiment was already forming itself and pacifist songs were chanted in New York. At the time of the negotiations about a test-ban treaty, Linus Pauling, a noted representative of the left in foreign affairs, picketed the White House and once the treaty had actually come to pass, the Norwegian Storthing gave Pauling the Nobel peace prize for having put pressure on Kennedy—a deliberate slap at Kennedy.

The formation of the Kennedy myth makes it possible for the left intelligentsia to mobilize in its struggle against Johnson the sentiments of loyalty, guilt, and grief stirred up by the memory of the young martyred president. They can now march under this prestigious flag.

But this is not all. The fact that Kennedy was killed in Texas, on a trip undertaken in order to help the vice-president politically, establishes a still more pointed connection. On the level of primary-process thinking, which prevails in the unconscious and permeates matters of great passionate concern, the following connections present themselves; the assassination of a president is an act of lawlessness; the frontier is lawless; Texas is a frontier country; Lyndon Johnson is a Texan, and a conscious Texan, to boot; hence, Lyndon Johnson is responsible for the assassination of Kennedy. This primary-process reasoning is reinforced by the fact that Lyndon Johnson actually gained from Kennedy's death by succeeding to the office that he otherwise had little chance of ever attaining. We know from many analyses how he who accepts the benefits from a superior's death (or disability) may feel guiltly of patricide, either because an unconscious wish had become true (omnipotence of thought) or merely because, by accepting the benefits from the event, he had welcomed it. Only a very few people have actually made the accusation that, on the level of reality, Lyndon Johnson killed John F. Kennedy. But is seems that the above-discussed *logique du coeur*, or primary-process operation, plays its part in the building up of the Kennedy myth among the enemies of Lyndon Johnson.

Once a myth has become thoroughly engrained, it becomes almost impossible to dislodge it, partly because the interests to hold on to it are too strong and partly because the roots of the myth stretch into the unconscious. "Nothing can be done against prejudices," said Freud; "the most sensible thing to do is to wait and to leave such prejudices to the eroding effect of time. One day the same people begin to think about the same things in quite different a way from before."[11] However, this seems to happen only when new prejudices have taken the place, or are about to take the place, of the old ones.

THE APPLICATION OF GROUP PSYCHOLOGY

A special case of the application of psychoanalytic thought to history and sociology is the psychoanalytic *Massenpsychologie*, or group psychology. As happens so often, the translation is inaccurate and misleading; the English language has no exact equivalent of the German "*Masse*"; "mass," in English, is perhaps nearest though sometimes "crowd" is the better translation. Freud's *Massenpsychologie* deals not with human groups in general but quite specifically with regressively formed groups, that is, groups whose members abdicate some of the judgment they would exercise and some of the norms they would observe as individuals or that they had exercised and observed before entering the group. The participants in a *Masse* are more dependent on external authority (person or public opinion) than they are otherwise. If insofar as we can see the maturation of an individual as a process of emancipation consisting in the progressive internalization of external standards accompanied by their gradual critical reevaluation, such group formations appear as brought about, or as causing, a regression in ego and superego development.

But this is not the case in all groups. There are groups in which men function no differently from the way they do as individuals. They enter a group on the basis of common interest, in order better to protect such egosyntonic concerns. A physician does not, as a rule, abdicate any of his views when he becomes a member of his professional organization. I once tried to articulate this difference by distinguishing between associations (nonregressive) and masses (regressive).[12] The majority of the historically most important groups, for example, nations, churches, and armies, must be looked on as at least partially regressive groups, as "masses"; this fact gives Freudian analysis of mass formation its particular importance for history and sociology.

The regressive process in the superego implies that such internalization of moral standards as has taken place is partly, or wholly, undone and replaced by external authority. "The Führer is my conscience," said Marshall Goering. The Communist playwright Bertolt Brecht showed in his play *The Measure*[13] how Communists fall into sin if they listen to their private consciences instead of to the order of the party.

As far as the ego is concerned, regression lies in the fact that people in danger rely on protection by others. This may at times be the wise thing to do; we rely on our physician in illness, on the police in an accident, or on a union in a wage struggle. But we have to do with regression if one attributes greater power to the protector than he actually has, as children do to their parents. Just as a child feels protected in a parent's arm whether the parent can actually shelter the child against the external danger, so does the member of the mass feel protected behind the leader. The morale of soldiers rises if their officer marches ahead of them into the fire—a behavior that meant physical protection in ancient times when the leader exposed himself to the dangerous animal or club-swinging enemy first, permitting his followers to take shelter behind his body, but that has only symbolic, or psychological, value under conditions of modern weaponry.

From this structure of the regressive group, the mass, the conditions of its functioning, its formation, and its decomposition (or demoralization) can be derived. The regressive group forms whenever a leader—under simple conditions a person but, in more sophisticated circumstances, an institution or an idea—can draw on himself such transferences as to make him a more suitable behavioral norm and thus a new incarnation of the superego a more suitable protector against danger and thus a "borrowed" ego, as it were, or both. The group disintegrates if the leader—person, institution or idea—conspicuously fails to fulfill these roles, if his demands conflict with old effectively internalized superego demands that have not been replaced in the regressive group formation (even the most charismatic leaders of our time would have lost their grip on their followers if they had asked them to sleep with their mothers), or if he fails to protect his followers, if not physically at least morally (symbolically) and abandons them to their fate while saving his own skin.

These are, of course, only the barest outlines and there are many complications and qualifications, not all of them worked out as yet. The first application of such line of thought was made by Paul Federn in a paper that must be counted among the classics in the field of applied psychoanalysis.[14] This paper was written in the now somewhat dated language of early psychoanalysis, but its conclusions are fundamentally sound. Written shortly after the collapse of the Austrian monarchy following the defeat in World War I, the paper discussed the fall of the dynasty in the German-speaking alpine part of the old Habsburg state in which there had been little or no national inspired opposition to the old state. Federn pointed out that the father (monarch) who can no longer protect the mother (fatherland) has forfeited his position as head of the family.

Experiences such as this are frequent in history; troops have panicked and fled after the fall, or the capture, of their leader, but the sudden emergence of a new self-appointed leader may have restored the situation. These conditions have sometimes been well understood and consciously manipulated by political and military leaders. Hernando Cortez, for instance, calculated correctly—up to a point—that if he only succeeded in seizing Montezuma, he would have seized with him the allegiance of his people. He only overplayed his hand—or, rather, was forced to overplay it—when, after the massacre caused in his absence by Fernando de Alvarado, the Indians were in full rebellion; Indian allegiance to their prince broke when the burden became too great. Again, in the battle of Otumba, Cortez concentrated on killing the Indian chief, correctly assuming that the Indian host would become demoralized and disintegrate.

There are, however, exceptions to this general pattern. Japanese allegiance to the emperor survived the defeat of 1945, a fact that suggests that the role played by the emperor and the imperial system in the minds of the Japanese people was different from that of the Aztec or the Habsburg emperor.[15]

Institutions, like dynasties, can take reverses better than rulers who rely only on their personal authority—on what Max Weber called charisma. The individual bearer of the crown, or pope, or commissar is but temporary administrator of a lasting estate, and his weaknesses and defeats need not cancel the impact of past triumphs and the confidence in the staying and regenerative power of the institution.

An appreciation of group psychology is necessary in understanding historical processes (and political events).

Examples of Psychoanalytic Interpretations in History

Psychoanalytic interpretations in history differ greatly in scope and in inventiveness. Some are visions of the entire sweep of history; others deal with specialized questions. Some are intuitive constructions that appeal to the imagination but are hard to prove otherwise. Others go only a little beyond the kind of psychological insight found in common sense and worldly experience.

The most impressive construction, at once sweeping in scope and profound in conception, is probably Freud's explanation of monotheism as the return of a repressed memory of the primeval father and his explanation of the myth of the sacrificial death of God's son as an atonement for the primeval crime of patricide. This is a beautiful theory, and it bears the earmark of genius. But it is difficult to see how it could ever be demonstrated to those in whom it does not invoke a sense of immediate evidence.

Psychological interpretations, it seems to me, can be ordered in a spectrum of increasing demonstrability and decreasing relevance, from imaginative and appealing grand theory, which cannot be proved, to demonstrable platitudes and irrelevancies. My inclination goes to the middle zone, somewhere between these extremes. I should like to discuss in the following two simple examples of this type.

The Revival of the Popularity of the British Monarchy

In conformity with this age's general trend toward the left, the popularity of the British monarchy seemed to decline during the late nineteenth and early twentieth centuries. But there was a remarkable resurgence of enthusiasm for the monarchy during the mid-century, reaching a spectacular climax in the popular absorption with the pageantry of the coronation of Elizabeth II.

Psychoanalytic considerations may help to understand this monarchic revival in the midst of a steady movement toward the left. During the nineteenth century Great Britain was the center of a worldwide empire, the ruler of the seas, the balance of power in Europe, and the actual, if unofficial, protector of the isolation of the western hemisphere. The sources of this overwhelming power had already been silently undermined during the later nineteenth century when Germany and the United States became the two industrial giants. But people were slow in realizing these changes.

The outbreak of World War I indicated already that Britain had not been able to maintain the balance without having to enter the arena herself. In the war itself, she no longer could confine herself to the exercise of her sea power and to minor land operations in support of her continental allies as she had done during the Napoleonic wars, but had to throw a major army, raised by draft, into the bloody battle. Even so, victory was won only after the intervention of the United States. World War I left England's power position badly shaken, but the disarmament of Germany, the self-exclusion of Russia from the European theater, and the withdrawal of the United States into isolation—all of them transient phenomena—tended to obscure this fact; England was still the greatest power in the temporarily restricted field of international politics. World War II carried the process further and made it finally unmistakably clear; England emerged victorious but as the weak ally of the United States and the Soviet Union. Moreover, the antiimperialist trend of the time, strongly supported by the two superpowers, made a retreat from the empire inescapable. After a long history of domination, this "scepter'd island" suddenly found herself a relatively small, crowded country, vulnerable in an atomic age and dependent on the protection of an ally more trusted for her intentions than for her wisdom.

Though the common people did not clearly understand this development, they were aware of feelings of unease and anxiety. Anxiety made them look for new security. The simplest solution, so it seemed, was the commonwealth. The empire, it was felt, was obsolete, but its substance would live on in a purer form—no longer as colonies held together by the force of an imperial center but as an association of free peoples who are looking to England for leadership. Britons were ready to congratulate themselves on their wisdom in understanding the times and on their skill in riding the currents of history.

The new commonwealth in its tremendous heterogeneity—Canadians and Ceylonese, Indians and Pakistanis, Africans and Afrikaners—needed some unifying force to cement, however loosely, the disparate elements into a whole; under the circumstances, this bond could only be the crown. According to the first concept, the queen was to be queen of Canada, of Australia, of South Africa, and of all the other emerging Asian and African sovereignties; the new commonwealth was to have the form of a personal union. This turned out unacceptable to many, particularly to the nonwhite members, who were still willing to recognize the queen as the head of the commonwealth.

Thus, the crown, which had lost more and more of its functions in the process of democratization, was now acquiring an entirely new one—to maintain some kind of unity of the commonwealth to which the British people looked for a continuation of their international role, and with it of their security, in a dangerous new world. What England could no longer do by virtue of her own power, she would now be able to do, it was hoped, by virtue of the combined power of all the free nations of the commonwealth who looked to England for moral leadership; the crown was necessary to make this commonwealth a reality. Thus, the monarch had suddenly become the protector of the British people against the anxiety of their loneliness. When they patiently camped on the street day and night to watch the coronation ceremony, they greeted not just the queen of England but the monarch of many countries, who would unite under English banner the many sovereign states of the commonwealth. Anxiety thus created the new popularity of the House of Windsor.

If this interpretation is correct one would expect the decline of monarchic sentiment as the commonwealth is progressively revealed as an illusion.

The Austrian Revolution of 1918

The Austro-Hungarian monarchy collapsed with the defeat in World War I. The non-Germanic and non-Magyar nationalities of the ancient state, encouraged by the victorious Allies, either joined the already existing nation-states (as did the Italians, Rumanians, and southern Slavs) or set up new states, either alone (as did the Czechs and Slovaks) or in conjunction with their conationals in other defeated countries (as did the Poles). In some places there were revolutionary acts, most outspoken in Prague where loyalty to the old state had been weakest and where politically articulate people had seen themselves as captives of the Habsburg empire. In other places, as among the Austrian Poles who had not considered themselves as oppressed but rather as the relatively most fortunate of the three sectors of partitioned Poland and who had lived in a kind of *mariage de convenance* with the Habsburg state, it was more a parting of ways, without hesitation but also without hatred.

But though the non-German and non-Magyar nationalities had not been fully identified with the multinational concept of the traditional Habsburg empire and had lived for half a century in varying degrees of alienation, the same cannot be said of the German Austrians. They had, on the whole, supported the war, at first enthusiastically, later with sinking morale; the Austro-German workers had been less enthusiastic—they had to bear the heavier burden, with less chance of escaping the trenches or supplying themselves with adequate food—but they, too, had been loyal to the state. There is little doubt that, up to the very end, all but an insignificant few hoped for victory.

And yet, when the old state collapsed, there was something like a revolution in Vienna. Some of this can, of course, be explained as the consequence of the fact that the old regime had been discredited by defeat and so had lost the position of leadership, as pointed out by Federn. But what happened went beyond this; it is one thing to discard leadership because it has led the people to disaster, and quite another thing to claim that one had always been oppressed and a captive. This curious illusion seems to me to be owing to the desire to escape, psychologically, the humiliation of defeat and so to protect one's narcissism. If facts had been faced as they actually were, the German Austrians would have had to admit to themselves that they had suffered complete defeat in an encounter they had been foolish enough to seek. But the "revolution" permitted them to think that it had not been they who had started and lost the war but only the house of Habsburg and that they had been victims of Habsburg rule as much as the Czechs or Rumanians; thus the final catastrophe was made to appear as delivery from Habsburg tyrannny. Of course, they only half-heartedly believe it, and one can easily detect signs of contradiction in their behavior. But this is so in all acts of denial; truth is known and must be fought off constantly.[16]

At the same time, Count Michael Karolyi who had been in bitter opposition to the war, became Hungarian prime minister; he immediately proclaimed Hungary neutral. He traveled with some members of his government to Belgrade to meet the commander of the advancing allied Balkan army and come to terms with him. At the meeting Karolyi declared: "Hungary is a neutral country." But Marshall Franchet d'Esperey, who embodied the military spirit of his age as much as the German generals, replied: "Hungary is not a neutral but a defeated country. You have fought together with the Germans and together with them you will be chastized." These remarks were personally unfair—Michael Karolyi had been a staunch friend of the Western powers all along—and they were political folly because they effectively undermined the home position of a friendly government. But the no-nonsense attitude of the old soldier clarified the psychological situation quite correctly.

The two discussed cases point at two of the most potent forces in history as in individual life: in the first example, anxiety; in the second, hurt pride, that is, the castration complex.

A SPECIFICALLY FREUDIAN HYPOTHESIS

There is a specific historical hypothesis that has been formulated by Freud.[17] In short, it says that just as childhood experiences have a great impact on the organism and make a disproportionate contribution to character, psychopathology, and destiny, so do experiences in the childhood of a nation, its formative period, lastingly and indelibly influence national character and outlook.

Childhood, in individual life, is a biologically well-defined period, whereas in nations or other stable groups we speak of childhood, infancy, or early history only figuratively. The lineages to which these people belong have existed before, and the experiencs and actions of what we call a nation's infancy were those of adults. What we mean then by the childhood of a nation (or a movement or other historically significant groupings) is *the time during which the group was formed and stabilized*—in which the ethos common to the group came into being and was accepted and the mutual identifications established.

It is possible for national, or other groups, to have more than one formative period, more than one childhood. Those who believe that Jewish history antedates the Egyptian captivity would have to seek the childhood of Judaism in the time of the patriarchs. Another formative period was, in any case, the time of the exodus, the laws of Moses, and the conquest of Canaan. The future may perhaps look on the early years of the state of Israel as a new formative period for those Jews who became Israelis.

Such periods, according to the Freudian hypothesis, are particularly sensitive periods, and experiences of these times have a lasting imprint on the future life of the group, an imprint as resistant to the corrective influences of later experience as is the imprint of childhood in individual life. The cause of this preeminent influence can be easily surmised; because it is the period in which the group is formed and stabilized it is also a time of success in terms of the group values. The behavior and the methods of the time have thus "worked" and become deeply engrained in the people's memory as the methods of choice, the obvious thing to do.[18] They are transmitted as memories from generation to generation; they are also reenacted in countless social situations from earliest childhood on and their efficacy is thus proved in what amounts to self-fulfilling prophecies. It is hardly possible for later adverse experience to dislodge convictions so deeply rooted, so well removed from the reach of new experience.

Freud's hypothesis was developed in the special case of the Jewish people and their early history, which, he believed, accounts for the Jewish characteristics. As is well known, Freud suggested that Moses was not a Hebrew but an Egyptian. This hypothesis is based partly on some historical data such as his Egyptian name or the fact that there has been a kind of subterranean tradition of his Egyptian origin (as, for example, in Posidonius). But its foremost basis is the myth of Moses' exposure, as an infant, in a box in the Nile, and his rescue by an Egyptian princess who reared him in the palace. The story of an infant exposed by his mother and reared by adoptive parents is not unique; the motif appears repeatedly in the life story of great rulers. It has been told, for instance, of Sargon, King of Agade, and of Cyrus, founder of the Persian empire. These stories can hardly be taken at face value and are more likely myths that provide the hero with the kind of ancestry needed to legitimize his later position. According to the myth, Sargon and Cyrus were not really upstarts, soldiers of fortune; the families in which they grew up were not their real families, and they actually came from royal seed.

To generalize these suggestive interpretations, it would appear that the myth of adoption provides a man with the legitimacy he lacks. If this principle is applied to the myth of Moses' adoption it would appear that here, too, a man who grew up in an Egyptian palace and became the leader of the Jewish people is provided with the ancestry he needs in his new role–which in this case does not mean royal but Hebrew ancestry.

This is a case in which a reconstruction of facts rests–largely though not exclusively–on psychological considerations concerning the probable motives of myth formation. The psychological reasoning itself will be convincing to some and rather persuasive to some others. But even those who consider it as psychologically sound will hardly take as sufficient evidence of the Egyptian origin of Moses; Freud always hoped that new excavations in Tel-el-Amarna would provide data about an Egyptian—Tutmose or Ahmose—perhaps a governor of the province of Gosen, whom he might identify as Moses. This hope was probably instrumental in postponing the publication of his hypothesis. In the absence of such independent evidence—except for whatever weight is allowed to the Egyptian name and the continuance of an unofficial tradition—it is almost a matter of personal taste how one will estimate the relative probability of this psychological reasoning as against the time-honored official tradition.[19]

It might be mentioned that rather comparable cases of myth formation, albeit in a modern, scientific, form, have occurred in our time. The commander of the German air force during the Hitler era, Air Marshall Milch, had a Jewish father and a Gentile mother. The Nazi laws disqualified him from serving in the German armed forces, not to mention the possibility of reaching one of their top positions. Milch's mother appeared before the court and testified under oath that during the time of her son's conception she had no longer entertained any sexual relations with her Jewish husband, that her son was conceived by a Gentile lover. There were many such affidavits sworn out by German women at that time. What should future historians think of this documentary evidence of adultery? Should we assume that German middle-class women at the turn of the century, the height of the Victorian age, frequently conceived their children out of wedlock, with the connivance of their husbands? Or should we rather assume that mothers perjured themselves in the interests of their sons' careers? Traditional, documentary evidence is opposed to psychological plausibility; no objective, irrefutable evidence is available, and it is a matter of individual judgment as to what we will consider more likely.

Freud's hypothesis, not all elements of which can here be fully elaborated, is as follows; Moses was a highly placed Egyptian of the middle fourteenth century B.C. a follower of the heretic king Akhenaten; during the turmoil following the latter's death he led an Asiatic tribe who had supplied corvées for the Egyptian government into Canaan, with a view to building there a permanent home for the worship of his god, which had now become heresy in Egypt. On this basic hypothesis, Freud erected a sequence of further hypotheses leading to a vast construction both of the formation of the people and the religion of Israel and of the origin of monotheism in general. Only one of these constructs will here be considered in order to demonstrate the hypothesis of the special role of the childhood of a nation for national character and national destiny.

There is the strange Hebrew idea of being a "chosen people," in the *literal* sense of the word, directly chosen by God for a special destiny—a belief that is not simply a case of the universal chauvinism, which "sees his own wit close at hand and others at a distance."[20] Freud sees in this deep-rooted belief the reflection of a historical truth. It was, in fact, true—if we accept Freud's reconstruction—that a humble tribe was chosen by one of the great of the earth, a god in the perspective of the lowly, to be his people and to serve his religion. It would be precisely this content of historical truth about which each generation learns in early youth and in the rites of the Passover ceremony[21] that has kept this belief alive through all the disasters of Jewish history—a history that might have suggested that selection (if selection there was) was rather for misery and tragedy.

Freud's hypothesis may be applied, for instance, to the interpretation of the firm hold that eighteenth-century (Lockean) rationalism has over the American mind. According to this doctrine, the world is, or at least can be, on its way to eternal harmony if everything is approached in a spirit of reason and good will (the latter seen only as an aspect of reason because cooperation is "in the end" the enlightened self-interest of everybody). The ideal government is therefore democracy and federalism, which, given time, can solve all problems. Applied on a world scale, it will assure peaceful progress for all.

This doctrine has its adherents everywhere in the West, but only in the United States has it become a self-evident truth—something that is taken for granted and never really challenged no matter how often experience may contradict the assumption. Every new disappointment is only taken as evidence that one has not tried hard enough. This unalterable belief may well be owing to the American experience during the nation's formative years. For it was on the basis of this philosophy that the settlers proclaimed their independence from the British crown and agreed on the constitiution of a new nation, which has since grown immensely in size and prospered. Every generation hears it from childhood on that this was the secret of American success. And the pattern is repeated time and again in private life where it functions with fair success because everybody has been conditioned in the same way.

Authoritarian and totalitarian systems can be introduced everywhere where there is sufficient force and the determination to use it. But democracy can work only if there is a large area of agreement, that is, if what people have in common with one another weighs heavier than what separates them. For only with this bedrock of agreement will the ins refrain from using their power to destroy the opposition so as to make its return to office impossible and will the outs refrain from actively sabotaging government by civil disobedience or violence. In the absence of this core of consensus, the introduction of the legal forms of democracy will lead either to a putsch from above or a revolution from below, or to anarchy and civil war. Despite these rather obvious conditions, American policy has persistently introduced democracy to countries where these conditions were entirely lacking. After World War I, the monarchy was overthrown and "democracy" introduced in Germany on American demand; the preconditions for a working democracy were largely lacking, and the fact that democracy came about as a result of defeat and at the request of the victor encumbered the small number of German democrats. The result was parliamentary paralysis, leading to authoritarian presidential rule, and, eventually, to the totalitarian dictatorship of Hitler.

Countless interventions in favor of democracy in Latin America were no more successful, and if the results were less disastrous it was only because these nations lacked the German potential for mischief-making. In many countries a basis for democracy simply does not exist, and the alternatives boil down to a traditional authoritarianism and revolutionary (or counterrevolutionary) totalitarianism. But American faith in the universal applicability of democracy seems unshakable, inaccessible so far to the corrective influence of experience. Whatever disappointments or disasters may be encountered in the ancestral pursuit of democracy is always counterbalanced by the memory of the successful adoption of the constitution in the thirteen colonies with the subsequent history of increasing power and wealth; the impact of this memory is reinforced many times by the experience in school and office, in local community and trade association or club house, in which the democratic process has actually worked to the satisfaction of the people (at least up to the most recent past). If it then did not work in, say, Germany or San Domingo, Vietnam or the Congo, Greece, Brazil, or Nigeria, it can only be that it has not been honestly applied, and the hunt for the chimera continues. That may well go on until, as may well be the case, democracy proves unworkable in the United States herself because the core of agreement on fundamentals has rotted away.

The related belief in federalism as the answer to conflict has led to the setting up of the League of Nations and the United Nations, both creations of American initiative. If they did not yield the results expected of them, it must be owing to this or that mistake—for example, the veto, or the absence of a military force of the United Nations, or the absence or half-heartedness of American support. One refuses to consider the possibility that federalism requires preexisting community and leads to absurd consesquences without it.

In the recently published psychoanalytic biography of Woodrow Wilson, Freud sketched Wilson's illusionist thinking in the introduction (which appears to be the part of the publication that actually comes from his hand):

> Wilson repeatedly declared that mere facts had no significance for him, that he esteemed highly nothing but human motives and opinion. As a result of this attitude it was natural for him to ignore facts of the real outer world, even to deny that they existed, if they conflicted with his hopes and wishes. He therefore lacked motive to reduce his ignorance by learning facts. Nothing mattered except noble intentions.[22]

Freud compared Wilson to a man "who wishes to restore the eyesight of a patient but does not know the construction of the eye and has neglected to learn the necessary methods of operation."[23] These features are in the subsequent book brought into connection with Wilson's childhood and his relation to his father, mixed of identification and passive surrender. Much of this interpretation may seem plausible as far as it goes. But liberal utopianism is not a rare phenomenon in America; it is probably shared by most American intellectuals. There are in the United States hundreds of thousands of Wilson's who believe that all that is necessary is to do the moral thing and the rest will take care of itself; morality, in their eyes, carries in itself the power to prevail. What distinguished the historical Thomas Woodrow Wilson from the rest of the group was only his political acumen, his ability to reach a position of power, that is, his relatively greater sense of reality.

If Wilson's utopianism is to be understood in terms of his childhold, are we to assume that all the others who are like him in this respect—only more so—have had comparable family situations? Or should we rather assume, in line with another Freudian hypothesis discussed in this chapter, that these traits are the consequence not of individual childhood conflicts but of a collective childhood, as it were, of the American people at the time of the formation of the nation, experiences transmitted from generation to generation through early indoctrination and conditioning?[24]

NOTES

1. As, for instance, K. R. Eissler's suggestion that Freud's "Moses and Monotheism" (1939) contained an interpretation of a "trauma" in early Jewish history and that this interpretation may have made it possible for the Jewish people to realize their 2,000-year-old dream and to restore Jewish statehood in Israel.

It seems hardly necessary to point out that the Zionist movement; the Balfour Declaration; the League of Nations mandate, and the large-scale Jewish immigration into Palestine under the terms of the mandate; and the emergence of Jewish cities and farms as well as the formation of an underground Jewish army preceded the publication of Freud's book, which, incidentally, found few believers. What, then, brought the matter to a climax was the tremendous need created by the Hitler exterminations. After the war, the guilt feelings of the Western nations who had done little to prevent the genocide and the brief moment of a virtually unchallengeable American power provided the unique opportunity. It is true that the Jews of Israel proved themselves equal to the opportunity, but it is difficult to see what Freud's book could have had to do with it. K. R. Eissler, "Freud and the Psychoanalysis of History," *J. Am. Psa. Assn.*, 11 (1963): 675–703.

2. Norbert Elias, *Über den Prozess der Zivilization: Wandlungen des Verhaltens in den weltlichen Oberschichten des Abendlandes* (Vorabdruck, 1937).

3. William Foxwell Albright, *From the Stone Age to Christianity* (Baltimore, Md., 1946), p. 166.

4. *Ibid.*, p. 194.

5. Robert Waelder, "Authoritarianism and Totalitarianism: Psychological Comments on a Problem of Power," in G. B. Wilbur and W. Muensterberger, eds., *Psychoanalysis and Culture* (New York, 1951).

6. Sigmund Freud, "Preface to Hermann Nunberg's General Theory of the Neuroses on a Psycho-analytic Basis" (1931), in J. Strachey, ed., *Standard Edition* (London, 1966), vol. 221.

7. Ricarda Huch, *Römisches Reich Deutscher Nation* (Berlin, 1934), p. 258.

8. The above-discussed myth formation, which is universal both in individual and collective life, should not be confused with the majestic lie, or "Newspeak," developed to perfection by modern totalitarians.

9. A. P. Thornton, *Doctrines of Imperialism* (New York, 1965), p. 14.

10. These individuals would have entered history as heroes if history were written by their own side—as Hermodios and Aristogeiton in ancient Athens, Wilhelm Tell in the saga of the Swiss independence or, in modern times, Gavrilo Pricip, the assassin of Sarajewo, in Yugoslavia; but they are called criminals or misfits when history is written by the other side. Vera Zasulich who shot at the governor of St. Petersburg is a heroine; Berta Kaplan who shot at Lenin is a misfit. Charlotte Corday is a heroine to monarchists and a misguided fanatic to the left. Others have changed their public image as the wheels of history have turned, for example, Planetta and Holzweber, the murderers of Dollfus in Austria, who were hanged in Schuschnigg's Austria, worshipped after the Anschluss, and returned to the status of criminals after the fall of the Third Reich, and Claus Schenk von Stauffenberg, who almost killed Hitler—"an intellectually subnormal creature" and a "worm" in the Third Reich and a hero in contemporary Germany and for most of the world.

11. Sigmund Freud, *Introductory Lectures* (1916-1917), in J. Strachey, ed., *Standard Edition* (London, 1966), 16:462.

12. Robert Waelder, "The Psychological Aspects of War and Peace," *Geneva Studies* 10 (1939).

13. Bertolt Brecht, *The Measure Taken* (New York, 1960).

14. Paul Federn, "Zur Psychologie de Revolution: Die Waterlose Gesellschaft," *Der Oesterreichische Volkswirt* 11 (1919): 571–574, 595–598.

15. The fact that Colonel Nasser's authority could outlive defeat in war with Israel is probably owing to the fact that the Arabs see these events as a lost battle rather than as a lost war.

16. Robert Waelder, "The Structure of Paramond Ideas," *International Journal of Psychiatry* 32 (1951): 167–177.

17. Sigmund Freud, "Moses and Monotheism" (1939), in J. Strachey, ed., *Standard Edition* (London, 1966), vol. 23.

18. As, for instance, the almost instinctive return of the Afrikaners to the *laager* in times of danger.

19. I have tried to show elsewhere that there is an irreducible personal factor in the different weight that various people attribute to various forms of evidence.

20. Thomas Hobbes, *English Works* (Oxford University Press, 1961).

21. Ernst Kris, suggested that the continued effectiveness of ancient events could be explained as owing to rites, the symbolic meaning of which is correctly, if unconsciously, understood by each successive generation.

22. Sigmund Freud and William C. Bullitt, *Woodrow Wilson: A Psychological Study* (Boston: 1967).

23. *Ibid.*

24. The Freud and Bullitt biography of Wilson brings to mind the habit of some painters—Corot among them—to put their signature to works of their pupils though the master may have contributed only a few brush strokes. Such habits are bound to be confusing to later art historians.

2

PROTEAN MAN

Robert Jay Lifton

I wish to discuss a set of psychological patterns that I believe to be characteristic of contemporary life and that I shall summarize under the concept of "protean man." I intend this to be no more than a preliminary statement of an idea I hope to pursue more thoroughly in the future, but I shall at least try to make clear what I mean by protean man. The essay is part of a long-standing attempt to combine depth-psychological and historical perspectives—an approach greatly influenced by the psychoanalytic tradition, notably by the work of Erik Erikson; by anthropological and sociological studies of national character, particularly those of Mead, Benedict, and Riesman; and by work from various sources that emphasize man's dependence on the symbol and the image, including that of Cassirer, Langer, and Boulding.

My stress is on change and flux. I shall therefore not make much use of such words as "character" and "personality," both of which suggest fixity and permanence. Erikson's concept of identity has been, among other things, an effort to get away from this principle of fixity; I have been using the term "self-process" to convey still more specifically the idea of flow. For it is quite possible that even the image of personal identity, insofar as it suggests inner stability and sameness, is derived from a vision of a traditional culture in which man's relationship to his institutions and symbols are still relatively intact—hardly the case today. If we understand the self to be the person's symbol of his own organism, then self-process refers to the continuous psychic re-creation of that symbol.

CROSS-CULTURAL STUDIES

I came to this emphasis through work in cultures far removed from my own, studies of young (and not so young) Chinese and Japanese. Observations I was able to make in America, between and following these East Asian investigations, led me to the conviction that a very general processs was taking place. I do not mean to suggest that everybody is becoming the same, or that a totally new "world self" is taking shape. But I am convinced that a universally shared style of self-process is emerging. It derives from the three-way interplay responsible for the behavior of human groups: the psychobiological potential common to all mankind at any moment in time; those traits given special emphasis in a particular cultural tradition; and those traits related to modern (and particularly contemporary) historical forces. My thesis is that this third factor plays an increasingly important part in shaping self-process.

My work with Chinese was done in Hong Kong, in connection with a study of the process of thought reform (or brainwashing) as conducted on the mainland. I found that Chinese intellectuals of varying ages, whatever their experience with thought reform itself, had gone through an extraordinary array of what I then called identity fragments—of combinations of belief and emotional involvement—each of which they could readily abandon in favor of another. I remember particularly the profound impression made on me by the extraordinary psychohistorical journey of one young man in particular. He began as a "filial son," or "young master," that elite status of an only son in an upper-class Chinese family, with all it meant within the traditional social structure. He then felt himself an abandoned and betrayed victim, as traditional cultural forms collapsed amid civil war and general chaos, and his father, for whom he was always to long, was taken from him by political and military duties. He became a student activist in militant rebellion against the traditional cultural structures in which he had been so recently immersed (as well as against a Nationalist regime whose abuses he had personally experienced). This led him to Marxism and to strong emotional involvement in the Communist movement; then, because of remaining "imperfections," he participated in a thought reform program that advocated a more thorough ideological conversion, but that, in his case, had the opposite effect. He was alienated by the process, came into conflict with the reformers, and fled the country. Then, in Hong Kong, he struggled to establish himself as an anti-Communist writer, and after a variety of difficulties, found solace and significance in becoming a Protestant convert. Following this, and only thirty years old, he was apparently poised for some new internal (and perhaps external) move.

Even more dramatic were the shifts in self-process of young Japanese whom I interviewed in Tokyo and Kyoto from 1960 to 1962. I shall mention one extreme example of this protean pattern, though there were many others who in various ways resembled him. Prior to the age of twenty-five he had been many things. He was a proper middle-class Japanese boy, brought up in a professional family within a well-established framework of dependency and obligation. Then, owing to extensive contact with farmers' and fisherman's sons brought about by wartime evacuation, he was a "country boy" who was to retain what he described as a life-long attraction to the tastes of the common man. Then, he was a fiery young patriot who "hated the Americans" and whose older brother, a kamikaze pilot, was saved from death only by the war's end. He then became a youngster confused in his beliefs following Japan's surrender, but curious rather than hostile toward American soldiers. He became an eager young exponent of democracy, caught up in the "democracy boom" that swept Japan, and, at the same time, a youthful devotee of traditional Japanese arts—old novels, Chinese poems, kabuki, and flower arrangement. During junior high and high school, he was an all-around leader, outstanding in studies, student self-government, and general social and athletic activities. Almost simultaneously, he was an outspoken critic of society at large and of fellow students in particular for their narrow careerism, on the basis of Marxist ideas current in Japanese intellectual circles. He was also an English-speaking student, which meant, in effect, being in still another vanguard and having strong interest in American things. Midway through high school, he experienced what he called a "kind of neurosis" in which he lost interest in everything he was doing and, in quest of a "change in mood," took advantage of an opportunity to become an exchange student for one year at an American high school. He became a convert to many aspects of American life, including actually being baptized as a Christian under the influence of a minister he admired—his American "father" —and returned to Japan only reluctantly. As a "returnee," he found himself in many ways at odds with his friends and was accused by one of "smelling like butter" (a traditional Japanese phrase for

Westerners). He therefore reimmersed himself in Japanese experience—sitting on *tatami*, indulging in quiet, melancholy moods, drinking tea, and so on. He became a *ronin*—in feudal days a samurai without a master, now a student without a university—because of failing his examinations for Tokyo University (a sort of Harvard, Yale, Columbia, and Berkeley rolled into one), and, as is the custom, spent the following year preparing for the next round rather than attend a lesser institution. Once admitted, he found little to interest him until becoming an enthusiastic Zengakuren activist, fully embracing its ideal of pure Communism and having a profound sense of fulfillment in taking part in the planning and carrying out of student demonstrations. But when offered a high position in the organization during his junior year, he abruptly became an ex-Zengakuren activist, resigning because he felt he was not suited for "the life of a revolutionary." Then, an aimless dissipator, he drifted into a pattern of heavy drinking, marathon Mah-jong games, and affairs with bar girls. Later, he had no difficulty gaining employment with one of Japan's mammoth industrial organizations (and one of the *bêtes noires* of his Marxist days) and embarking on the life of a young executive, or *sarariman* ("salaried man")—in fact he did so with eagerness, careful preparation, and relief, but at the same time had fantasies and dreams of kicking over the traces, sometimes violently, and embarking on a world tour (largely Hollywood-inspired) of exotic and sophisticated pleasure-seeking.

There are, of course, important differences between the protean life styles of the two young men, and between them and their American counterparts—differences that have to do with cultural emphases and that contribute to what is generally called national character. But such is the intensity of the shared aspects of historical experience that contemporary Chinese, Japanese, and American self-process turn out to have striking points of convergence.

I would stress two general historical developments as having special importance for creating protean man. The first is the worldwide sense of what I have called "historical (or psychohistorical) dislocation," the break in the sense of connection which men have long felt with the vital and nourishing symbols of their cultural tradition—symbols revolving around family, idea systems, religions, and the life cycle in general. In our contemporary world one perceives these traditional symbols (as I have suggested elsewhere, using the Japanese as a paradigm) as irrelevant, burdensome, or inactivating, and yet one cannot avoid carrying them within or having one's self-process profoundly affected by them. The second large historical tendency is the flooding of imagery produced by the extraordinary flow of postmodern cultural influences over mass communication networks. These influences cross readily over local and national boundaries and permit each individual to be touched by everything, but at the same time cause him to be overwhelmed by superficial messages and undigested cultural elements, by headlines, and by endless partial alternatives in every sphere of life. These alternatives, moreover, are universally and simultaneously shared—if not as courses of action, at least in the form of significant inner imagery.

THE PROTEAN STYLE

We know from Greek mythology that Proteus was able to change his shape with relative ease—from wild boar to lion to dragon to fire to flood. But what he did find difficult, and would not do unless seized and chained, was to commit himself to a single form, a form most his own, and carry out his function of prophecy. We can say the same of protean man, but we must keep in mind his possibilities as well as his difficulties.

The protean style of self-process, then, is characterized by an interminable series of experiments and explorations—some shallow, some profound—each of which may be readily abandoned in favor of still new psychological quests. The pattern in many ways resembles what Erik Erikson has called "identity diffusion" or "identity confusion," and the impaired psychological functioning these terms suggest can be very much present. But I would stress that the protean style is by no means pathological as such and, in fact, may well be one of the functional patterns of our day. It extends to all areas of human experience—to political as well as sexual behavior, to the holding and promulgating of ideas, and to the general organization of lives. I would like to give a few illustrations of the protean style, as expressed in America and Europe, drawn both from psychotherapeutic work with patients and from observations on various forms of literature and art.

One patient of mine, a gifted young teacher, spoke of himself in this way:

> I have an extraordinary number of masks I can put on or take off. The question is: is there, or should there be, one face which should be authentic? I'm not sure that there is one for me. I can think of other parallels to this, especially in literature. There are representations of every kind of crime, every kind of sin. For me, there is not a single act I cannot imagine myself committing.

He went on to compare himself to an actor on the stage who "performs with a certain kind of polymorphous versatility"—and here he was referring, slightly mockingly, to Freud's term, "polymorphous perversity" for diffusely inclusive (also protean) infantile sexuality. And he asked: "Which is the real person, so far as an actor is concerned? Is he more real when performing on the stage—or when he is at home? I tend to think that for people who have these many, many masks, there is no home. Is it a futile gesture for the actor to try to find his real face?" My patient was by no means a happy man, but neither was he incapacitated. And though we can see the strain with which he carries his polymorphous versatility, it could also be said that, as a teacher and a thinker, and in some ways as a man, it served him well.

In contemporary American literature, Saul Bellow is notable for the protean men he has created. In *The Adventures of Augie March*, one of his earlier novels, we meet a picaresque hero with a notable talent for adapting himself to divergent social worlds. Augie himself says: "I touched all sides, and nobody knew where I belonged. I had no good idea of that myself." And a perceptive young English critic, Tony Tanner, tells us: "Augie indeed celebrates the self, but he can find nothing to do with it." Tanner goes on to describe Bellow's more recent protean hero, Herzog, as "a representative modern intelligence, swamped with ideas, metaphysics, and values, and surrounded by messy facts. It labors to cope with them all."

A distinguished French literary spokesman for the protean style—in his life and in his work—is, of course, Jean-Paul Sartre. Indeed, I believe that it is precisely because of these protean traits that

Sartre strikes us as an embodiment of twentieth-century man. An American critic, Theodore Solotaroff, speaks of Sartre's fundamental assumption that "there is no such thing as even a relatively fixed sense of self, ego, or identity—rather there is only the subjective mind in motion in relationship to that which it confronts." And Sartre himself refers to human consciousness as "a sheer activity transcending toward objects," and "a great emptiness, a wind blowing toward objects." Both Sartre and Solotaroff may be guilty of overstatement, but I doubt that either could have written as they did prior to the last thirty years or so. Solotaroff further characterizes Sartre as "constantly on the go, hurrying from point to point, subject to subject; fiercely intentional, his thought occupies, fills, and distends its material as he endeavors to lose and find himself in his encounters with other lives, disciplines, books, and situations." This image of repeated, autonomously willed death and rebirth of the self, so central to the protean style, becomes associated with the theme of fatherlessness—as Sartre goes on to tell us in his autobiography with his characteristic tone of serious self-mockery:

> There is no good father, that's the rule. Don't lay the blame on men but on the bond of paternity, which is rotten. To beget children, nothing better; To have them, what iniquity! Had my father lived, he would have lain on me at full length, and would have crushed me. Amidst Aeneas and his fellows who carry their Anchises on their backs, I move from shore to shore, alone and hating those invisible begetters who bestraddle their sons all their lifelong. I left behind me a young man who did not have time to be my father and who could now be my son. Was it a good thing or bad? I don't know. But I readily subscribed to the verdict of an eminent psychoanalyst: I have no superego.

We note Sartre's image of interchangeability of father and son, of "a young man who did not have time to be my father and who could now be my son"—which, in a literal sense refers to the age of his father's death, but symbolically suggests an extension of the protean style to intimate family relationships. And such reversals indeed become necessary in a rapidly changing world in which the sons must constantly "carry their fathers on their backs," teach them new things that they, as older people, cannot possibly know. The judgment of the absent superego, however, may be misleading, especially if we equate superego with susceptibility to guilt. What has actually disappeared—in Sartre and in protean man in general—

is the classical superego, the internalization of clearly defined criteria of right and wrong transmitted within a particular culture by parents to their children. Protean man requires freedom from precisely this kind of superego—he requires a symbolic fatherlessness—in order to carry out his explorations. But rather than being free of guilt, we shall see that his guilt takes on a form different from that of his predecessors.

There are many other representations of protean man among contemporary novelists: in the constant internal and external motion of beat generation writings, such as Jack Kerouac's *On the Road;* in the novels of a gifted successor to that generation, J. P. Donleavy, particularly *The Ginger Man;* and of course in the work of European novelists such as Günter Grass, whose *The Tin Drum* is a breathtaking evocation of prewar Polish-German, wartime German, and postwar German environments, in which the protagonist combines protean adaptability with a kind of perpetual physical-mental strike against any change at all.

In the visual arts, perhaps the most important postwar movement has been aptly named "action painting" to convey its stress on process rather than fixed completion. And a more recent and related movement in sculpture, "kinetic art," goes further. According to Jean Tinguely, one of its leading practitioners, "Artists are putting themselves in rhythm with their time, in contact with their epoch, especially with permanent and perpetual movement." As revolutionary as any style or approach is the stress on innovation per se that now dominates painting. I have frequently heard artists, themselves considered radical innovators, complain bitterly of the current standards dictating that "innovation is all," and of a turnover in art movements so rapid as to discourage the idea of holding still long enough to develop a particular style.

We also learn much from film stars. Marcello Mastroianni, when asked whether he agreed with *Time* magazine's characterization of him as "the neo-capitalist hero," gave the following answer:

> In many ways, yes. But I don't think I'm any kind of hero, neo-capitalist or otherwise. If anything, I am an *anti*-hero or at most a *non*-hero. *Time* said I had the frightened, characteristically 20th century look, with a spine made of plastic napkin rings. I accepted this—because modern man is that way; and being a product of my time and

an artist, I can represent him. If humanity were all one piece, I would be considered a weakling.

Mastroianni accepts his destiny as protean man; he seems to realize that there are certain advantages to having a spine made of plastic napkin rings, or at least that it is an appropriate kind of spine to have these days.

John Cage, the composer, is an extreme exponent of the protean style, both in his music and in his sense of all of us as listeners. He concluded a recent letter to the *Village Voice* with the sentence: "Nowadays, everything happens at once and our souls are conveniently electronic, omniattentive." The comment is McLuhan-like, but what I wish to stress particularly is the idea of omniattention—the sense of contemporary man as having the possibility of receiving, or taking in, everything. In attending, as in being, nothing is off limits.

CONSTRICTED SELF-PROCESS

To be sure, one can observe in contemporary man a tendency that seems to be precisely the opposite of the protean style. I refer to the closing off of identity or constriction of self-process, to a straight-and-narrow specialization in psychological as well as in intellectual life, and to a reluctance to let in any extraneous influences. But I would emphasize that where this kind of constricted, or one-dimensional, self-process exists, it has an essentially reactive and compensatory quality. In this it differs from earlier characterological styles it may seem to resemble (such as the inner-directed man described by Riesman, and still earlier patterns in traditional society). For these were direct outgrowths of societies that then existed, and in harmony with those societies, whereas at the present time a constricted self-process requires continuous psychological work to fend off protean influences that are always abroad.

Protean man has a particular relationship to the holding of ideas that has, I believe, great significance for the politics, religion, and general intellectual life of the future. For just as elements of the self can be experimented with and readily altered, so can idea systems and ideologies be embraced, modified, abandoned, and re-embraced, all with a new ease that stands in sharp contrast to the inner struggle we have in the past associated with these shifts. Until relatively recently, no more than one major ideological shift was likely to occur in a lifetime, and this one would be long remembered as a significant individual turning point accompanied by profound soul-searching and conflict. But today it is not unusual to encounter several such shifts, accomplished relatively painlessly, within a year or even a month; among many groups, the rarity is a man who has gone through life holding firmly to a single ideological vision.

In one sense, this tendency is related to "the end of ideology" spoken of by Daniel Bell, because protean man is incapable of enduring an unquestioning allegiance to the large ideologies and utopian thought of the nineteenth and early twentieth centuries. One must be cautious about speaking of the end of anything, however, especially ideology, and one also encounters in protean man what I would call strong ideological hunger. He is starved for ideas and feelings that can give coherence to his world, but here too his taste is toward new combinations. Though he is by no means without yearning for the absolute, what he finds most acceptable are images of a more fragmentary nature than those of the ideologies of the past; these images, though limited and often fleeting, can have great influence on his psychological life. Thus political and religious movements, as they confront protean man, are likely to experience less difficulty convincing him to alter previous convictions than they do providing him a set of beliefs that can command his allegiance for more than a brief experimental interlude.

THE SENSE OF ABSURDITY

Intimately bound up with his flux in emotions and beliefs is a profound inner sense of absurdity, which finds expression in a tone of mockery. The sense and the tone are related to a perception of surrounding activities and belief as profoundly strange and inappropriate. They stem from a breakdown in the relationship between inner and outer worlds—that is, in the sense of symbolic integrity—and are part of the pattern of psychohistorical dislocation I mentioned earlier. For if we view man as primarily a symbol-forming organism, we must recognize that he has constant need of a meaningful inner formulation of self and world in which his own actions, and even his impulses, have some kind of fit with the outside as he perceives it.

The sense of absurdity, of course, has a considerable modern tradition, and has been discussed by such writers as Camus as a function of man's spiritual homelessness and inability to find any meaning in traditional belief systems. But absurdity and mockery have taken much more extreme form in the post-World War II world and have in fact become a prominent part of a universal life style.

In American life, absurdity and mockery are everywhere. Perhaps their most vivid expression can be found in such areas as pop art and the more general burgeoning of pop culture. Important here is the complex stance of the pop artist toward the objects he depicts. On the one hand, he embraces the materials of the everyday world, celebrates and even exalts them—boldly asserting his creative return to representational art (in active rebellion against the previously reigning nonobjective school), and his psychological return to the real world of things. On the other hand, everything he touches he mocks. Thingness is pressed to the point of caricature. He is indeed artistically reborn as he moves freely among the physical and symbolic materials of his environment, but mockery is his birth certificate and his passport. This kind of duality of approach is formalized in the stated duplicity of camp, an ill-defined aesthetic in which all varieties of mockery converge under the guiding influence of the homosexual's subversion of a heterosexual world.

Also relevant are a group of expressions in current slang, some of them derived originally from jazz. The "dry mock" has replaced the dry wit; one refers to a segment of life experience as a "bit," "bag," "caper," "game" (or "con game"), "scene," "show," or "scenario"; one seeks to "make the scene" (or "make it"), "beat the system," or "pull it off" or else one "cools it" ("plays it cool") or "cops out." The thing to be experienced, in other words, is too absurd to be taken at its face value; one must either keep most of the self aloof from it, or if not one must lubricate the encounter with mockery.

A similar spirit seems to pervade literature and social action alike. What is best termed a "literature of mockery" has come to dominate fiction and other forms of writing on an international scale. Again Günter Grass' *The Tin Drum* comes to mind, and is probably the greatest single example of this literature—a work, I believe, that will eventually be appreciated as much as a general evocation of contemporary man as of the particular German experience with Nazism. In this country the divergent group of novelists known as black humorists also fit into the general category—related as they are to a trend in the American literary consciousness that R. W. B. Lewis has called a "savagely comical apocalypse" or a "new kind of ironic literary form and disturbing vision, the joining of the dark thread of apocalypse with the nervous detonations of satiric laughter." For it is precisely death itself, and particularly threats of the contemporary apocalypse, that protean man ultimately mocks.

The relationship of mockery to political and social action has been less apparent, but is, I would claim, equally significant. There is more than coincidence in the fact that the largest American student uprising of recent decades, the Berkeley free speech movement of 1964, was followed immediately by a Filthy Speech Movement. Though the object of the Filthy Speech Movement—achieving free expression of forbidden language, particularly of four-letter words—can be viewed as a serious one, the predominant effect, even in the matter of names, was that of a mocking caricature of the movement that preceded it. But if mockery can undermine protest, it can also enliven it. There have been signs of craving for it in major American expressions of protest such as those of black power and the opposition to the war in Vietnam. In the former a certain chord can be struck by comedian Dick Gregory, and in the latter by the use of satirical skits and parodies, that revives the flagging attention of protesters becoming gradually bored with the repetition of their "straight" slogans and goals. And on an international scale, I would say that, during the past decade, Russian intellectual life has been enriched by a leavening spirit of mockery—against which the Chinese leaders are now, in their current reactivation of thought reform programs, fighting a vigorous but ultimately losing battle.

NURTURANCE VS. AUTONOMY

Closely related to the sense of absurdity and the spirit of mockery is another characteristic of protean man, which I call "suspicion of counterfeit nurturance." Involved here is a severe conflict of dependency, a core problem of protean man. I originally thought of the concept several years ago while working with survivors of the atomic bomb in Hiroshima. I found that these survivors both felt themselves in need of special help and resented whatever help was offered them because they equated it with weakness and inferiority. In considering the matter more generally, I found that this equation of nurturance with a threat to autonomy was a major theme of contemporary life. The increased dependency needs resulting from the breakdown of traditional institutions lead protean man to seek out replacements wherever he can find them. The large organizations (government, business, academic, and so on) to which he turns, and which contemporary society increasingly holds out as a substitute for traditional institutions, present an ambivalent threat to his autonomy in one way, and the intense individual relationships in which he seeks to anchor himself, in another. Both are therefore likely to be perceived as counterfeit. But the obverse side of this tendency is an expanding sensitivity to the inauthentic, which may be just beginning to exert its general creative force on man's behalf.

Technology (and technique in general), together with science, have special significance for protean man. Technical achievement of any kind can be strongly embraced to combat inner tendencies toward diffusion, and to transcend feelings of absurdity and conflicts over counterfeit nurturance. The image of science itself, however, as the ultimate power behind technology and, to a considerable extent, behind contemporary thought in general, becomes much more difficult to cope with. Only in certain underdeveloped countries can one find, in relatively pure form, those expectations of scientific-utopian deliverance from all human want and conflict characteristic of the eighteenth and nineteenth-century Western thought. Protean man retains much of this utopian imagery, but he finds it increasingly undermined by massive disillusionment.

More and more he calls forth the other side of the god-devil polarity generally applied to science, and sees it as a purveyor of total destructiveness. This kind of profound ambivalence creates for him the most extreme psychic paradox: the very force he still feels to be his liberator from the heavy burdens of past irrationality also threatens him with absolute annihilation, even extinction. But this paradox may well be—in fact, I believe, already has been—the source of imaginative efforts to achieve new relationships between science and man and, indeed, new visions of science itself.

AMBIVALENT FEELINGS

I suggested before that protean man was not free of guilt. He indeed suffers from it considerably, but often without awareness of what is causing his suffering. For his is a form of hidden guilt—a vague but persistent kind of self-condemnation related to the symbolic disharmonies I have described, a sense of having no outlet for his loyalties and no symbolic structure for his achievements. This is the guilt of social breakdown, and it includes various forms of historical and racial guilt experienced by whole nations and peoples, both by the privileged and the abused. Rather than a clear feeling of evil or sinfulness, it takes the form of a nagging sense of unworthiness all the more troublesome for its lack of clear origin.

Protean man experiences similarly vague constellations of anxiety and resentment. These too have origin in symbolic impairments and are particularly tied in with suspicion of counterfeit nurturance. Often feeling himself uncared for, even abandoned, protean man responds with diffuse fear and anger. But he can neither find a good cause for the former nor a consistent target for the latter. He nonetheless cultivates his anger because he finds it more serviceable than anxiety, because there are plenty of targets of one kind or another beckoning, and because even moving targets are better than none. His difficulty is that focused indignation is as hard for him to sustain as is any single identification or conviction.

Involved in all these patterns is a profuond psychic struggle with the idea of change itself. For here too protean man find himself ambivalent in the extreme. He is profoundly attracted to the idea of making all things, including himself, totally new—to what I have elsewhere called the "mode of transformation." But he is equally drawn to an image of a mythical past of perfect harmony and prescientific wholeness, to the "mode of restoration." Moreover, beneath his transformationism is nostalgia, and beneath his restorationism is his fascinated attraction to contemporary forms and symbols. Constantly balancing these elements amid the extraordinarily rapid change surrounding his own life, the nostalgia is pervasive and can be one of his most explosive and dangerous emotions. This longing for a golden age of absolute oneness, prior to individual and cultural separation or delineation, not only sets the tone for the restorationism of the politically rightist antagonists of history: the still-extant emperor-worshipping assassins in Japan, the colons in France, and the John Birchites and Ku Klux Klanners in this country. It also, in more disguised form, energizes that transformationist totalism of the left that courts violence, and is even willing to risk nuclear violence, in a similarly elusive quest.

Following on all that I have said are radical impairments to the symbolism of transition within the life cycle—the *rites de passage* surrounding birth, entry into adulthood, marriage, and death. Whatever rites remain seem shallow, inappropriate, fragmentary. Protean man cannot take them seriously and often seeks to improvise new ones with whatever contemporary materials he has available, including cars and drugs. Perhaps the central impairment here is that of symbolic immortality—of the universal need for imagery of connection predating and extending beyond the individual life span, whether the idiom of this immortality is biological (living on through children and grandchildren), theological (through a life after death), natural (*in* nature itself, which outlasts all), or creative (through what man makes and does). I have suggested elsewhere that this sense of immortality is a fundamental component of ordinary psychic life and that it is now being profoundly threatened by simple historical velocity, which subverts the idioms (notably the theological) in which it has traditionally been maintained, and, of particular importance to protean man, by the existence of nuclear weapons, which, even without being used, call into questions all modes of immortality. (Who can be certain of living on through children and grandchildren, through teachings or kindnesses?)

Protean man is left with two paths to symbolic immortality, which he tries to cultivate, sometimes pleasurably and sometimes desperately. One is the natural mode we have mentioned. His attraction to nature and concern at its desecration has to do with an unconscious sense that, in whatever holocaust, at least nature will endure—though such are the dimensions of our present weapons that he cannot be absolutely certain even of this. His second path may be termed that of "experiential transcendence"—of seeking a sense of immortality in the way that mystics always have, through psychic experience of such great intensity that time and death are, in effect, eliminated. This, I believe, is the larger meaning of the drug revolution, of protean man's hunger for chemical aids to expanded consciousness. And indeed all revolutions may be thought of, at bottom, as innovations in the struggle for immortality, as new combinations of old modes.

We have seen that young adults individually, and youth movements collectively, express most vividly the psychological themes of protean man. And though it is true that these themes make contact with what we sometimes call the "psychology of adolescence," we err badly if we overlook their expression in all age groups and dismiss them as mere adolescent phenomena. Rather, protean man's affinity for the young—his being metaphorically and psychologically so young in spirit—has to do with his never-ceasing quest for imagery of rebirth. He seeks such imagery from all sources—from ideas, techniques, religious and political systems, mass movements, drugs; or from special individuals of his own kind whom he sees as possessing that problematic gift of his namesake, the gift of prophecy. The dangers inherent in the quest seem hardly to require emphasis. What perhaps needs most to be kept in mind is the general principle that renewal on a large scale is impossible to achieve without forays into danger, destruction, and negativity. The principle of death and rebirth is as valid psychohistorically as it is mythologically. However misguided many of his forays may be, protean man also carries with him an extraordinary range of possibility for man's betterment, or more important, for his survival.

Three important questions about the over-all concept of protean man have been repeatedly raised and are worth considering a bit further. First, is protean man—with his continuous psychic movement and shifts in identity and belief—exclusively a young man? Second, is he really a new man or merely a resurrection of a type we are familiar with from many periods in the past? And third, despite his fluidity, just what in him, if anything remains stable?

I would, very briefly, answer these questions as follows. He is most prominent among the young—or to put the matter another way, the young are most protean—but it would be a great mistake for the rest of us to hide behind this truism, because no one is immune to the larger influences at play and, in greater or lesser degree, protean man inhabits us all. Similarly, such men have indeed existed in earlier historical times also out of joint because of extreme dislocation and rapidly changing symbols and ideas. But contemporary influences have converged to render him a much more clear-cut and widespread entity than ever before. About his stability, it is true that much within him must remain constant in order to make possible his psychological flux—among which I would mention certain enduring elements in the mother-child relationship (what I refer to elsewhere as the "emotional-symbolic substrate"), certain inner consistencies of style (including his sense of absurdity and mockery, his approach to individual and group relationships, and various aesthetic emphases), and even the continuous expectation of change itself. Surely the whole issue of stability amid change needs much more exploration within a specifically psychohistorical framework.

3

PSYCHOANALYSIS AND LITERARY CRITICISM IN HISTORICAL PERSPECTIVE

Ronald Grimsley

I

Though psychoanalysis first appeared as a strictly scientific theory based on the results of clinical experience, its widespread acceptance as an explanation of hitherto imperfectly understood aspects of human nature and the rapid extension and application of its main principles to other branches of knowledge undoubtedly owed a great deal to the existence of a cultural climate already sympathetic to its general spirit, if not to its particular doctrines. The European Romantic Movement, which had originated in the frustrations and dissatisfactions of an excessively rationalistic culture, gave priority to emotion and imagination as the source of ultimate aesthetic values and so prepared the way for a broader conception of human personality.

Already in the eighteenth century an important precursor, Jean-Jacques Rousseau, had called attention to the incompatibility of society and man's original nature: civilized man, he affirmed, had made reflection subservient to his pride and passions instead of using it to attain a proper understanding of his place in the universal order. Consequently, appearance differed from reality, and men who had become the slaves of opinion were no longer capable of heeding the voice of nature; what they consciously strove to become no longer corresponded to what they really were. If Kant set definite limits to the valid exercise of reason, later thinkers, such as Schopenhauer and Nietzsche, actually rejected reason in favor of an outlook that identified the meaning of human existence with the activity of the will. Kierkegaard also challenged the rationalist pretensions of Hegelianism in the name of Christian freedom, which accorded priority to faith and grace instead of reason and nature. Before Freud, the German philosopher Eduard von Hartmann, drawing freely on Hegel, Schopenhauer, and Schelling, had elaborated "the philosophy of the unconscious."[1] Hartmann attached a particular philosophical meaning to the term, identifying the unconscious with a higher, almost divine mode of creative being, which was treated as the absolute source of all existence. Henri Bergson, a contemporary of Freud, believed that intuition and duration as well as change and movement were more authentic aspects of ultimate truth than the intellectual conclusions of the mathematical and experimental sciences. Novelists such as Stendhal and Dostoevsky had stressed the importance of will and energy as the source of human activity, which often ran counter to the principles of everyday morality. Balzac's characters were also driven on by violent, obsessive passions; Balzac himself was fascinated by occultism and illuminism. The German Romantics had already proclaimed the value of poetry as a means of penetrating the deeper mysteries of existence, whereas later French poets, such as Baudelaire and Rimbaud and those of the Symbolist movement, appeared to add a new dimension to the aesthetic consciousness by exploring new aspects of the poetic imagination. Because of the rapid spread of these influences, nature was no longer envisaged in a static, abstract manner but was viewed as an organic, dynamic unity.

Freud on Art

In view of this growing interest in mysterious and irrational aspects of nature in general and of human nature in particular, it is not surprising that the advent of psychoanalysis should have made a striking impact on literature. Not only did it attract the attention of such creative writers as James Joyce, Thomas Mann, D. H. Lawrence, and Franz Kafka,[2] but it also began to interest critics concerned with the explanation and interpretation of literary works. Indeed, Freud himself had led the way by some modest but significant excursions into the field of literary criticism. When taken within the context of his writings as a whole, Freud's discussions of literature may seem comparatively limited in scope, but his psychoanalytic principles conveyed a view of art that led to far-reaching consequences. Freud insisted that literature, appealing though its aesthetic effects might be, ultimately had to be interpreted as a form of neurosis. The artist was a man whose inability to accept the reality of everyday experience caused him to turn to the creation of a world of fantasy that compensated for the inadequacy of his frustrated feelings. Literary skill gave wide diffusion to these fantasies because they reflected feelings already experienced—though only dimly or unconsciously—by the readers themselves. In Freud's words:

> The artist is originally a man who turns from reality because he cannot come to terms with the demand for the renunciation of instinctual satisfaction as it is first made, and who then in phantasy-life allows full play to his erotic and ambitious wishes. But he finds a way of return from this world of phantasy back to reality; with his special gifts he moulds his phantasies into a new kind of reality, and men concede them a justification as valuable reflections of actual life. Thus by a certain path he actually becomes the hero, king, and creator, favourite he desired to be, without pursuing the circuitous path of creating real alterations in the outer world. But this he can only attain because other men feel the same dissatisfaction as he with the renunciation demanded by reality and because this dissatisfaction, resulting from the displacement of the pleasure-principle by the reality-principle, is itself a part of reality.[3]

In another essay, "The Relation of the Poet to Day-Dreaming," Freud brought out the regressive, almost infantile nature of the artist's inspiration when he put forward the hypothesis that "imaginative creation, like day-dreaming, is a continuation of and a substitute for the play of childhood."[4]

The same essential points were restated in *Introductory Lectures on Psycho-Analysis*, in which Freud affirmed that

> An artist is in rudiments an introvert, not far removed from neurosis. He is oppressed by excessively powerful instinctual needs. He desires to win honour, power, wealth, fame and love of women; but he lacks the means for achieving these satisfactions. Consequently, like any other unsatisfied man, he turns away from reality and transfers all his interest, and his libido too, to the wishful constructions of his life of phantasy, whence the path might lead to neurosis.[5]

The artist, however, differs from other men because, being able to eliminate what is too personal about his daydreams, he makes them accessible to the enjoyment of others; he also tones them down in a way that masks their real origin; he possesses "the mysterious power of shaping some particular material until it has become a faithful image of his phantasy."[6] Ultimately, therefore, what might have become a cause of pain becomes a source of pleasure for those who unconsciously identify themselves with the artist's own fantasies.

Freud admitted that he was not offering a complete explanation of the artistic process. "Since artistic talent and capacity are ultimately connected with sublimation we must admit that the nature of the artistic function is also inaccessible to us along psychoanalytic lines."[7] Being "no connoisseur in art, but simply a layman," Freud conceded that "he had often observed that the subject-matter of works of art had a stronger attraction for him than their formal and technical qualities, though to the artist their value lay first and foremost in these latter."[8] This prudent reservation was frequently ignored by later followers who made exaggerated claims for the relevance of Freud's principles to literary criticism.

If the inspiration of the literary work is similar in several fundamental respects to the fantasy-weaving of the child or neurotic, it also reflects the ambiguity of such processes. Certainly the creation of the work of art is a deliberate and conscious act, as Freud acknowledged, but according to the psychoanalytic view, the artist's specific intention cannot express the full meaning of an inspiration that is largely drawn from his unconscious self. In this respect the interpretation of art involves the same difficulty as the interpretation of dreams in which the latent content lies concealed beneath the manifest content and may be made even more inaccessible through the distorting process of secondary elaboration, that is, the conscious attempt to reconstruct the dream in waking life. In order to understand the meaning of both the dream and the literary work it is not enough to accept them at their face value. Even though the literary work obviously represents a more controlled creative effort than the mere dream, it may still contain puzzling or incomprehensible elements. To take an example which became the subject of a very ingenious essay by Freud's biographer and disciple, Ernest Jones,[9] we may quote the problem in *Hamlet*. Many generations of earlier critics had struggled—usually without success—to explain the reason for Hamlet's failure to kill his uncle when he apparently had the motive, the means, and the opportunity of doing so. The psychoanalytic view explained the real obstacle as a psychological one: in spite of his professed intentions, Hamlet is inhibited by the guilt associated with his unconscious emotional dependence on his mother. In a similar vein Freud himself, in "The Theme of the Three Caskets," tried to unravel the true significance of King Lear's reactions to his daughters, who were alleged to represent the three Fates; the ultimate meaning of the play involves the idea that "eternal wisdom, in the garb of primitive myth, bids the old man renounce love, choose death and make friends with the necessity of dying."[10]

The general effect of this kind of early psychoanalytic criticism was to focus attention on the personality and temperament of the artist himself. If Hamlet revealed the Oedipus complex, it was because this also constituted a problem for Shakespeare, who presumably sought to alleviate it by making it the subject of tragedy. *Hamlet* was not to be judged simply as a play, because it provided a "clue to much of the deeper workings of Shakespeare's mind." This kind of psychological approach to literature naturally tended to see an author's output as the result of some inner emotional disturbance. This is very evident in the more important of the earlier psychoanalytical studies such as those of Marie Bonaparte on Edgar Allan Poe and René Laforgue on Baudelaire.[11]

If at first sight this somewhat clinical approach to literature tended to treat the author as a sick man who turned to literary creation as a compensation for the frustration of real-life emotions, Freud tried to give such fantasies a wider significance by linking them with the idea of universal myths. The private myth elaborated by the writer frequently reproduced the themes illustrated by popular mythology and folk lore.[12] Thus Hamlet's subservience to the Oedipus complex was held to be merely one instance of a psychological pattern going back to ancient and primitive cultures; Cordelia was not simply a character involved in her father's attempt to struggle with the problems of his emotional life; she was also one of the Fates, or Parcae—Atropos ("the inevitable") or Death.

Jung's Archetypes

Followers of Jung sought to broaden the basis of psychoanalytic interpretation still further by relating these archetypal themes to the "collective unconscious." Jung had insisted that "great poetry draws its strength from the life of mankind, and we completely miss its meaning if we try to derive it from personal factors."[13] "The artist," he affirms,

> Is not a person endowed with free will who seeks his own ends, but one who allows art to realize its purposes through him. As a human being he may have moods and a will and personal aims, but as an artist he is "man" in a higher sense—he is "collective man," a vehicle and moulder of the unconscious psychic life of mankind.[14]

If, therefore, the work of art has value, it is not because of any personal idiosyncrasies it may contain; its greatness consists "in its rising above the personal and speaking from the mind and heart of the artist to the mind and art of mankind."[15] Jung is firmly opposed to the Freudian view that "all artists are undeveloped personalities with marked infantile autoerotic traits."[16] This kind of judgment is perhaps applicable to them as men, but certainly not as artists. Art is a kind of "innate drive" that "seizes" the individual and uses him for its own purposes. "The creative process consists in the unconscious activation of an archetypal image and in elaborating and shaping the image into the finished work."[17] If certain archetypes emerge at particular historical moments, it is because they are called into being by the "onesidedness of life," which has refused to give adequate expression to the impulses they represent.

A number of critics have found this notion of archetypal myth more congenial than the strictly Freudian view. An interesting attempt was made to relate the Jungian archetypes to poetry by Maud Bodkin in her *Archetypal Patterns in Poetry*,[18] in which such well-known poems as Coleridge's *Ancient Mariner* and T. S. Eliot's *Waste Land* were treated as examples of the rebirth myth. More recently the idea of myth criticism has attained a certain popularity among American critics, even though it does not necessarily involve the acceptance of the idea of the collective unconscious. Northrop Frye, with his *Anatomy of Criticism*,[19] is one of the most distinguished representatives of this kind of approach to literature. As in the case of Freudian psychoanalysis, the result of this myth criticism has been to broaden the significance of the work of art and relate it to fundamental nonaesthetic aspects of the human psyche. The literary use of myth is considered to be just one example of a basic aspect of the human consciousness which can express itself in philosophy and religion as well as in art.

The Work of Art

This concern with the notion of archetype indicated a dissatisfaction with the excessive Freudian emphasis on the personality of the author. Indeed, it soon became apparent that to be really fruitful, even psychologically orientated criticism had to concentrate primarily on the work of art itself. Freud himself had indicated a particularly effective way of relating psychoanalytical principles to criticism when he had discussed what must obviously be one of the writer's main concerns—the problem of language. The title of one of his most famous works, *On the Interpretation of Dreams*,[20] indicated the importance he attached to the elucidation of the patient's private fantasy world, and another study, "The Psychopathology of Everyday Life,"[21] called attention to the significance of apparently trivial verbal slips; it was the analyst's task to decode those irrational uses of language at variance with the conscious habits of voluntary speech. The review entitled "The Antithetical Sense of Primal Words" indicated one of Freud's most fundamental views—that language as the expression of emotion becomes charged with ambiguity and contradiction; it is the natural tendency of a word to call up the idea of its opposite.[22] In this article Freud drew attention to the similarity between the antithetical aspects of primitive languages and the peculiarity of dreams, which "show a special tendency to reduce two opposites to a unity or to represent them as one thing."[23]

It was not difficult to extend this idea to the literary work itself, especially when it was believed that it issued from the depths of the unconscious, whether of the individual or the "life of the collective." The work of art contained, it was affirmed, the same ambiguity as that of the dream world and revealed the same need for interpretation. Jung insisted on a similar point when he stated that "a great work of art is like a dream; for all its apparent obviousness it does not explain itself and is always ambiguous."[24] Because both the work of art and the dream are more than they seem to be insofar as the manifest content may contain a latent meaning, it is the critic's business to bring this hidden element to the surface by a careful examination of its verbal formulation. More recent psychoanalytic studies have also insisted on the importance of the linguistic aspects of psychotherapy. Dr. Rycroft, for example, sees the psychoanalyst as a man who "knows as it were the grammar and syntax" of symptoms, gestures, and dreams and "is therefore in a position to interpret them back again into the communal language of consciousness"; a great deal of the psychoanalyst's activity must be devoted to "research into the private notes of patients and the way in which their cryptic and disguised utterances and gestures can be understood and translated back into common and communicable language."[25] A psychoanalyst, therefore, is in a position surprisingly similar to that of "a linguist who encounters a community which speaks an unfamiliar language." The critic, too, "translates" the meaning of the work to those who are not yet fully aware of its true significance. Both psychoanalysis and literary criticism can thus be considered as "theories of meaning."

If psychoanalysis has shown that the ambiguity of language, being largely influenced by unconscious or repressed emotion, involves certain psychological mechanisms more characteristic of the dream than waking life, it has also demonstrated that the life of fantasy is not purely arbitrary but follows certain laws and principles of its own. Because the mechanisms of the imagination tend to conform to a definite pattern, the ultimate effect of psychoanalytic criticism has been to show that there exists a law of the imagination different from the rational activity of the conscious self and yet containing a definite form and structure of its own. The world of imagination, though drawn largely from the hidden resources of the unconscious, is as meaningful in its own way as the apparently more direct and lucid expressions of the intellect.

Baudouin

Charles Baudouin[26] was one of the first French critics to make extensive use of psychoanalytic principles for the interpretation of literary works. In his opinion, the meaning of a specific work could be identified with the writer's unconscious self, the literary symbols being the expression of personal "complexes." Yet Baudouin was careful to insist that the work of art represented a kind of sublimated ascent from mere instinctual elements to the higher regions of the self; the literary symbol, as the work of the imagination, represented a kind of dynamic thrust of the personality toward a higher form of expression. The critic's task was to "read" these symbols and images in terms of their original emotional significance.

If, therefore, literary activity was held to be similar in many ways to that of the dream (for example, in the way in which, through the liberation of repressed tendencies from the unconscious, it remained attached to certain basic drives, such as sexuality and aggression), the literary work differed from the dream inasmuch as it involved a more refined process of "sublimation." As we have seen, Freud had already admitted that psychoanalysis had little to say about the artistic gift as such and Baudouin also insisted that it merely served to demonstrate the continuity of primitive, infantile impulses and the higher expressions of the mind and heart; it was not a question of reducing the work of art to something lower than itself, but of explaining its personal genesis.

Baudouin admits that interpretation can be a delicate task, requiring a good deal of sensitivity, perspicacity, and prudence. Because of the peculiar structure of the imagination, the real meaning of the work of art may be expressed only indirectly. The mechanisms of symbolization, condensation, displacement, and transference will often cause the apparently insignificant detail or image to become charged with great significance. Baudouin's study of Hugo, for example, places great emphasis on the theme of the watching eye as a clue to the poet's fundamental complex. The imagination thus no longer remains a merely capricious activity but is determined by the needs of the affective life—the "sentiments, emotions and instincts that accompany the images."[27] Imagination and emotion exert a reciprocal influence. "Condensation," which causes various emotions to become grouped around a single object, will help to explain the frequent polyvalence of the literary image. Inversely, the phenomenon of transference will often cause an emotion to become dispersed and attached to various images—hence the "symbolic" significance of the emotionally charged object. "Displacement" may cause the affective stress to be removed from the real object with which it was originally associated to some apparently more innocuous object, so that what seems to be of minor importance may actually provide the clue to the whole emotional situation. However, displacement is only one aspect of a complex process involving condensation, transference, and subconscious activity.

Baudouin wishes to break down the barrier between aesthetic and other forms of the imagination on the ground that there is simply "imagination" in the general sense of the term. No doubt the artist brings a special talent or genius to bear on his work, but the quality of his imagination as such is not different from that of other men, save perhaps in its intensity; it is the artist's sensibility and will that, in Baudouin's view, give his activity its particular characteristics. Yet, however intricate and elaborate the literary work may be, it originates in the spontaneity of the imagination and draws its inspiration from the depths of the author's unconscious. Though the final symbol may be modified by the sensibility and the will, it always retains this intimate link with the artist's deeper self, and it is for this very reason that the true significance of the work cannot be fully accounted for by an examination of the author's conscious intention. "The poet's work, apparently objective, is the involuntary symbol of a subjective reality more or less unconscious." The critic's function is to try to elucidate these unconscious elements. "The essence of the analytic method . . . is found in unravelling the condensations of an imaginative creation, in disentangling displacements and repressions.." The result will be a clarification of "the inner psychological meaning of the most obscure symbols," and, ultimately, the disclosure of "the secret soul of the man of genius." Baudouin is convinced that such an approach to art need not lose contact with life or "forfeit the sense of beauty."[28]

Mauron

A more recent and subtle form of this approach to literature is the so-called psychocriticism of Charles Mauron.[29] Mauron's object is not to give a complete explanation of the meaning of literary works but to call attention to an aspect neglected by the kind of classical criticism that concentrated almost exclusively on their rational characteristics. Psychocriticism closely follows the psychoanalytic method by seeking the "associations of involuntary ideas" that lie beneath the "manifest structures" of the work; it proposes to examine relationships, which are the result of impulses originating in the author's unconscious. At the same time, by concentrating on the text itself, Mauron seeks to correct the excessive emphasis placed by psychoanalytic critics on the author's personality. Though the study of unconscious processes, even when closely related to their literary expression, will inevitably involve some reference to the author's psychic life, Mauron insists that the critic's main purpose will be aesthetic rather than psychological. He considers the biographical aspect of the problem to be of comparatively minor importance; at most it can help to confirm solutions derived from the analysis of the literary material. In this respect Mauron sees an important difference between his own position and that of an earlier psychoanalytic critic, such as Marie Bonaparte, who, he believes, gave undue prominence to the biographical and personal elements. Even so, his emphasis on the importance of the unconscious undoubtedly means that the study of the primitive prelogical inspiration of the work is an essential prerequisite to a full understanding of its ultimate literary significance.

Mauron's method involves four distinct stages of critical examination. He always begins by superimposing an author's various texts on one another in order to trace the networks of associations and the groups of recurrent and "obsessing" images contained in them. Though significant for the comprehension of the works concerned, these relationships will probably be hidden from the author himself because they are brought into being by the power of his unconscious life, not by his conscious will; they are affective, not rational, structures, and so differ from the deliberate use of metaphor, allegory or symbol. Thus Mauron examines the theme of the sunset in various poems of Mallarmé, a theme that can be rationally explained within the context of each individual poem but that emerges as an unconscious feminine symbol as soon as it is seen as part of a wider network of relations involving the entire poetic production. On closer inspection various poems will be found to contain the same network of obsessive associations, which are linked to a unique unconscious dynamism. Mauron believes that the literary critic can derive considerable help from the important research carried out by the British psychoanalysts Susan Isaacs and Melanie Klein on the imagination of young children; for the child the meaning of external objects is inseparable from a close dependence on the demands of his inner self, so that though he accepts these objects as existing in their own right, he at the same time treats them as part of an inner world endowed with powerful emotional significance; as internal objects, they are closely related to the conflicting demands of his own personality and his subsequent attempts to overcome them through various kinds of adaptation. In all this the activity of the infantile imagination, based on the complementary processes of projection and introjection, is very different from that of the conscious will; but it may continue to operate in the unconscious life of the maladjusted adult. The "obsessing" images discovered in the literary work have to be related to this primordial, unconscious aspect of the author's imagination.

When once these fundamental images and relationships have been made explicit, it is the critic's task to observe their subsequent repetition and modification through the movement of the artist's imagination, and, as Freud has already pointed out, this kind of imaginative process bears a striking resemblance to the life of dreams. Mauron, however, lays particular emphasis on the way in which the "obsessing" images gradually assume the form of dramatic figures or situations. Each of these figures, in his view, does not have a genuinely independent existence of its own; it derives its significance from its relation to the others, the whole group being ultimately identified with the conflicting elements in the author's unconscious self. At the same time the constant recurrence of the associative network of images shows that these conflicts are a permanent feature of the author's inner life. We are thus led to "the hypothesis of an internal, personal dramatic situation, incessantly modified by the reaction to internal or external events, but persistent and recognizable."[30] This is what Mauron calls "the personal myth."

So far, therefore, psychocriticism involves the following steps: the detection of the "obsessing" metaphors, their elaboration into patterns of relations, and, finally, their transformation into characters involved in a dramatic situation. This progressive elaboration is made possible through the impetus of the affective imagination, which, because it expresses the conflicting emotions of the personality, never remains purely passive or static but constantly organizes its impulses with a view to modifying them. In this way each author's myth is given its own individual meaning.

The final stages of Mauron's psychocritical method turn on the interpretation of the personal myth by means of a study of the development of the author's unconscious self. Because his life involves him in some kind of active contact with the external world, the precise forms of the figures in the myth will often be determined by those features of his real-life situation that have become charged with particular emotional significance; in other words, because the dramatic figure refers to certain aspects of the author's material circumstances as well as to the demands of his inner life, it may be helpful, as a last stage in the interpretation of the myth, to seek confirmation and verification in his personal life. Thus Mauron's analysis of the network of unconscious associations in Mallarmé's poetry leads to the conclusion that the mythical figure of woman becomes identified in Mallarmé's mind with the dancer, who is alleged to represent his unconscious emotional attachment to his mother and sister. Mauron finds confirmation of this hypothesis in the fact that the figure of the dancer became especially significant at a time when Mallarmé was upset by the death of his mother and sister. According to this view, therefore, the real meaning of the myth is to be found in the poet's infantile attachment to these two women, Hérodiade (the heroine of the famous unfinished poem of that name) representing the figures of his infantile libido, from whose influence, even as an adult, he was never able to free himself.

Mauron has applied his method to a number of French writers, ranging from such dramatists as Racine and Molière to such poets as Nerval, Mallarmé, and Valéry. His studies undoubtedly represent one of the most important recent efforts to apply psychoanalytical principles to literary criticism, and it is interesting to compare his often sophisticated analyses to the much cruder and heavy-handed efforts of earlier critics to grapple with the same problems.

II

We have so far been considering the type of literary criticism that has been more or less directly inspired by orthodox psychoanalysis, and before we attempt a critical assessment of its value, it may be useful to give some brief indications of more recent viewpoints which though claiming to be broadly related to the psychoanalytic tradition, diverge from it in very fundamental ways. In particular, there has been considerable resistance on the part of many critics to the idea of using the notion of the unconscious as the basis of literary interpretation; it has been argued that this method explains the superior by the inferior; as the product of unconscious irrational impulses the work of art is reduced to the status of a mere substitute for reality. It is argued that inasmuch as art is in fact the very opposite, namely, one of the highest expressions of man's mind and imagination, the theory that tries to depreciate it in this way must be unsound in its basic assumptions. More especially, many critics felt that the emphasis placed by early Freudian criticism on the artist's personality tends to obscure the intrinsic characteristics of the work of art, to blur its distinctive outlines, and to associate it with a vague mass of primordial impulses that have no distinctive and independent existence outside man's elemental psychic life.

Bachelard

Though Gaston Bachelard (1884–1962)[31] uses the word "psychoanalysis" in the title of some of his works, it owes little to its strictly Freudian meaning. Bachelard blames Freud for conceptualizing the unconscious in a way that makes it refer exclusively to repressed feelings, for if the literary object, as Freud believed, derives its significance from its relationship to the author's unconscious, then the literary symbol, as an attempt at emotional adaptation and sublimation, can never free itself from its dependence on regressive, infantile emotions. Though agreeing that the literary image is an active, dynamic expression of the unconscious, Bachelard refuses to limit the idea of the unconscious to a psychic life enclosed on itself. On the contrary, he believes that, through the unconscious, man is brought into vital contact with the physical world. Far from being a merely subjective experience derived from the frustrated resources of the author's inner life, the poetic image expresses the movement of the unconscious toward the primal elements of the material universe—earth, fire, air, and water. The unconscious, which reveals itself through the activity of the poetic imagination, operates at a cosmic level and precedes all reflection, even all sexual differentiation. From this point of view Bachelard's view would seem to be much closer to the Jungian archetype than to the Freudian conception.[32] In any case, the unconscious is treated as a primordial aspect of human nature that brings man into a fundamental relationship with things rather than people.

The activity of the "materializing" imagination, being of an elemental kind, involves no definite break between the conscious and the unconscious levels of experience. The imagination moves towards the material object with which it feels itself to be in close affinity. The "psychoanalysis of matter" would thus appear to be much closer—as Bachelard himself admitted in his later works[33]—to phenomenology than to Freudianism, for the imagination is intentionally directed on an object in a way that seeks to penetrate its essential being. Poets especially have this highly developed kind of perception, for between imagination and perception there does not seem to be any absolute qualitative distinction. The image is "not an object or still less a substitute-object" but a kind of prolongation of the archetype residing in the depths of the unconscious. The material world reverberates as it were in the unconscious, and through a process of "absolute sublimation" the poet sets in motion a force that transcends all merely psychological impulses because it is "without antecedents." The poetic consciousness therefore does not depend on a causal relationship with the source of the image; it is completely absorbed by it.

Bachelard establishes an important distinction between dreaming and reverie; whereas the former may well be a mere psychological phenomenon explicable in terms of the conflicts and frustrations of man's psychic life, reverie is considered to be the expression of man's response to the world of things. In this respect Bachelard insists that the preoccupation of psychoanalysis with dreams betrays a serious limitation because it deals only with the world of man and their broken relationships; reverie, on the other hand, is most effective when it expresses the reaction of the solitary man to the world of objects. He who is prepared to reestablish contact with things and to rediscover his essential relationship with cosmic substances may find in this way a more rapid cure for his neurosis than frequent visits to the analyst's couch. Contact with things means, for Bachelard, a "working" participation in the world, which will undoubtedly benefit the soul.

To the poet belongs the function of completing and extending this kind of reverie before nature. Apart from his primordial contact with the material world, he possesses in language a means of giving creative expression to his reverie. Through the help of poetry the image inspired by the material universe is able to go beyond it; language helps to activate matter, as it were, and reveal it as substance in metamorphosis and movement. When expressed through language, reverie thus leads to a new perception of the universe. Moreover, the imagination's contact with matter usually shows the ambiguity and ambivalence of primordial substances: fire is an element that heals and destroys; air too is a source of protection and danger. The imagination cannot escape the material antinomies of the universe, which reveal themselves in the conflict of substances with one another. Yet such is the power of the imagination, especially when embodied in the word, that it remains a source of fulfilment, completing the world and man's active participation in its material substance. It leads to reconciliation with the universe and the achievement of a new form of unity through the liberation and expansion of a fundamental human quality. The image, therefore, is not a mere substitute for reality, but a reality in its own right.

Imagination is not the same as mere fancy in the conventional literary sense; it is a dynamic power associated with man's unconscious participation in primordial aspects of the material universe. Bachelard admits that an author's choice of a particular element as the organizing principle of his work cannot be purely arbitrary but will be determined by his "oneiric temperament," which will impel him to this primordial identification of his unconscious with a particular form of material substance. Because poetic reverie is not merely detached impersonal observation, but active participation, images possess a momentum, growing and proliferating through their own intrinsic power, especially when they are expressed through the medium of language. The fertility and abundance of the imagination are due mainly to its materiality and the fact that true reverie begins with matter.

The poetic image has for Bachelard a particularly privileged role, for, as the "spoken imagination," it expresses the creativity of "the speaking being." The word is a compound of being and spirit, not just an intermediary between subject and object. Through the word the universe is revealed in its true reality. Obviously the imagination, being rooted in matter, does not depend on man alone, but it is through man that it becomes temporalized and attains its highest expression. "Everything speaks in the universe, but it is man, the great speaker (*parleur*) who utters the first words. . . . The imagination, temporalized through the word (*le verbe*) is the humanizing faculty *par excellence*.[34] The imagination becomes enriched because, through language, it is associated with one of man's primordial characteristics.

Perhaps Bachelard's exalted conception of the role of language explains his neglect of and even contempt for the visual, which in his view is not capable of expressing the dynamic, ambivalent, and conflicting aspects of the imagination. The visual has not the same power of expansive abundance, the same capacity for energetic expression. In Bachelard's opinion, the reverie expressed through language can remake nature and lead to an active dialogue between man and the material substances of the universe. So intimate is this relationship that it is often difficult to know who is speaking, man or the universe; man's fusion with "original matter" becomes so complete at this exalted level of experience that the usual distinctions between self and nonself become meaningless. Poetry for Bachelard, therefore, is not simply a translation of life, but its transmutation into a new mode of being. Through poetry man re-creates not only himself but the cosmos too.

Bachelard's high opinion of the poetic imagination probably explains his refusal to allow true greatness to works of art that are not rooted in the authentic unconscious; it is the primordial contact with the material world that gives life and purpose to the literary work. Without a "complex" based on the activity of the material imagination a work of art remains "cold, artificial and false."[35]

Sartre

Whereas Bachelard interprets the idea of the unconscious in a very personal way that owes little to orthodox psychoanalysis, the existential psychoanalysis of Jean-Paul Sartre claims to dispense with it altogether.[36] If Sartre still uses the term "psychoanalysis," it is because he agrees with Freud that the empirical aspects of the psychic life are not self-explanatory, but have to be deciphered in the light of more fundamental principles. Man is not a mere aggregate or collection, of particular parts; his existence must be interpreted by means of a global principle that treats it as a totality. Sartre and Freud are in agreement on yet a further point—that this ultimate principle of explanation is not accessible to immediate reflection; the conscious pattern of reactions is determined by a factor that defies any conscious effort to grasp it. At this point, however, the two thinkers begin to diverge. The hidden determinant of human behavior is, according to Freud, to be located in the repressed emotions of the unconscious, that is, in the domain of pure affectivity; the key to the personality's reactions is thus to be found in a complex of which the individual himself is unaware. The analyst hopes to elucidate the meaning of the patient's behavior by relating it to past emotional experiences that have been of particular significance for his psychological development. If Sartre also emphasizes the insufficiency of mere reflection and seeks a more fundamental, prelogical principle, he defines it in a completely different way. According to him, psychoanalysis has made the mistake of assuming that certain emotional drives, such as sexuality and aggression, are ultimate and irreducible. In Sartre's view, all such feelings must depend on a factor that is still more important—on the activity of a "prereflective *cogito*," which expresses itself through the "original project" by which each individual freely chooses the meaning of his own existence.

As the expression of man's free choice, the original project cannot be understood in terms of his past; it is a question of a "return from the future to the present." The originality of the choice means that the individual seeks in some way to transcend his past by moving towards an as yet unrealized possibility of the future. This choice, therefore, does not represent a "state" or a "datum buried in the darkness of the unconscious" because the individual is never the passive instrument of forces over which he has no control. His freedom means that he must accept the absolute responsibility of a choice that cannot be explained by anything other than itself. The original project is a nonsubstantial absolute, unique and irreducible.

The work of art, according to Sartre, is to be understood in the light of the same freedom, though the activity of the imagination gives it special characteristics of its own. As the psychoanalysts have already stressed, the particular aspects of the literary work, its images and symbols, do not necessarily carry their own self-evident meaning, but have to be interpreted symbolically. Yet, in Sartre's view, psychoanalysis has made the mistake of assuming that these symbols have some kind of universal significance insofar as they are determined by fixed psychological laws; Freudians believe that it is possible to establish a definite correlation between certain physical elements or objects and their psychological meaning. Sartre denies this and argues that every choice being unique, the meaning of secondary structures or symbols through which it is expressed will also have to be interpreted in an individual way.

Though it would seem that both orthodox and existential psychoanalysis tend to locate the ultimate meaning of the work of art in the artist's personality, they do so in radically different ways. Whereas Freudianism seeks to stress the unconscious conditions determining the artist's choice of symbols, existential psychoanalysis insists that the artist is involved with expressing a mode of possible being—not an abstract mode of being, but one revealed through a particular situation. Art is but one special way through which the individual seeks to express his mode of being-in-the-world. Through his choice of being the individual confers meaning on both his own existence and the world with which he is actively concerned. Ultimately, therefore, the meaning of the work of art must be sought in the ontological rather than the psychological sphere. The artist's individual choice of an imaginative world cannot be interpreted in merely psychological terms, because it is rooted in the "original upsurge of human freedom," not in the complexes and emotions of a maladjusted inner life. In this way Sartre tries to lift the free aspects of human behavior, including the creation of works of art, above the causal determinism imposed on them by the strict application of psychoanalytical principles.

III

It is probably not very profitable to try to assess the significance of psychoanalysis for literary criticism by means of some absolute assumption about the ultimate aims of the two disciplines. No doubt many psychoanalysts would now hesitate to say in what precise sense their activities were intended to effect a cure, whereas a number of literary critics would not agree that their primary function was to judge particular works. Rather than start with some fixed presupposition about their aims it seems better to consider both psychoanalysis and literary criticism in the light of the total situations from which their theoretical concepts are derived. In spite of the philosophical use to which psychoanalysis has been put, it began as a clinical experience involving the active interrelation of two people[37]; literary criticism likewise depends on a situation involving an individual reader in the presence of specific literary texts. This wider frame of reference to which all theoretical considerations must finally be applied means that both disciplines deal with a form of reality that cannot be exhaustively understood in terms of a single abstract attitude. The patient's life has a meaning for him outside the consulting room, however thorough and prolonged the treatment may be; ultimately it is he who has to decide how to apply the insights obtained from the analysis to the total pattern of his personal existence. In the same way the work of art, though it obviously has no genuinely personal existence, can never be completely grasped by conceptual analysis; it has a richness and density that defy intellectual elucidation. All interpretation must in the end be subordinated to the actual experience of the living individual who encounters the work in its immediacy and decides on its significance for his own consciousness.

In their confident belief that they had found a key that would open many doors hitherto closed to human understanding, early Freudian critics too readily assumed that the meaning of the literary work was like that of any other scientific object—that it did not exist in its own right but merely as the symbolic expression of something other than itself, namely, the author's unconscious emotions. It was affirmed that the artist who had failed to live out his dreams in real life, found compensation in the creation of a fantasy world. The work of art was thus held to illustrate a psychological law derived from the analysis of abnormal aspects of human behavior. More especially, this scientific approach to literature tended to stress the role of psychic determinism and causal explanation. However obscure it might seem to be, the work of art, it was affirmed, could ultimately be understood as the product of impulses that were reducible to psychological laws. This critical approach was deemed to have the further advantage of simplicity, for it was asserted that the work of art had one fundamental meaning to which everything else could be related; it was the outward, objective expression of an emotional conflict in the author's personality.

The New Approach

If psychoanalysis was at first excessively clinical in its treatment of literature, it helped to raise, if only by implication, a question of far-reaching significance: in what precise sense was the work of art an "object"? No doubt psychoanalysts overhastily assumed that the work of art was some kind of scientific object capable of conceptual explanation in terms of psychological laws, but it was also made clear that these laws were not those of physical science or traditional psychology; the unconscious did not fit in with the type of explanation usually applied to the activities of the conscious mind; its language was not that of rational discourse. This new psychological approach also threw out a challenge to classical literary criticism by suggesting that the meaning of the work of art was not what it seemed, that what the author deliberately said and intended was not to be identified with the ultimate meaning of what he had created. The internal structure of the work was determined by unconscious impulses lying beyond the control of his will; its manifest content did not properly account for its latent meaning. The significance of the whole could thus be discovered only by a method of analysis that explored the depths of the author's personality.

One particularly important consequence of this new approach to literature was the emphasis henceforth to be placed on the ambiguous nature of the work of art, and to Freudian psychoanalysts undoubtedly belongs the merit of having discovered, as Lionel Trilling well puts it, the "rich ambiguity" of literature.[38] Their major error was to suppose that this ambiguity was completely amenable to scientific explanation. Even so, the psychoanalytic emphasis on the meaningfulness of the unconscious showed that its activities, far from being capricious, followed—again in Trilling's phrase—a "directing purpose," which had to be explained by principles different from those used by traditional psychology and criticism.

The Problem of Meaning

By showing that the work of art required an analysis of its unconscious affective content as well as its outward rational form psychoanalysis reopened the whole question of its essential nature. No longer could a literary work be considered as a simple homogeneous reality, for it was henceforth revealed as a complex object requiring explanation at more than one level. The principles applicable to the analysis of its formal voluntary structure might not be valid for the examination of its unconscious elements. Perhaps their overriding interest in the problem of the unconscious caused psychoanalysts to forget the importance of the conscious elements, but it was henceforth made clear that a proper understanding of the work of art had to reckon with its conscious and unconscious aspects. In this respect the effect of psychoanalysis on the interpretation of the work of art was similar to its influence on the conception of human personality. Both the living person and the work of art appeared as the embodiment of a number of different impulses that were not amenable to a single kind of explanation. Just as the individual personality revealed itself through a pattern of physical and psychological reactions, so was the work of art given physical identity by its linguistic elements; but the whole work could not be explained by a single physical principle that was merely a vehicle for the transmission of various kinds of meaning.

The very fact that both psychoanalysis and literary criticism are so frequently concerned with the problem of meaning suggests that the most fruitful point of contact between them may be in the semantic sphere. Attention has already been called to the emphasis placed by some modern psychoanalysts on this aspect of their activities. Though the purpose of the analyst's linguistic interest is presumably to lead the patient to a better understanding and eventual improvement of his condition, this process of verbal explanation is deemed to be a useful and often necessary preliminary to some kind of personal action. Likewise, the reader of a literary work has to become aware of its meaning as a definite linguistic structure before he can enjoy or judge it intelligently. No doubt it will be objected that the analyst may effect cures and the reader obtain enjoyment without any deliberate analysis of the situation and that both can adopt a successful intuitive attitude toward the whole problem, but, in general, informed understanding will surely be a help rather than a hindrance to both psychoanalysis and literary criticism.

Early psychoanalytical criticism often made the mistake of supposing the explanation was enough in itself, thus forgetting that critical activity, in the form of reflection about literature, is simply one aspect of a total process that ultimately involves the adoption of a personal attitude. No explanation, however detailed or ingenious, can be a substitute for the direct experience of the work itself and its acceptance or rejection by the individual. Any explanatory process that does not help to stimulate an active personal response is ultimately without value.

Because it sees literary works in a limited psychological perspective, treating them as objects of a specific kind, psychoanalytic criticism can never represent more than one of a number of possible attitudes toward literature. It will undoubtedly help to broaden the reader's understanding by explaining obscure or ambiguous elements and especially by showing that language cannot be completely separated from its psychological roots. In this way it makes possible a fuller appreciation of the work of art as a complex whole; it shows, for example, that the work is not a mere linguistic structure existing in a void, or something that has been created *ex nihilo*, but that it draws many of its elements from its creator's inner life. Every work thus contains features that escape the attention of the author himself, because they are derived from his unconscious self. Yet it is difficult to admit that the organization of the material and the ultimate linguistic elaboration of the work have been determined solely by its unconscious origins. In this respect psychoanalysis stands in the same relation to literary criticism as do Marxism and other theories that interpret aesthetic values by means of nonaesthetic principles. Like psychoanalysis, the sociological method also directs attention to the extraliterary source of inspiration by suggesting that the work may contain a social or historical meaning of which the author is not fully aware and that this mirrors in some way the consciousness of the social group or larger society to which he belongs. This means that by the very fact of establishing its own claim to recognition as a valid approach to literature, psychoanalysis implicitly affirms the right of other disciplines to make equally useful contributions to literary criticism. The complete explanation of the work of art will henceforth involve the use of a number of nonaesthetic disciplines, such as psychology, sociology, and history.

On the other hand, if they were rigidly applied, such methods would destroy literature as an autonomous activity. For example, by reducing it to the mere expression of psychological laws, psychoanalysis suggests that we are dealing with an attitude that could be more effectively realized in living experience. The critic's insistence that the literary work must always look beyond itself should not make him deny or ignore the importance of its intrinsic characteristics, the exact analysis of which requires the use of specific stylistic and other literary techniques. A literary work exists both in its own right and as an entity grounded in something other than itself. The essential point is to recognize the many-sidedness of images and symbols, which can be interpreted in various ways. Though they constitute particular entities, with characteristics of their own, they also form part of a larger cultural world that helps to determine their complete significance.

The Readers

Perhaps the most difficult problem is that of deciding how to relate these nonliterary principles to the complete process of interpretation. In any case, the final synthesis of these explanatory methods will probably not be possible at a purely theoretical level; though reflection is necessary to critical interpretation and rightly seeks to account for the various elements in the literary work, it cannot function in isolation from the rest of the human personality. The reader's total response to the work will involve his sensibility, emotions, and imagination as well as his reason. Even though the work undoubtedly exists in its own right, it does not achieve complete unity of being until it has been re-created or interpreted by the living individual. In other words, the complete experience of the work goes beyond mere knowledge or explanation of its constituent elements. The work of art contains more than its skeletal verbal structure, however objective this may be; it also involves more than the elements described and analyzed by nonliterary disciplines; it possesses a unique essence that reveals itself only to the individual consciousness.

Reading is not simply a kind of passive acceptance of linguistic patterns or the reflective analysis of character and plot. In trying to become conscious of the literary work in the fullest sense the reader has to cooperate actively in its re-creation. This process is not an arbitrary act, for there is a fixed linguistic structure that must provide the permanent basis of any particular reading or performance. The work cannot be made to mean anything the reader wishes; to a large extent the text must be allowed to speak from its own resources. Admittedly, help may be required in the elucidation of the linguistic, historical, psychological, and other difficulties; there is a hard core of meaning that has to be made explicit to the reader's understanding if his ultimate response to the work is to be at all adequate. Mere subjective impressionism itself can never be an adequate substitute for an informed comprehension of the objective meaning of the text. Yet when due allowance has been made for the need to respect the objective aspects of the work, the reader still has to find a more fundamental meaning that has relevance to him. It is not enough to retrace the psychological genesis of the work or to reestablish the original meaning of the text, whether this be understood as the reconstitution of the author's own intention or as the meaning the work had for his contemporaries. However psychologically or historically minded the reader may be, any such reconstruction, if taken as an end in itself, will necessarily be incomplete, because, even when it seeks to be exhaustive, it ignores the essential fact that the work exists here and now and that the reader cannot, and should not, treat it as a mere historical or scientific object. Through his original act of creation the writer brought into being an aesthetic entity that, though rooted in psychological, sociological, and historical reality, has a unique existence of its own and contains essential characteristics that will yield their true meaning only to a living consciousness.

Because the work of art is the result of a genuinely creative act, it will always contain an element of spontaneity that challenges the reader to decide on its significance for his own existence. The appearance of any serious literary work involves the freedom of both its creator and its reader. However earnestly he may seek to benefit from the detailed explanations offered by literary critics, the reader himself has ultimately to decide what the work means for him. Knowledge of the work's meaning can never be a substitute for an active response to its value. In the last resort every individual's judgment has to be based on his experience of the work in its immediate reality, and this experience involves more than a mere knowledge of its constituent elements. Naturally this does not mean that the reader's free choice cannot profit from an informed understanding of the work's objective significance or a reflective appraisal of its aesthetic qualities; the effectiveness of the artist's vision must depend largely on his ability to express it in concrete form. Nevertheless, admiration for technical excellence can never replace a spontaneous acceptance of its deeper imaginative content. Any final judgment will depend on the extent to which the individual is willing to accept the world of the literary object as a possible extension of his own imaginative conception of existence. This possible world is not the world as he thinks it ought to be, for that would make literary appreciation subservient to didactic or moral purposes, nor does the aesthetic picture have to be one of which he would approve in everyday life; it is simply a world with which he can imaginatively identify himself during his experience of the work.

The richness, density, and complexity of the great work of art may not always be apparent at the first encounter. Even the accurate perception of the aesthetic structure may require several readings for the merely objective meaning of the language to become fully comprehensible, whereas still further readings may be required for the more subtle emotional overtones or the full implications of the use of certain key images to become fully accessible to the reader's sensibility and imagination. The almost infinite variety and abundance of literary works make it impossible to establish a single type of appreciation response capable of embracing them all. The existence of great works of art requiring a considerable depth of understanding need not exclude lesser works that can still give pleasure for their merely formal excellence or their imaginative portrayal of some minor aspect of the human condition. All works cannot claim the metaphysical dimension, which seems to belong to the greatest.[39] Yet at whatever level literary judgment is exercised, it will always involve some measure of freedom; there must always be a point at which the individual's free experience of the work leads him to bestow a decisive meaning on the understanding and knowledge of its various elements.

The Impact of Psychoanalysis

When it is seen within this wider context, the contribution of psychoanalysis to literary criticism may appear to be less extensive than its early exponents would have wished. A fuller comprehension of the broader aspects of aesthetic experience has made many critics reluctant to accept the rigid dichotomy between the conscious and unconscious aspects of literary creation, on the ground that this involves literary criticism in two apparently incompatible modes of interpretation. Moreover, by according priority to the unconscious as the final criterion of literary meaning, psychoanalysis seems to eliminate the essential element of freedom on which all judgment must ultimately rest. If it were strictly adhered to, the psychoanalytic method would lead to an unwarranted restriction and impoverishment of literary experience. On the other hand, even though later criticism has moved away from the oversimplified picture of literary creation presented by the first psychoanalytical critics, there is no doubt that their effort to reexamine the very nature of aesthetic consciousness has led to a broadening of the critical horizon. Even such philosopher-critics as Bachelard and Sartre, who do not accept the psychoanalytic view of the unconscious, are often indebted to psychoanalysis on many points. Today, it is true, there are few psychoanalytic literary critics of international repute, but there are equally few who have not been influenced by psychoanalysis and benefited from its fertilizing effects on the understanding of a vast range of cultural phenomena. Indeed, the success of psychoanalysis in illuminating hitherto perplexing aspects of man's behavior has inevitably led to a fuller comprehension of his purely aesthetic achievements.

NOTES

1. See Eduard von Hartmann, *The Philosophy of the Unconscious* (London, 1884).
2. F. J. Hoffman, *Freudianism and the Literary Mind* (Louisiana, 1945).
3. Sigmund Freud, "Formulations regarding the two principles in mental functioning" in *Collected Papers* (New York, 1959), 4:19.
4. Sigmund Freud, "The Relation of the Poet to Day-Dreaming" (1908), *ibid.*, 4:182.
5. Sigmund Freud, "Introductory Lectures on Psycho-Analysis" (1915-1917) (New York, 1943).
6. *Ibid.*
7. *Ibid.*
8. Sigmund Freud, "The Moses of Michelangelo" (1914), in *Collected Papers*, 4:257.
9. Ernest Jones, *The Life and Work of Sigmund Freud* (New York 1953).
10. Sigmund Freud, "The Theme of the Three Caskets" (1913), in *Collected Papers*, 4:244–256.
11. Marie Bonaparte, *Edgar Poe* (Paris, 1933); René Laforgue, *L'Échec*

de Baudelaire (Paris, 1931), and *La Psychopathologie de l'Échec,* rev. ed. (Paris, 1950).

12. See Sigmund Freud, *Totem and Taboo* (1913) (New York, 1931), for Freud's attempt to extend psychoanalytic principles to anthropology. Several of these ideas were subsequently developed by Otto Rank.

13. Carl Jung, *Collected Works,* Vol. 15, *The Spirit in Man, Art and Literature,* R. F. C. Hull, trans. (New York, 1966), p. 98. See, especially, the essays "On the Relation of Analytic Psychology to Poetry" and "Psychology and Literature."

14. *Ibid.,* p. 101.

15. *Ibid.*

16. *Ibid.*

17. *Ibid.*

18. Maud Bodkin, *Archetypal Patterns in Poetry* (New York, 1934).

19. Northrop Frye, *Anatomy of Criticism* (Princeton, 1957).

20. Sigmund Freud, *On the Interpretation of Dreams* (1900) (New York, 1949).

21. Sigmund Freud, "The Psychopathology of Everyday Life" (1901).

22. Sigmund Freud, "The Antithetical Sense of Primal Words" (1910), in *Collected Papers,* 4:184–191.

23. *Ibid.*

24. Jung, *Man, Art and Literature,* p. 104.

25. Charles Rycroft, "Introduction: Causes and Meaning," in Charles Rycroft, ed , *Psychoanalysis Observed* (London, 1966), p. 18.

26. Charles Baudouin, *Psychanalyse de l'art,* (Paris, 1929), *Le symbole chez Verhaeren* (Paris, 1924), *Psychoanalysis and Aesthetics,* E. and C. Paul, trans. (London, 1924), and *La psychanalyse de V. Hugo* (Paris, 1943).

27. Baudouin, *Hugo, Ibid.*

28. Baudouin, *Psychoanalysis and Aesthetics,* p. 31.

29. See, especially, *Des métaphores obsédantes au mythe personnel: introduction à la psychocritique* (Paris, 1964) *Introduction to the Psychoanalysis of Mallarmé* (1950), A. Henderson, Jr., and W. L. McLeason, trans. (Berkeley, 1963). A brief critical discussion of Mauron's views is found in John Cruickshank, "Psychocriticism and Literary Judgement," *British Journal of Aesthetics* 4(1964):155–159.

30. Mauron, *Métaphores,* p. 195.

31. From the point of view of literary criticism his most important works are *Psychanalyse du feu* (Paris, 1938), *L'eau et les rêves* (Paris, 1942), *L'air et les songes* (Paris, 1943), *Le terre et les rêveries de la volonté* (Paris 1940), *La terre et les rêveries du repos* (Paris, 1948), *La poétique de l'espace* (Paris, 1957), *La poétique de la rêverie* (Paris, 1961), and *La flamme d'une chandelle* (Paris, 1961).

32. See Pierre Quillet, *Bachelard,* Philosophies de Tous les Temps (Paris, 1964), pp. 155–157 et passim.

33. *La poétique de l'espace,* especially pp. 2–3.

34. Bachelard, *ibid.*

35. Bachelard, *ibid.*

36. Jean-Paul Sartre, *Being and Nothingness: An Essay on Phenomeno-*

logical Ontology (1943), Hazel E. Barnes, trans. (London, 1957), especially pp. 557 ff.

37. Geoffrey Gorer, "Psychoanalysis in the World," in Rycroft, ed., *Psychoanalysis Observed*, p. 49, rightly points out that the abstract and philosophical interpretation of psychoanalysis ignores the fact that "the theories are deduced from the observation of the interaction between two people in specified roles."

38. Lionel Trilling, "Freud and Literature," in Lionel Trilling, *The Liberal Imagination: Essays on Literature and Society* (London, 1951), p. 51.

39. See Roman Ingarden, *Das literarische Kunstwerk* (Halle, 1931).

4

SENSE AND NONSENSE IN HISTORY

Benjamin B. Wolman

HISTORY AS A SCIENCE

The common denominator of all sciences is the search for truth. The results of such a scientific search, called research, are presented in a set of propositions that tell the truth about certain parts or aspects of the universe. Sciences often overlap one another; astronomy, for instance, studies celestial bodies; geology is confined to our earth; but chemistry discovers the elements of which the entire universe is composed. Biology deals with all living organisms; anatomy, physiology, neuroanatomy, and neurophysiology study certain aspects of life but overlap one another considerably.

The ascertainment of empirical facts is usually the first step in scientific inquiry, and all sciences strive toward presenting their findings in an orderly way, in a system of validated and generalized propositions. Scientists abstract from particular individual characteristics of a given object or event and group together objects and events on the basis of at least one common denominator. Certainly each piece of iron, each seagull, and each thunderstorm is different. However, on the basis of certain similarities scientists describe not single pieces of iron, nor a particular seagull, nor a given thunderstorm, but a class of objects called iron, a class of birds called seagulls, and a class of events called thunderstorms. A physicist puts together in the class of acceleration the motion of trains, falling bodies, and flying rockets; a chemist puts amino acid and lysergic acid in the class of acids, despite the obvious differences between the two acids. Under the term "conditioning" psychologists group together a galaxy of mental processes that occur in a variety of people and animals. All scientists proceed to formulate empirical generalizations pertaining to a certain class of objects and events, and classification and generalization are usually the second major step in their work.

Some philosophers maintain that the subject matter of history differs from all other things that sciences study. According to Windelband[1] all sciences are nomothetic, for they seek to establish general laws (*nomos*). Historical events are however unique, unrepeatable, and defy generalization; they are idiophenomena, and history must therefore remain an idiographic science.

It may be worthwhile mentioning that no other branch of human knowledge produced as many general theories as history. Vico, Hegel, Marx, Spengler, Croce, Toynbee, to mention only a few, profusely and eloquently interpreted historical events in terms of general laws. It could be also argued that all sciences, and not only history study idiophenomena. The fact is that there was just one, unique, and unrepeatable American Declaration of Independence in 1776, one George Washington, and one, unique, and unrepeatable defeat of Napoleon at Moscow in 1812. But the same holds true in regard to physical and biological events; there was just one particular eruption of Vesuvius that destroyed Pompei; it was a particular hurricane, Camille, that caused so much damage in the Gulf area in August 1969; there is just one river Nile; and just one earth with one natural satellite, the moon. And yet scientists have been making generalized statements about volcanoes, hurricanes, rivers, and celestial bodies, as they have made generalized statements concerning gravitation, liberation of nations, osmosis, occupations, and military defeats.

Most historians, especially those concerned with biographies and political history, stress the role of the individual and describe particular events. Historians of social and economic development pay more attention to generalizations, such as social classes, social structures, and levels of income productivity. Nordau maintained that only such a generalized history of social institutions and movements makes sense,[2] but there is no reason to conclude that biography and political history are necessarily less scientific and less objective than the history of social movements. Scientific inquiry is judged not by its subject matter but by its scientific method, and that events studied by the scientist may be irrational does not make their study irrational.

METHODOLOGICAL PROBLEMS

Individual and generalized empirical propositions are either true or false; instance, the statements, "This lion lives in Africa" (an individual proposition) and "Lions are carnivorous animals" (a generalized proposition) are either true or false depending on the results of empirical test. Empirical propositions are verifiable, and the search for evidence is the most significant attribute of scientific inquiry.

The search for proof can proceeed along several paths. Sciences use planned observation, measurements, surveys, statistics, and other methods. The most reliable and precise method is controlled experimentation. The historian, however, is at a definite methodological disadvantage in comparison with other research workers.

Natural scientists deal with things that exist. A physicist, chemist, neurophysiologist, psychologist, and economist study observable or inferrable phenomena. They can observe and measure the same phenomena several times. A historian deals with a peculiar subject matter. He studies the events that lead to conquest of the Persian empire by Alexander, the destruction of the Jewish Temple by the Romans, the acceptance of Christianity by Emperor Constantine, the decline of the Roman empire, the rise of the feudal system, the Crusades, the Industrial Revolution, and World War II. But all these events that led to other events do not exist any longer. Historians study ruins and documents and try to recapture the past glories and calamities and to prove and interpret something they never saw.

In this aspect the methodological troubles of psychology are mild in comparison to the complexities of historical research. Psychology deals with individuals and groups and tries to assess their behavior. Simple, naturalistic observation does not do justice to the necessary rigorous pursuit of truth, and case studies and clinical interviews, whether as part of therapeutic, diagnostic, or purely research procedure, are heuristically useful but often lack objective evidence.[3] Freud's iconoclastic ideas were derived from incisive clinical studies, but their main value lies in opening new horizons rather than in adducing final proof. The most rigorous scientific method is controlled experimentation and, whenever possible, Freud's hypotheses have been subject to experimental test.[4]

Obviously history is not an experimental science, but it is not the only nonexperimental science. Astronomy and ethology are also not experimental, but they can apply repeatedly observational methods and measurement. It is futile to ask the question what would have happened if Cleopatra's nose were one inch longer, and it may be futile to try to "watch" the feelings, thoughts, and actions of Queen Elizabeth I, Gregory Hildebrand, and Abdul-Rashid.

Time is of utmost significance in the historical science. Irrelevant in mathematics, converted into a fourth dimension in physics, reduced to a minor role in astronomy, time has still retained its reign and rule over history. Time is like a strange hydra with millions of heads. This hydra eats its own heads and grows new ones. Historical time knows no mercy. Whatever happened happened once and does not exist any longer. There are sequences, outcomes, and aftermaths of the battle at Marengo, of the invasion of the lords of Attila, of the death of Cromwell, of Joshua's conquest of Canaan, of the congress in Nice, of the reform of Akhenaton, of the October Soviet Revolution, of the landing on the moon, and of the bomb at Hiroshima, but all these events belong to the past, and no power in the world can revive them.

Historians use a variety of methods appropriate for their particular subject matter, but their prime aim is searching for sources that could enable the reconstruction of facts. Excavations, papyrology, comparative philology, hermeneutics, heraldry, and the like are the various methods historians use in their efforts aimed at the findings of the historical truth.

HISTORICAL TRUTH

Even at this initial step historians face unpredictable hardships. Prior to Champollion's discovery of the Rosetta stone, historians were unable to decipher hieroglyphic texts and held erroneous notions of the history of ancient Egypt. The publication of the Sykes-Picot 1915 agreement and the opening of the tsarist archives by

Trotsky shed new light on the struggle of great powers for the Middle East. Today's secret American, Soviet, and Chinese documents hide a great deal of truth despite the avalanche of mass communication. A historian who will live in the thirtieth century, or probably an archeologist who will excavate the ruins of our brave, self-destructive era, may discover things unknown to the historians in the twenty-first century. Thus historical truth does not correspond to the concept of truth as by other empirical sciences that abide by the rules of critical epistemological realism.[5] No scientist has a final say and every scientific discovery may be superseded by a new and more precise one, but in history such a process is a daily occurrence.

THEORY FORMATION IN HISTORY

The historian has the task of (1) discovery and critical analysis of historical sources, (2) reconstruction of the past and its description (historiography), (3) generalization of historical facts, and (4) interpretation of these facts. This last task of a historian is historiosophy, or the science of history.[6]

No science is a mere collection of data as no house is a mere pile of bricks, Poincaré wrote.[7] Scientists endeavor to link the empirical data in a meaningful system. On the basis of thorough and empirically proven knowledge, scientists formulate hypothetical interpretations. The knowledge of facts is a prerequisite of their interpretation, and scientists proceed from empirical fact-finding and generalization to theory formation.

A theory is a set of hypothetical propositions that bind the empirical data in a causal, teleological, or any other interpretative system. The rule of empirical evidence does not apply in a simple and equivocal manner, to scientific theories. Probably one can interpret the same set of phenomena in more than one way, for examples, the corpuscular and wave theories of light, Pavlov's and Hull's theories of conditioning, and Freud's and Sullivan's theories of the unconscious. A theory is not necessarily true or false in the empirical sense. Methodologists of science usually expect a theory to meet three requirements, namely, (1) inner consistency, that is, freedom from self-contradictory statements (the principle of immanent truth), (2) agreement with proven empirical data (the principle of transcendent truth), and (3) heuristic advantage over other theories in promoting further research.[8]

RECONSTRUCTION

In most sciences empirical study of facts and theoretical interpretations are two distinct areas, but writing history (historiography) and interpreting historical facts (historiosophy) are not two clearly separated areas. Certainly the scientific task of historians is complex, for unlike other scientists, they cannot apply observational or experimental research methods. Historians must decipher the past from whatever was left behind from bygone epochs and reconstruct the past, filling the inevitable gaps and selecting issues and concepts that seem relevant to a particular historian or particular philosopher of history.

However, even the very reconstruction of the past is inevitably selective. No historian in the world can describe the entire story of everything that happened in the past. Usually historians choose what seems to them to be of particular relevance and importance. Certain aspects of historiographical omissions and inclusions are related to a particular aspect, time, or place. A political historian selects events that have bearing on government and intergovernmental relations, whereas a historian of science is concerned with research methods and discoveries. A historian of Cuba may hardly mention Belgium, and an ancient historian will safely omit the United States. But even within these clearly established tasks, scientific objectivity is hardly more than a glorious goal rarely and certainly never fully attained by historians. Consider political history. Was Napoleon an usurper who shed human blood to satisfy his megalomania or, using right or wrong methods, did he fight against reactionary forces and dream about a United States of Europe? Why, indeed, did Brutus murder Julius Caesar? What was the true cause of the Crusades—piety or greediness? Should historians of science describe celebrities only or include thousands of laboratory technicians? Should historians delve into the private life of a Hartley, Lavoisier, Newton, Helmholtz, Joule, or Sechenov? How far should they go in searching the impact of personal life on creative thought? Does the hero make history, or does history produce the hero? Is the Soviet regime what it is because of the peculiarities of the Russian mentality, or was the Russian mentality shaped by Mongolian and German invaders, by Ivan the Terrible, the Black Friday, and the Russian climate? What are, then, the relevant factors?

THE PRESENT AND PAST

Students of history are keenly aware of the inevitability of interpolating factual knowledge with hypothetical statements, but not all of them are aware of the subjective nature of their hypotheses.

> The historian aims to give us unitary pictures, and this requires the filling in of gaps in our verifiable knowledge. It requires engaging in a synthesis that depends on imaginative constructions. A good deal of historiography is necessarily speculative. Were the Crusades caused by the blocking of the path to the Holy Land or by the overflow of European population?
>
> The indisputable records of the past are relatively scant, partial and fragmentary and these fragments cannot all be embraced by the historian and instead he is forced to make some selection in which operative subjective considerations cannot be eliminated![9]

But all great historians, such as Lamprecht, Mommsen, Ranke, and Seignobos, insisted that the task of the historian is to tell the truth, the entire truth. Inasmuch as this is not entirely possible, some guidelines might be advisable. And there is advice given to American historians:

> The historian is not and cannot be concerned with all that did happen. He is and must be concerned with those particular events that did happen which turn out to be "basic" for his history. He is not concerned with the entire past, with all its infinitesimal detail; he is only with the "basic" or significant past. And it is precisely this "basic" past, this meaning and significance of the past, that is continually changing, that is cumulative and progressive. Writing the

> history of the United States, the historian uses what is basic and significant in that history-that-happened for 1927, or for 1944, is the principle that will control his selection of material. What is significant in American history he will understand in one way in 1927, and in somewhat different way in 1944.[10]

Apparently one should not read history books without checking the date of publication, the name of the author, and his whereabouts. French historiography of the Napoleonic period was not the same during the Napoleonic wars as it was during Restoration, and later during the rule of Napoleon III. There is more than one history of the conflict between Elizabeth and Mary Stuart, or the Fashoda conflict, or the biography of Descartes, or the Thirty Years War. Often there are more than two sides of the coin, and sometimes no one knows the entire truth. In most cases the historians believe in what they write and write what they believe in, but even good intentions cannot prevent bias. Quite often historians are exposed to public opinion or straight governmental pressures and are forced to write things they do not believe. I, for instance, find Soviet history very interesting, and I like to read and reread it, for it is never the same.

However, the lack of objectivity in historiography cannot be reduced to political pressures. Historians must select, and since the times of Dilthey[11] they search for a meaning.

> The "meaning" of any historical fact is what it does, how it continues to behave and to operate, what consequences follow from it. . . . We understand any history-that-has-happened in terms of the future: our principle for selecting what is basic in that history involves a reference to its predicted outcome. Our "emphasis" will be determined by what we find going on in the present. But what we find there is not yet fully worked out. Rather, the present suggest what will eventuate in times to come. Thus we understand what is basic in a history in terms of what we call some "dynamic element" in the present, some present tendency directed toward the future.
>
> The historian must thus choose among the various possibilities of the present that tendency, that predicted future, which he judges to be dynamic or controlling.[12]

Certainly historiography is influenced by the present time, that is, the time when the historian writes, but this does not mean that the past is influenced by the future. Past events can be evaluated differently in different times, depending on their present impact.

The results of the past change and the chain of consecutive events is never ending and continuously changing. Consider the Locarno Treaty of 1925. Historians could not have described and interpreted it in the same manner in 1930, before Hitler's rise to power, as during World War II. It is not only a matter of attitudes. It has much to do with the real consequences, as they emerge and as people realize their influence. The flux of history is incessant, and no historian, unless he is also a prophet, can predict the future impact of the war in Vietnam and of the landing on the moon.

HISTORY AS A STUDY OF BEHAVIOR

Some historians and philosophers of history inspired by the mythological tradition of man's alleged uniqueness, sought some special and lofty qualities in the latest stages of evolution of a certain species during the last couple of thousands of years. Overlooking or ignoring hundreds of thousands of years of evolution of this particular species, such men as Vico, Hegel, Marx, Spengler, Croce, and Toynbee attributed to the last few thousand of years of mankind some peculiar tendencies, aims, and destinies not discovered by biologists in regard to the history of other species nor found by anthropologists and archeologists in the earlier and prehistorical stages of the human species.

Methodologically speaking, the search for more complex phenomena in the higher evolutionary levels is a legitimate scientific task, but discoveries must be made rather than taken for granted. The fact that at a certain evolutionary level a certain species became capable of communicating with the use of symbolic signs is a highly important event, but, as such does not necessarily herald a radical change in behavioral patterns of the particular species. Thus, too often history records a description of lives that pretend to be more than they really were.

Comparative psychology, sociology, and anthropology bear witness to the fact that the so-called progress and alleged changes in human behavior have not been so large and significant as some thinkers would like them to be. There have been substantial changes in the technique and tools used in production of food, housing, and clothing, but today as well as 100,000 years ago, people have toiled for food, clothing, and shelter. Atomic warheads and ballistic missiles are not exactly a copy of a dagger and a bow, but ultimately, they serve the same purpose. Regardless of the pill, human beings are born as a result of the ancient method of sexual intercourse, and they grow, mature, decline, and die as ever. Cavemen and skyscraper dwellers, lonely prehistorical shepherds and ultramodern private jet-owners are born, eat, drink, and die in practically the same way, and all of them fear death.

Preciously little has changed. What has changed was not to please Hegel's dialectical fantasies or Croce's humanistic ideas or Marx's economic contradictions. The changes that took place have been, as always, a result of interaction between man and his social and physical environment. History is a story of events that transpired along multiple lines studied by physics, geology, biochemistry, neurophysiology, and human behavior in its multiple forms and ramifications.

It seems therefore that the only way of seeing the past in an objective way is to dethrone the human species and to depedestal history, and finally accept the Copernican point of view. Man is not the center of the universe, and he better take care lest his magnificent progress turn against him and destroy him together with his pretentious aspirations. The entire history of the human species is just a small segment of the natural history and historical events that follow the causal rules pertinent to other natural phenomena. The fact that men build houses and bridges does not make human history less natural, nor does it exclude historical science from the group of biological sciences. Birds build nests, and beavers build bridges; some fish and wolves live in families, and the rebellion against parental authority is not a particularly human privilege.

The all-embracing laws of historical development are often tacitly or even unconsciously assumed, and,

> no historical description or explanation can possibly dispense with abstractions. To be sure, the individual man Caesar will never occur again, but all that we know about him depends upon the assumption of certain laws. In this respect human history does not differ from natural history. . . . Indeed, every physicist in the laboratory as well

as the engineer engaged in testing a bridge or particular engine is engaged with an individual object. But just as natural history depends upon general physical science, so does human history depend upon and presuppose general knowledge of the laws of human conduct. Take any attempt at historical description or explanation (explanation is but a developed description). We say Caesar was killed because he was ambitious or too generous to his former enemies, and Brutus conspired because he was patriotic or because he was a greedy usurer who could not resist the opportunity to gather revenues of provinces, etc. Do not these and other historic explanations assume certain laws or uniformities in human conduct? To be sure, in human history these laws are assumed tacitly, while in natural history they are explicit; and this is true partly because the laws of physics dealing with phenomena capable of indefinite repetitions, are simpler and more readily verified.[13]

It seems therefore that the interpretation of history must descend from its Olympus and join other natural sciences that analyze the behavior of individuals and groups. Freud has largely contributed to such an approach to history. He tore down the sacrosanct stories about the alleged human kindness and morality and exposed the true human nature from its animalistic roots to its most sublime cravings. Man is neither beast nor angel, but his nature is a strange, irrational, and often incomprehensible mixture of both. Culture to Freud meant restraint, and "much of our most highly valued cultural heritage has been acquired at the cost of sexuality and by the restriction of sexual motive forces," stated Freud in his last and final summary of psychoanalysis.[14]

BELLIGERENCE

One of the outstanding features of the past and present behavior of the human species is its belligerence. All animals fight for survival, and eating implies the destruction of what is eaten; thus, animal belligerence is primarily determined by hunger and other needs related to survival. Animals fight when there is a danger to their life; it is either a danger of starvation or a danger of being killed; it is either a danger of not having anything to eat or a threat of being eaten by by another animal. Thus animals partake in aggressive fights for food and defensive fights to prevent becoming someone's food.

Most fights in the animal world are interspecific, that is, one species fights against another. Wolves attack deer and sheep, but rarely fight to death among themselves. Even when food is scarce, animals rarely engage in intraspecific fights to kill. All animals compete with one another for food, access to water, place to rest, sex, and so on. In most cases pecking order develops, and the stronger animals secure a better access to food, water, and other needs. On rare occasions of severe overcrowding, intraspecific fights may become fatal;[15] in most situations, however, the weaker members of the species escape, and only in some rare cases they are killed.

> Aggressive encounters between members of the same species occur in most vertebrates and in many invertebrates. . . . [However] overt fighting to the death very rarely occurs in vertebrates, and it is doubtful whether it ever occurs in mammals under natural conditions. . . . Fighting is ritualized into display, threat, submission and appeasement. . . .[16]

The animal world knows little intraspecific wars.

> There are very few animals which, even when threatened with starvation, will attack an equal sized animal of their own species with the intention of devouring it. I only know this to be definitely true of rats and a few related rodents.[17]

Human beings are one of the few species that engage in intraspecific murderous fights. Men do not kill men to eat them; cannibalism is rather a rare phenomenon, but men kill men to take away food and to enslave other men.

A perusal of human history indicates that the human species has overdone all prey animals in belligerence. The history of humanity is full of peace-preaching speeches, slogans, and prayers, but it knows hardly any peaceful times. Between 1820 and 1945, 59 million people were killed in wars. Human history started with wars, and it seems to continue in the same vein. Of course every war comes to an end when the enemies are killed or surrender. Carthage was a threat to Rome, therefore "Carthago delendam esse" ("Carthage must be destroyed") was the slogan as long as Carthage existed. After the war, the victors are usually on the side of peace;

for it is impossible to perpetuate a war against a nonexisting enemy. On the smoldering ruins of Babylon, Carthage, and Jerusalem, the victorious armies marched with arms of war and slogans of peace. No victor ever wanted to have "his peace" disturbed; no emperor or dictator planned to continue fighting after completing his conquest. The eagles of war have always carried in their claws an innocent dove of peace, but no peace, not even the Pax Romana, lasted too long.

Most insects, mammals, and all human beings practice territorial wars.[18] They either invade a foreign territory or defend their territory against invaders. Human tribes, groups, and nations led by autocratic rulers and democratic leaders have always fought for fertile lands, gold mines, and iron ores or for an access to open seas and control of land and water routes.

INTRAGROUP FIGHTS

As mentioned before, rats, some insects, and practically all human beings engage in fratricidal wars. Group living has never been a deterent against intragroup fighting. Certainly living together offers numerous opportunities for cooperation, as described by the anarchist philosopher Peter Kropotkin.[19] Such an intraspecific cooperation increases the chances for survival of the members of the group. In many instances, herbiverous animals form a defensive ring against predatory beasts. On the other hand, a pack of wolves has a better chance of killing a deer than a single wolf.

However, such a unity does not last too long. When a herd runs over a cliff escaping from danger, a stronger animal pushes a weaker one down into the abyss. As soon as the hunt is over, wolves fight one another for a bigger share.

Human beings do the same, but they often outdo animals. As soon as the persecutions of Christians in Rome came to an end, the Christians began to persecute others. The "great" French revolutionaries who rebelled against the king's tyranny sent to death not only their enemies but also their most ardent supporters, the Herbertists. Soon the Reign of Terror had its Thermidor and Robespierre was a victim of his favorite guilliotine. The victorious

Bolsheviks soon got rid not only of the counter-revolutionary "white" armies, but also of the anarchists and the left wing Social-Revolutionaries who had helped them in the October Revolution. After Lenin's death his faithful disciples engaged for decades in the mass murder of their most devoted comrades.

The Biblical myth of Cain and Abel is a case in point; so is the story of Romulus and Remus. Territorial wars were called "patriotic"; intragroup wars were called other fancy names. In the religious wars of the sixteenth and seventeenth centuries good Christians who prayed (in Latin) to the god of mercy murdered other good Christians who prayed to the same god (in another language). During the American Civil War (1861–1865) more lives were lost than in any other war the Americans fought.

THE SO-CALLED PROGRESS

Weakness seems to provoke aggression; balance of power (a euphemism for the fear of retaliation) restrains it. The mighty Roman empire, at least for a while came to terms with the Parthians, but it destroyed the Jewish Temple and tortured the Christians. The great Catholic Church perssecuted Jews and heretics (Albigenses, Waldenses, Hussites, and others) who have never represented a real threat to the Church. But there was the Greek Orthodox Church that dared to break away and challenge the papal authority, yet the Roman Catholics, so eager to burn John Huss, never set Constantinople or Moscow afire. They intrigued the best they could and incited the Polish kings Stefan Batory and Zygmunt Waza against the Greek Orthodox Christians, but they never declared a holy war nor did they institute an inquisition against them. Wars become "holy" when one is sure of victory and there is lots of looting; otherwise it is just a "necessary" war.

Obviously some Germans "needed" Polish wheat, French iron, and Caucasian oil. Some other Germans needed to prove their military power. Today, after they have lost the war, the Germans are economically and in any other way better off than they were ever before, even at the peak of their national glory. The war was, as it usually is, an insane act leading to mass destruction and mass murder with no real gain for anyone. Were Germans a pack of wolves, no Hitler-type leader could have driven them to do what they did. But in the subanimal abyss of human nature there is room for most paradoxical phenomena. Germany was overpopulated in 1939 and needed *Lebensraum;* after the war the Germans from Silesia and Sudeten immigrated to Germany and there is no overpopulation today. In the Thirty Years War the emperor of the Holy Roman empire wanted to put his hand on the property that became secularized, and the pious Protestant lords joined Luther in order to confiscate property that formerly belonged to the Church. The Holy Crusades, started by the inspiring words, "C'est le Dieu qui veut" ("God wills it"), invoked the good Lord for the sake of the merchants from Venice and the Byzantinian rulers who paid well for the "holy" enterprise.

Mankind is definitely making progress. In the past, one had to use a clumsy sword to kill one "enemy" at a time; the indolent and ineffectual Crusaders killed a couple of hundred thousand Jews; the total loss of human life in the Hundred Years War was less than in today's Vietnam. In modern times, 6 million Jews and 4 million other people were gassed in a spectacularily short time, and millions were murdered elsewhere. In the "primitive," barbaric past prior to the great advent of modern technology, world wars were unthinkable. By now, we have had two world wars in one century, and a most spectacular third one lurks around the corner.

WHO HATES WHOM?

Men do not hate chickens; they "love" to eat them. Julius Caesar did not hate the Gauls; he simply subjugated them. Napoleon did not hate the Spaniards; he merely wanted his family to rule the world. But if chickens have human feelings they surely hate their murderers. The Gauls hated Julius Caesar and fought against him. The Spaniards fanatically hated Napoleon and offered a desperate resistance to his armies. Apparently, the defenders hate the aggressors; do the aggressors hate their victims?

Quite often conquerors make up excuses for their acts of aggression. Hitler never professed hatred for Austria and Czechoslovakia.

When he attacked Poland on September 1, 1939, he ordered some of his henchmen to shoot at his own border guards. At sunrise he announced on the radio that the Poles opened fire on German soldiers "und es wird zurückgeschossen" ("the fire has been returned"). The apparent lie had a purpose: to prevent or at least to slow down allied help to Poland.

Hanna Arendt, who dismissed Eichmann's guilt in a cavalier manner, apparently misunderstood why the Jews only resisted the Nazis at the end. The civilian, scattered, unarmed Jewish population has never had a greater chance for a successful resistance to the German army than did the united armies of Poland, Holland, Norway, France, Belgium, and a half dozen other armies. However, the mighty 80 million Germans did not disclose their murderous plans to the scattered Jewish refugees. Almost to the last moment the Nazis successfully hid the truth about the extermination camps. The emaciated Jews in ghetto Warsaw, decimated by hunger and typhoid fever, were told that they were being sent to labor camps, because otherwise they might rebel and cause the Nazis more difficulties than their handful of partisans in the ghetto uprising of 1943.

How much the Nazis hated the Jews is another question, but they certainly "loved" Jewish money, gold extracted from Jewish teeth, soap cakes made of Jewish bones, and lampshades made of Jewish skin. It is quite possible that they hated the Japanese more than the Jews, but the Jews have always been an easy scapegoat.[20] The French may dislike the British and vice versa, but the chances of a war across the channel could be substantially increased if one of the two nations would become an easy target. The Russians hate China more than they hate Czechoslovakia, but in 1968 they occupied Prague and not Peiping. The Czechoslovakians raised their fists in helpless hatred; the Russian tanks opened fire unemotionally.

THE GREAT HISTORICAL LEADERS

The mass hatred and mass violence that occurred on several occasions resemble animal "mobbing." At the sight of an intruder, birds attack the common enemy en masse, no matter who he is. The fights between Moslems and Hindus in India, Protestants and Catholics in Belfast, and the persecution of Kurds and Armenians are not recollections from the Stone Age or from intrahuman races.

Human cruelty to minorities has been substantially increased by a few dozen especially aggressive individuals who have gained an uncanny, almost hypnotic control over large numbers of people. History is full of chieftains, prophets, saviors, gurus, dictators and other megalomaniacs who somehow managed to obtain the support from some people in order to enslave them. Almost every historical hero strove to his own immortality and made sure to destroy as many human lives as he could before his own death. Pursuing their particular goals, most "heroes" fostered hostile feelings to neighbors and incited violence. Some of them seem to have believed in their historic mission and thought of themselves as saviors of perplexed humanity. Fanatics obsessed by supranatural delusions of grandeur, overwhelmed by persecution complex, driven by an unsatiable desire of power pushed millions of people to mass murder and self-destruction. The story of leadership is probably the most weird part of the bizarre history of humanity. Anxiety-ridden individuals, paranoiac such as Stalin, paranoid schizophrenics such as Tiberius and Calvin, sadists such as Torquemada and Hitler exercised more power than rational leaders.

THE DEATH INSTINCT

Observations on sadism and masochism and the atrocities practiced by the Germans during World War I in 1920 forced Freud to revise his theory of instincts. Freud postulated then two basic instincts, Eros and Thanatos. The aim of Eros is to bind and preserve, and the aim of Thanatos is to undo and destroy. "We may suppose," Freud wrote in 1938, "that the final aim of the destructive instinct is to reduce living things to an inorganic state. For this reason we also call it the death instinct."[21] According to Freud, destructiveness is primarily directed toward oneself in a drive toward death.

> It is indeed a strange instinct that is occupied with the destruction of its own organic home. . . . If it is true that once in an inconceivable past life arose out of inanimate matter, then in accordance with our

> hypothesis, an instinct must at that time have come into being whose aim it was to abolish life once more and to re-establish the inorganic state of things. . . .[22]

Basically, the death instinct turns inwardly and is self-destructive. But "if these forces are turned to destruction in the external world," Freud wrote in 1932 in reply to Einstein,

> the living creature will be relieved and the effect must be beneficial. As a result of a little speculation, we have come to suppose that this instinct is at work in every living being and is striving to bring it to ruin and to reduce life to its original condition of inanimate matter. Thus it quite seriously deserves to be called a death instinct, while the erotic instincts represent the effort to live. The death instinct turns into the destructive instinct if, with the help of special organs, is directed outwards, on to objects. The living creature preserves its own life, so to say, by destroying an extraneous one. Some portion of the death instinct, however, remains operative within the living being, and we have sought to trace quite a number of normal and pathological phenomena to this internalization of the destructive instinct. We have even been guilty of the heresy of attributing the origin of conscience to this diversion inwards of aggressiveness. You will notice that is by no means a trivial matter if this process is carried too far: it is positively unhealthy. On the other hand if these forces are turned to destruction in the external world, the living creature will be relieved and the effect must be beneficial. This would serve as a biological justification for all the ugly and dangerous impulses against which we are struggling. It must be admitted that they stand nearer to Nature than does our resistance to them, for which an explanation also needs to be found.[23]

Freud's hypothesis concerning the destructive instincts have been widely criticized. According to this hypothesis all life should end in suicide, unless or until external outlets were found. However, animal and human infants fight for their own lives; hostility and destructiveness are not derivatives of death insinct but of the drive for own survival. Death is never the goal of fight; the goal is destruction, either in order to eat or to avoid being eaten. Hostility is initially object directed; how it turns inward is a problem to be discussed later on.

The unborn organism is endowed with instinctual forces, Eros and Ares, love and hate, both serving the protection and preservation of life and both capable of cathexes of the mental energies, libido and destrudo, at their disposal.[24] Neonates have no object relations, neither object love nor object hate. Gradually, all subjects serving the child's survival, such as mother's breasts or the bottle, elicit object cathexis of libido, and whatever is a threat to him evokes object cathexis of destrudo. Threat evokes fear and fear sounds an alarm bell. Fear produces one or both of the reactions, fight or flight. Aggressors are people who fear they may die unless they devour someone; defenders are people who fear aggressors. *Those who fear, hate, and those who hate, fear.*

In normal ontogenetic development the libido becomes gradually, and to a great extent, object cathected. In normal adults, the libido is distributed between self and object cathexis, that is, between care of oneself and care for others. Destrudo is always the same, archaic, primordial, and primary, and there cannot be developmental stages analogous to the developmental stages of libido because there is no progress in destrudo. Destrudo serves self-defense and survival; when object love fails, part of it turns into secondary narcissistic love, part into destrudo. Destrudo and libido can be presented as two types of mental energy, sort of kinds of fuel that seem to be transformable into each other. In states of greatest emergencies, severe deprivation, starvation, exhaustion, and pain, the destrudo takes over. Destrudo is the more primitive energy of the organism, always present and leading to outbursts of rage in animals and to temper tantrums in infants. It is however put under the control of the ego and discharged in self-defense in normal adults.

In states of serious regression in schizophrenia the destrudo is the sole controlling drive of the organism.[25] In normal adults it is partially fused with libido, partially suppressed by the ego, partially sublimated, and is never a pure, uncontrolled, savage freedom. An uninhibited, free, object-directed destrudo is genocidal and a menace to others; when destrudo is self-directed, it is a menace to oneself.

All available empirical data point to the survival origin of hostility. Consider xenophobia. Men and animals fear strange and unfamiliar creatures, but experience may modify behavior, and fear of the unknown can be reinforced, mollified, or even extinguished. Kittens raised for four months together with rats did not kill them, but 85 percent of the kittens raised by mothers who killed rats did likewise.[26] If Freud were right, kittens and infants would be born endowed with self-hate, which might eventually turn outwardly. According to the Thanatos theory, aggression is merely an outwardly directed self-destructive instinct of death. All empirical data prove that, with very rare exceptions, the entire animal and human behavior is directed to survival and not toward death. Were Freud right, suicide should have been the primary and universal behavioral pattern and genocide the secondary outcome or restraint in self-destruction. Accordingly, whenever an animal or a human would fail to kill itself, it would turn the wrath against others.

Apparently, nothing of that kind ever happened. All animals struggle for survival, and no animal strives to die. Death is a fact and not a goal, but protection of life is the main goal of all animal and human behavior. Apparently all living nature resists destruction, and the lust for life is the main driving force. The lust for life has two channels, love and hate. In the fight for survival, fight is the first and main behavioral pattern; thus Ares, the drive for war is more primitive, more archaic drive. In the phylogenetic evolution, fight comes much earlier than love; all animals devour, but only a few species develop consideration and love. Ares is universal, Eros is limited to a few higher species and mankind. Human beings are driven by both impulses, by hate and by love.

THE FEAR OF DEATH

All animals fight for survival, but it seems that only human beings are aware of the inescapable dead end of life. Worrying about food has always been the most important and time absorbing action of human beings, whether they were hunters, fishermen, shepherds, farmers, or modern factory workers. Plenty of food has represented good life and good chances for survival, and lack of food has meant starvation and death. Human societies therefore always have been divided along the lines of those who have more and those who have less. The fear of death by starvation has been always on human minds, and in periods of history people acted out their fear of want and death by a frenetic accumulation of possessions and by striving to become rich and thus protected. The property motive did not change much in the last 50,000 years. When one has little, he may lose it and starve soon, but whoever has plenty does not worry about possible little losses. When one is poor, he may fall prey to draught, shortage, and depression, but whoever owns lands, mines, and factories can survive the worst economic crises. He may increase his security by surrounding himself with slaves, servants, guards, and henchmen whose livelihood depends on his wealth and cunning. If they are armed well, he may sleep in peace.

The most frequent causes of death are hunger, war, and old age. People have always been obsessed with the fear of death, and most of their behavior has been motivated by this fear. Large posessions allay the fear of death by starvation, and large armies allay the fear of death from the hands of enemies. Dead people can not carry arms, thus murder of true or alleged enemies has been the traditional method used by great kings and little gangsters.

Human belligerence seems to be related to human weakness and cowardliness. Members of all biological species die, but they are unable to think about it. They cope with danger to their life as it comes and they fight whenever they are hungry or threatened. Human being are superbly endowed in the ability to worry about their future. The feeling of security is a manmade term derived from man's insecurity. Were men immortal, immune against diseases, protected against pain and injury, and sure of a bountiful supply of oxygen, water, food, and all other needs, mankind would probably calm down and renounce wars. Because such a perfect state is impossible, Charles Fourier, Karl Marx, and many others dreamed about a future paradise where there will be no wars and no worries. These fantasies are replicas of older prophesies about the hereafter—the messiah and an imaginary omniscient, omnipotent, and loving being that will bring redemption and eternal love and peace.

One may evade death by starvation and murder, but no one can live forever. Denial has always been the choice defense mechanism in dealing with the fear of death. Since the very beginning of the human species, people have made up elaborate stories about the hereafter, trying hard to believe that life must not come to an end. The Egyptian pyramids and the Greek sarcophagi bear witness to man's desire to stay alive forever.

It seems that in many ancient and prehistoric civilizations men were more concerned with imaginary perpetuation of life after death than with life proper. The gradual changes in man's ideas concerning immortality have been reflected in the philosophies of Plato, Philo, St. Augustine, Mohammed, Maimonides, St. Aquinas, Luther, Calvin, and many others. The essential idea remained, however, the same. The fear of death has created the defense mechanism of denial. Men can not accept the inevitable and fantasize about eternal life. Sometimes they pattern the future hereafter after the most peaceful period of life—life in the womb. Sometimes they give vent to their sadistic and masochistic impulses and paint the hereafter in the bleak colors of a purgatory and inferno. In either case, the human soul never dies.

ESCAPE INTO MAGIC

Modern times brought additional refinement to the age-old fear of death and to defense mechanisms erected against this fear. However, these new ideas and, especially,

> the Hegelian philosophy of history, is substantially a metaphysical adaptation of the Christian view. God is one and history is the unfolding of God. He unfolds himself on the human scene. God is primarily a logician unfolding Himself on Hegel's logic. But the world-drama requires antagonists. Therefore the Absolute must create His own antithesis in the process of unfolding, and in that struggle the synthesis is created, and so history moves on in an unending spiral. Applied to symbolic, classic and romantic art, to all other human institutions, and to history in general, the Hegelian dialectic made historians sensitive to three-stage patterns. . . . Substituting economic production for God, Marx got dialectical materialism.[27]

It seems that the search for a particular sense in history beyond the empirical facts of human behavior is another way of denying the apparent lack of consistency and plan in all natural history including the story of the human species. If there are laws of historical development, they certainly are not terribly lofty nor necessarily acceptable to man's wishful thinking of himself as the center of the universe and rational living.[28]

Toynbee tried to deny the inevitably unflattering interpretation of human history by the use of an old technique often applied by

Greek playwrights—the *deus ex machina.* The entire story that Toynbee is telling does not necessarily bear witness to God's providence as the driving power in history. Toynbee introduced God at the critical moment, saying that "We cannot say for certain that our doom is at hand; and yet we have no warrant for assuming that it is not."[29] Thus, it is obvious that the doom is at hand and only wishful thinking can deny it. Then Toynbee introduced the hope that "We may and must pray that a reprieve which God has granted to our society once will not be refused if we ask for it again in a contrite spirit and with a broken heart."[30]

This statement is indeed a denial of Toynbee's entire life work. Toynbee's religious philosophy of history is a denial of Toynbee's historical laws, and Toynbee's historical law leaves no room for his surprising "occasionalism."[31] Anyway, one cannot have both in the same system of thought.

I do not intend to analyze in this essay the ideas of C. A. Beard, R. Aron, A. O. Lovejoy, H. Butterfield, and others. The point that I am trying to make is that history of mankind is a history of behavior of a certain species that calls itself *Homo sapiens.* The evidence concerning "sapiens" is rather ambiguous.

THE ORIGINS OF COOPERATION

The greatest conquerer of ancient times, Alexander the Great, was in a sense, a forerunner of the idea of universal brotherhood. In his banquet at Opis in 324 B.C., Alexander called for a union of the victorious Macedonians with the defeated Persians. "He proclaimed for the first time, through a brotherhood of peoples, a brotherhood of man."[33] This idea was not entirely new; Isaiah prophesized peace and cooperation centuries before Alexander. In fact, the Ten Commandments, dated about 1500 B.C., advocated "Thou Shalt Not Kill."

The origin of aggression and hostility can be easily traced in the animal world because all animals eat (destroy) and resist being eaten (destroyed). Nothing comparable to this simple story can be said about cooperation, friendship, and love. Ares, the god of war, is primeval. Eros, the god of love, was born much later and his origins are shrouded in mystery and are probably rooted in two related factors, namely group living and sexuality.

There is no doubt that many living creatures live in herds, groups and colonies. Consider corals, fish, birds, sheep, wolves. Living together does not necessarily produce cooperation defined as acting in a manner that protects everyone's life. When sheep escape danger, the weak ones fall prey to predatory animals. Slow-moving fish in a school are eaten by bigger and faster fish. Physical proximity is not a guarantee for cooperation in the animal world nor among human being. Though the formation herds, flocks and schools usually increases the security of the individual against external, extraspecific enemies, it does not protect the individual from a pecking order and outright oppression from within the species herd, tribe, and nation.

History provides numerous examples of unity against external enemies combined with internal oppression. The sheer fact of living in Sparta protected the helots from the swords of Athenians, but it did not protect them from being persecuted by the ruling class of Spartians and their secret police, the Kripteia. The Soviet army defended the Russian people against Hitler's mass murder, but it did not protect them against Stalin's madness. Thus one must seek the origins of cooperation beyond physical proximity and territorial neighborhood, though the role of such proximity in the development of cooperation cannot be dismissed. Most probably the members of flocks, herds, and packs are blood relatives, who stay together not out of great love for one another, but because they started life in the same place and, by the rule of inertia, stay together.

The origins of affection and care are linked to procreation by sex and parental behavior. One can hardly imagine any emotional involvement in species that procreate in a nonsexual way. However, sex is not love; insects for instance, procreate sexually, but we can hardly find deep emotional involvement in insects. On higher evolutionary levels mating may become associated with care and protection. Nature is not too orderly nor systematic and high evolutionary levels are not necessarily accompanied with better marital relations. Male wolves, for instance, are loyal to their females, but not all mammals, including humans, follow this example. On the whole sexual behavior in higher species includes less rape and more courtship, less mechanical motion and more emotion, and the inter-individual relations, such as joint search for food and mutual protection, last much longer than the mating period. Many species develop lasting male-female relationships and stay together after copulation. Thus marriage is not a human artifact, but a product of evolution that evokes tender feelings and loyalty.

There is no one universal pattern of parenthood, though most birds take care of their offspring; wolves are good fathers, but their cousin species, the bears, are bad fathers, and often the mother bear has to protect the young against their own father. Most families are composed of both parents and children, but many families do not include fathers. Human families offer a spectacular variety of types, matriarchal and patriarchal, polygamous and polyandrous, group and individual. The Lesu practice all of them, the Tibetans perfer polyandry, whereas most ancient Oriental tribes favor polygamy.

Sexual attachment usually prevents or at least mollifies hostility. In higher biological levels there is an unmistaken trend toward an increased cooperation between the mates and increased child care. This evolutionary process introduces a new direction of libido cathexis. Instead of all libido being cathected in the survival of the individual, part of it becomes invested in other individuals. In the process of the phylogenetic evolution, selfish love came first. At a certain evolutionary stage this love branched off. Part of the libido energy remained and will always remain self-directed, part of it became cathected in others in a sexual and desexualized way. One cannot therefore say that sex is love, love being defined as protection of life. Sex can be practiced as a mechanical copulation with no feelings for the partner. Prostitution, rape, sadism, and sexual murder do not include much love.

Yet love originates in the phylogenetic evolution of sexuality. Love, defined as the willingness to protect life, was impossible as long as procreation was nonsexual. Sexuality is partnership, and the two who interact in sex may also interact in other areas. When they stay together after copulation, defend each other, and help each other in the search for food, in a more or less stable relationship, they form a "marriage." Affection, kindness, and loyalty are not always a part of a sexual relationship, but they originate in sexuality and evolve out of sexual relations. Sometimes they may transcend sexuality:

> When we are in love a considerable amount of narcissistic libido overflows on to the object. It is even obvious, in many forms of love choice, that the object serves as a substitute for some unattained ego ideal of our own . . .
>
> If the sexual overestimation and the being in love increase even further . . . the tendencies whose trend is toward direct sexual satisfaction may now be pushed back entirely . . . the ego becomes more and more unassuming and modest, and the object more and more sublime and precious, until at last it gets possession of the entire self-love of the ego, whose self-sacrifice thus follows as a natural consequence . . . Traits of humility, of the limitation of narcissism, and of self-injury occur in every case of being in love.[33]

PATTERNS OF INTERACTION

Human interaction can be divided roughly into life protective and life destructive, that is, friendly (erotic) and hostile (aretic) patterns. The aretic behavior appears earlier in the phylogenetic evolution, but the higher species including the human race are capable of life-protective and life-destructive relationships.

Instrumentalism

Friendly attitudes can be divided into three types, according to the objectives of the participating individuals. When an individual uses another individual or a group of individuals for the satisfaction of his own needs, that is, for protection and improvement of his own life, such a relationship is instrumental. Slaves-owners used their slaves, and their attitude to their slaves was instrumental. As a rule, slave-owners took care of their slaves, just as a craftsman takes care of his tools and instruments. An instrumental attitude is not hostile or destructive; it is merely exploitative.

Simultaneously with slavery and especially after its abolishment several other instrumental patterns developed. Using other people's skill, labor and resources is perhaps the most general pattern of human relations, often covered up by pious speeches and other types of disguise. When a "free" farmer hires a "free" farmhand, he hires him not because the poor farm-worker needs money, but because the farmer needs help and he intends to pay his employee less than his product is worth. He would not hire him if he were not sure of that. But, alas! The farmhand offers his services not because he cares for the farmer's profits but because by working he can earn his living. His attitude is as instrumental as that of his employer, and who is going to use whom and how much depends on a variety of factors, such as supply and demand, the relative force of industry and labor unions, and public opinion and political forces. Marx's theory of class struggle is a gross oversimplification of the issues involved, for the interaction of instrumental forces follows a variety of behavioral patterns and not just the Hegelian-Marxian dialectic. Consider the struggle between Themistocles and his opponents in Athens, or the story of the strife between the Plebeians and the Patricians in Rome, or the opposition of many labor unions to equal rights for Negro workers in the United States, or the complete domination of the labor unions by the Communist party in the U.S.S.R.

Instrumentalism is probably the most frequent pattern of human relations; it starts in the ontogenetic evolution in intrauterine life. The neonate, the infant, the child "loves" his mother because and as long as she satisfies his needs. All people use others and are used by others to a lesser or greater extent.

Mutuality

Though instrumentalism is not hostility, it easily leads to hostile clashes. Everybody being instrumental inevitably clashes with someone's instrumentalism. Slaves resent being enslaved and rebel against their owners who resent rebellious slaves. Exploited workers resent being exploited and form unions struggling for the biggest possible share of their products. One may doubt the possibility of a final solution for all human ills, but there have been serious efforts to alleviate them.

The awareness of the unescapable conflicts of instrumentalism often leads to a higher level of human relationship. Instead of trying to use others and avoiding being used by others, people come to agreements of mutual aid. Instead of hoping to get everything without giving anything in return, people agree on a give and take, mutual type relationship. The rationale of this relationship stems from the principle of equal rights.

Sexuality and physical proximity play significant roles in the development of mutuality. In many animal species sex is basically an act of rape; rape is a common pattern in monkeys, apes, and other infrahuman beings. The so-called feminine surrender is a mythological excuse for male brutality. But even in ancient times women were not entirely at the mercy of males who tried to coerce them. Fathers and brothers of unmarried women and husbands of married women defended their females against other males. The Romans had to come to some agreement with the male relatives of the Sabine women, and Israel's patriarchs had to pay off their future in-laws.

Freud's *Totem and Taboo* is a case in point.[34] Sex can be a purely instrumental act when a man coerces a woman. But, inasmuch as many men may desire the same woman, some sort of social agreement becomes a necessity; otherwise a destructive war of all against all may ensue. Small wonder that ancient Israel lawmakers instituted the "Thou shall not covet" rule among the Ten Commandments. Modern marriage is a social agreement based on equal rights. A man cannot buy, sell, or force a woman to become his wife; other men (and women) would not allow it. The principle of mutuality, that is of a give-and-take relationship, based on equal rights for both sexes, is gradually winning universal support for sociological and psychological reasons. Sociologically, no society can tolerate an unlimited and unrestrained inner strife, and a reasonable amount of cooperation is a prerequisite for survival of all. Thus all societies regulate marital relations and establish a set of laws aimed at the prevention of intrasocietal clashes and violence. Psychologically, infantile sexuality is instrumental masturbation whereas adult sexuality is a mutual relationship. Some individuals perpetuate their immature behavioral patterns and use others sexually; mature individuals seek satisfaction for both parties involved. A marriage between two mature individuals is a give-and-take, mutual relationship.

Sexual and nonsexual relationships based on the desire to avoid clashes and destruction must take into consideration the rights of both partners. Mutuality enters all areas of human life. Good neighborhood relations, business partnerships, union memberships, cultural, religious and political associations, and the entire role of democratic government and public administration are based on mutuality. Mutuality is not always pure love; most often it is a calculated agreement aimed at the avoidance of destruction. Mutual tolerance is not always a sign of love or a sentimental dove of universal peace; most often it is the recognition of the fact that the only way for survival is to allow everyone the same amount of freedom. It is a prudent choice between all freedom for some or some freedom for all. It is not a product of the moralistic superego, but a decision of the realistic ego. When it includes international relations, it leads to the formation of such imperfect yet useful bodies as the United Nations.

Vectorialism

Love may become desexualized and unselfish. When a mother bird protects her young against aggressors, she does it in an unselfish manner, risking her own life to protect the life of her children. The willingness of giving without asking anything in return, called "vectorialism"[35] has played a significant role in human history. There have been numerous instances when people willingly gave their lives to defend their family, nation, religion, or ideas. The idea of self-sacrifice and service for others is rooted in parenthood, but it may transcend parenthood and encompass entire mankid. Rabbi Akiba, Christ, Giordano Bruno, and many other great men willingly accepted suffering and death. The Jewish idea of *kiddush hashem* ("sacrifice for the Lord") and the Christian martyrdom reflect the vectorial, unselfish love that has motivated many men and women in their efforts to be of service to others.

The human race is apparently a product of a strange marriage between the highest and lowest behavior, between heavenly ideals and animalistic impulses, represented in the Freudian superego-id model, with the ego trying to control the unpredictable impulsiveness of the human nature.

WILL HUMANITY EVER GROW UP?

The analogy between the development of individual life and the historical process has been a favorite theme for many thinkers. A child can not survive unless protected by adults; and old man must die whether protected or not. There is no reason to assume that any biological species grows old, but it seems that a great part of human behavior is an anachronistic replica of behavioral patterns that made sense thousands of years ago.

Quite often people perpetuate behavioral patterns that were useful in their childhood; instead of facing hardships in an adult way, they regress to infantile behavior. Regression is the core of every neurosis; an adult who reacts to frustration with a temper tantrum or helpless despair reacts in a neurotic way. Can one apply the term neurosis to the behavior of millions? If it is so, history resembles a huge display of *folie en masse.* Violence, robbery, rape, kidnapping, torture, murders, Indians and cowboys, bloody revolutions, and holy wars reflected certain stages in human behavior. They were never terribly rational, but their irrationality becomes insanity in the age of space conquest and split atoms. One could practice a "run" in the good old times when a judge or a sheriff fired a pistol and everbody ran with a horse and buggy to capture free land. But in the United States today, no land is free, and there is no place to run. Even today a revolution can kill many people and destroy property, but it can hardly bring absolute freedom and equality, for no one can be absolutely "free" today; no one can drive in New York on the left side and in London on the right without jeopardizing many lives, including his own. No one can be free from taxes, and labor regulations and thousands of rules and laws are necessary for survival of all. Even the wealthiest men cannot fire and hire workers at will, and even the most despotic parent can be arrested for applying to his children the Roman law of *ius vitae necisque* ("right of life and death"). The modern technological society leaves no room for Raubritters, conquerors, and adventurers, and all modern societies regulate imports and exports, real estate, public health, education, welfare, and family life. The alternative to a democratic, willing acceptance of limitations of individual's rights is chaos or dictatorship.

One can hardly imagine any improvement of the social order that can be brought about by the use of force. Interracial or interfaith strife can only add fuel to the fire but cannot solve any controversy. A war between nations can kill and destroy, but it cannot offer any real advantages to anyone, for the price of war in blood and dollars is too high. It seems that the use of force is becoming obsolete, for it cannot bring the hoped for results in a crowded technological world.

Infants are destructive. In well-adjusted adults the destrudo is partially sublimated, partially aim-inhibited, and partially suppressed. In a normal ontogenetic development, "binding and neutralizing" of the destrudo takes place. According to Anna Freud, in people who failed to grow up and are aggressive:

> The pathological aggressiveness stems not from the aggressive tendencies themselves but from the lack of fusion between them and libidinal (erotic) urges. The pathological factor is found in the realm of erotic, emotional development which has been held up through adverse external or internal conditions. . . . Owing to the defects on the emotional side, the aggressive urges are not brought into the fusion and thereby bound and partially neutralized, but remain free and seek expression in the forms of pure, unadulterated independent destructiveness.[36]

WHO MAKES HISTORY

As long as people are mortal there is no hope for a perfect social order. The sword of Damocles hangs over human heads, and wars, worries, and dreams cannot remove it. The only sensible question one can ask is not how to evade death but how to live as long as life is possible. No one can stop death, but must people willfully destroy life?

History is not a matter of optimism, pessimism, or fatalism. No one else makes history but the people of the world. There are no other laws in history but the laws that underlie human behavior. We are the makers of history, and *we are responsible for history in the making*. The laws of nature cannot change, but human behavior can. Both the sober and the drunken driver follow the same laws of nature, but whoever prefers to live, stays sober. The future of mankind is not determined by Hegel's dialectic, Marx's materialism, or Spengler's pessimism. People of today are writing the prescript for the future.

NOTES

1. W. Windelband, *Praeludien* (Leipzig, 1907) and *Introduction of Philosophy* (London, 1921).
2. M. Nordau, *Der Sinn der Geschichte* (Zurich, 1909).
3. Benjamin B. Wolman, "Evidence in Psychoanalytic Research," *Journal of the American Psychoanalytic Association* 12, no. 4(October 1964).
4. B. A. Farrell, "Scientific Testing of Psychoanalytic Findings and Theory," in H. Brand, ed., *The Study of Personality* (New York, 1954); Sidney Hook, ed., *Psychoanalysis, Scientific Method, and Philosophy* (New York, 1959); and R. R. Sears, *Survey of Objective Studies of Psychoanalytic Concepts* (New York, 1943).
5. See M. R. Cohen, *The Meaning of Human History* (La Salle, Ill., 1961), and Benjamin B. Wolman and Ernest Nagel, eds., *Scientific Psychology: Principles and Approaches* (New York, 1965).
6. P. Barth, *Die Philosophie der Geschichte als Soziologie* (Leipzig, 1922).
7. Henri Poincaré, *La science et l'hypothese* (Paris, 1903).
8. Benjamin B. Wolman, *Contemporary Theories and Systems in Psychology* (New York, 1960), ch. 14.
9. Cohen, *Human History*, pp. 21–23.
10. J. H. Randall and G. Haines, "Controlling Assumptions in the Practice of American Historians," *Social Science Research Council Bulletin* 46 (1946).
11. W. Dilthey, *Einleitung in die Geisteswissenschaften* (1883) (Leipzig, 1924).
12. Randall and Haines, "Controlling Assumptions," pp. 20–21.
13. M. R. Cohen, *Reason and Nature* (New York, 1931), pp. 14–15.
14. Sigmund Freud, *An Outline of Psychoanalysis* (1938) (New York, 1949), p. 85.
15. L. H. Matthews, "Overt Fighting in Mammals," in J. D. Carthy and F. J. Ebling, eds., *The Natural History of Aggression* (New York, 1964), pp. 23–32, p. 25.
16. Carthy and Ebling, eds., *Natural History of Aggression*, pp. 1 ff.
17. K. Z. Lorenz, *King Solomon's Ring* (New York, 1962), p. 21.
18. D. I. Wallis, "Aggression in Social Insects," in Carthy and Ebling, eds., *Natural History of Aggression*, pp. 15–22.
19. P. Kropotkin, *Mutual Aid* (London, 1902).
20. Gordon W. Allport, *The Nature of Prejudice* (Boston, 1954).
21. Freud, *Outline of Psychoanalysis*, p. 20.
22. Sigmund Freud, *New Introductory Lecture in Psychoanalysis* (New York, 1933), pp. 145–147.
23. Sigmund Freud, "Why War?" (1932), in *Collected Papers* (New York, 1959), vol. 5.
24. Benjamin B. Wolman, *Call No Man Normal* (New York, 1970).

25. Benjamin B. Wolman, *Vectoriasis Praecox or the Group of Schizophrenics* (Springfield, Ill., 1966).
26. A. Y. Kuo, "The Genesis of the Cat's Response to the Rat," *Journal of Comparative Psychology* 2(1930): 1–35.
27. Cohen, *Human History*, p. 83.
28. Benjamin B. Wolman, "Historical Laws—Do They Exist?" *Proceedings of the Tenth International Congress of Philosophy* (1948).
29. Arnold J. Toynbee, A *Study of History* (London, 1939), 6:320.
30. *Ibid.*
31. I use the term "occasionalism" to describe Guelinx' interpretation of Descartes's philosophy.
32. W. W. Tarn (1932), quoted in S. Baron, *Social and Religious History of the Jews* (New York, 1953), 6:437.
33. Sigmund Freud, *Group Psychology and the Analysis of the Ego* (1921) (New York, 1949), pp. 74–75.
34. Sigmund Freud, *Totem and Taboo* (1913) (New York, 1931).
35. Wolman, *Vectoriasis Praecox.*
36. Anna Freud, "Aggression in Relation to Emotional Development: Normal and Pathological," in *Psychoanalytic Study of the Child* (New York, 1949), pp. 3–4, 37.

PART II

Biographical Studies

5

JOSEPH V. STALIN: PARANOIA AND THE DICTATORSHIP OF THE PROLETARIAT*

Gustav Bychowski

I

We may recall that the psychological background of the first Russian revolution evolved from defeats in the long war and from hunger, weariness, and growing anarchy in the country as well as in the army. The corruption among the ruling classes had contributed toward annihilating the basis of former ideals; the imperial dynasty had lost its prestige. In these respects the situation was similar to that of the French Revolution.

Thus the first socialist revolution, hailed as an act of liberation, claimed to achieve the great ideals of the French Revolution together with abolition of the capitalistic system along the lines of a democratic socialism to be realized in the future. This promising situation altered after the arrival of Lenin and his staff from Swiss exile. The Germans permitted the Bolshevist chiefs to enter Russia so the disruptive influences could be exerted on the Russian war effort. They were not mistaken in their expectations. Lenin made short shrift of honoring Russia's alliance with the bourgeois powers. The Bolshevists induced the soldiers to throw their arms down and enter discussions on a separate peace with the Germans.

They were successful in these maneuvers despite the opposition of the provisional Social Democratic Government of Kerensky. From then on the principle of violence, applied by a well-organized minority, became the major tenet of Bolshevist policy. The constituent assembly, consisting not of capitalists but of workers, peasants, and democratic intellectuals, was dispelled by Lenin and his loyal sailors. The Bolshevists took advantage of the forbearance of the

* Dr. Bychowski's chapter is based on his book, *Dictators and Their Disciples*. (New York: International Universities Press, 1948). Section I of this chapter was written in 1948. The author, the editor, and the publisher gratefully acknowledge the permission of International Universities Press to reprint the following material.

democratic leaders, who felt that they could not put under arrest representatives of a socialist party. They had to pay dearly for this yielding to the bourgeois predjudice of humanitarianism.

Dictatorship of a Minority

After Lenin had sapped the power of the constituent assembly, he initiated the practical application of the so-called dictatorship of the proletariat. This idea was originally promulgated by Marx, who looked on it as a necessary stage of transition between the capitalistic society and the socialist democracy of the future. The element of violence contained by implication in these concepts helped to distort the entire socialist ideal. According to Lenin's concept, "democracy is not identical with the subordination of the minority to the majority."[1] Democracy is a state recognizing the subordination of the minority to the majority, that is, an organization of the systematic use of violence by one class against the other, by one part of the population against another. "We set ourselves the ultimate aim of destroying the state, i.e., every organized and systematic violence, every use of violence against men in general."[2] In addition to the force these concepts exercised on Lenin, he was strongly influenced by Sorel, who in turn, had been "saturated by some of Nietzsche's ideas."[3]

> Sorel had written:
> Proletarian violence not only makes the revolution certain; but it also seems to be the only means by which the European nations—at present stupefied by humanitarianism—can recover their former energy. . . . The violence of the proletariat exercised as a pure and simple manifestation of class feeling, and class struggle, appears in this light to be a very beautiful, a very heroic thing. . . . The concept of the class struggle tends to purify the concept of violence. . . . The idea of the general strike, continuously revitalized by the emotions which proletarian violence provokes, fosters an absolutely epic state of mind.[4]

Official Bolshevist theory is based on the premise that the means are justified by the end. Lenin remarked aggressively that "great questions in the life of nations are settled only by force."[5] Trotsky wrote in his *Defense of Terrorism:* "No other ways of breaking the class-will of the enemy except by the systematic and energetic use of violence."[6]

The socialist Martov and the Marxist theoretician Plechanov had pointed out that terror and violence employed in the interests of a proletarian dictatorship, particularly where capitalism had not entered a stage of violent reaction, would become ends in themselves. The socialist Kautsky, opposing the concept of a proletarian dictatorship on virtually the same grounds, was branded by Lenin as a traitor—a procedure that rapidly became a familiar weapon of Bolshevism and was liberally applied to every dissident, heretic, or critic. The high ethical principles, so characteristic of socialism, were eliminated by Lenin from politics even prior to the revolution. With the seizure of power and establishment of terror, such bourgeois prejudices as individual liberty and freedom were completely overthrown.

In vain did Gorky, the defender of the poor and the oppressed, appeal to the Communists:

> Evidently killing is easier than persuasion, and this very simple method is very easy for people who have been brought up amongst massacres and educated by massacres. . . . All you Russians are still savages, corrupted by your former masters, who have infused you with their terrible defects and their insensate despotism.[7]

Terror became an easy substitute for freedom of speech, press, opinion, and so forth. Were those ideals of a defunct capitalistic system anything more than convenient tools of capitalistic exploitation? This devious and characteristic Bolshevist reasoning could invoke for its justification the great authority of the *Communist Manifesto*, which says:

> When the Christian ideas succumbed in the Eighteenth Century to Rationalism, feudal society fought its death battle with the revolutionary bourgeoisie. The doctrine of religious freedom and liberty of conscience simply gave expression to the rule of free competition within the domains of knowledge.[8]

It was an easy matter for Lenin and his followers to debase and ridicule all the democratic principles that are the common ideals of Western civilization. With some semblance of justice, he proclaimed, for instance, that there could not exist any freedom of assembly in a society where the main buildings in which a meeting could be held were owned by capitalists. Therefore, the seizure of those buildings was the necessary prerequisite for freedom of assembly. Marx devoted the greater part of his life, writings, and scientific investigations to disparaging freedom, equality, and the will of the majority by claiming that every kind of freedom is a fraud unless it serves the interest of the emancipation of labor from the oppression of capital. He stated that humanity could not attain socialism other than through dictatorship of the proletariat.

> Dictatorship of the proletariat is inevitable; it is necessary and undoubtedly essential for the transition from Capitalism. Dictatorship does not only mean violence, although it is impossible without violence, it also means an organization of labor, which is higher than the preceding organization.[9]
>
> Dictatorship of the proletariat will mean substitution of the dictatorship of the proletariat for the actual dictatorship of the bourgeoisie. . . . It will mean substituting democracy for the poor for the democracy for the rich. It will mean a substitution of the right of assembly and freedom of the press for the majority of the population—the toilers, for the right of assembly and freedom of the press for the minority—the exploiters. It will mean an enormous world-historic expansion of democracy, its transformation from a lie into a truth, the emancipation of mankind from the fetters of capital.[10]

Dictatorship of a small minority, identifying itself with "the oppressed," invoking the great socialist ideal of liberation of the exploited and oppressed workers, became an objective that would ultimately, it was believed, lead to a classless society. Thus suppression of freedom has become an essential attribute of a system aiming at the establishment of liberty. We see here the operation of the rationalization of power drives and egotistic desires in the disguise of millennial benefits for the masses.

To achieve such power, it was required that theory be translated into action by a leader fully aware of its implications and with the ability to lure or coerce the masses into accepting his program. Certainly Lenin knew not only how to handle the masses, but had the magnetic qualities of a true leader. He had prepared in a lifetime of hardship for the moment of seizure of power and meant to use it without restraint. His convictions were absolute and unswerving, based on what he believed to be utter truth. He was the man to bring Marx's predictions to fulfillment. He never doubted that his mission and the mission of revolutionary Russia was to initiate the fall of capitalism throughout the world, and thus save mankind: "Proletarian revolution alone is capable of saving perishing culture and perishing mankind."[11]

It was Engles who had asserted that Revolution must arise from war:

> We are entitled to be proud and to consider ourselves fortunate that it has been our lot to be the first, in one part of the globe, to fell that wild beast—capitalism, which has drenched the earth in blood, and reduced humanity to starvation and demoralization and whose end is near and inevitable, no matter how monstrous and savage its frenzy in the face of death.[12]

And it was Lenin, cognizant of Engel's theories, who had, from the atmosphere of revolution and armed intervention, brought Russia to a pitch of revolutionary fervor.

Lenin became the leader of the Russian masses and was hailed throughout the world as the leader and savior of the proletariat, the herald of a new era of social justice and liberty. He seemed to incorporate in his person the suffering of centuries of oppression. A faithful follower gave her impressions of her visit to Lenin in terms of utter devotion:

> An impression of unspoken and unspeakable suffering was on his face. I was moved, shaken. In my mind I saw the picture of the crucified Christ . . . Lenin appeared to me burdened, oppressed with all the pain and all the suffering of the Russian people.[13]

Thus, representing endless suffering and presumably giving voice to the torments of the oppressed classes, Lenin was able to stimulate and fan the hatred of these classes for their alleged persecutors. Combining personal grievances and the sanction of the theory of class society, Lenin could channel this hatred and violence to a direct and observable opponent—the bourgeoisie.

Freud wrote in 1930,

> It is understandable that the attempt to build up a new communistic culture in Russia finds its psychological backing in the persecution of the bourgeoisie. Only one cannot help wondering what the Soviets will undertake once they finish exterminating their bourgeoisie.[14]

We are now in a position to answer this question. The unleashed aggression found new objects, which at the same time served as scapegoats for all the disillusionment of the masses. Their constant deprivation and increasing frustrations could be blamed on the machinations of saboteurs, old liberals, Mensheviki socialists, and foreign agents.

Thus, in exterminating all these enemies of the proletariat, the ruling group could satisfy not only their own aggressive impulses, but also could divert the aggression of the masses and enforce its power by demonstrating its Bolshevist vigilance and loyalty to the ideals of the revolution. The machinations of the scapegoat became an excellent device for strengthening the ties between the rulers and the people; the struggle against common enemies and salvation from common danger provided an important factor for the formation of new ego ideals, incarnated in the person of the leader and his disciples.

What has become of the ideal set by Engels, and advocated with such enthusiasm by Lenin? After the seizure of power by the oppressed proletarians the state was supposed "to wither away." Engels predicted

> banishment of the whole state machine to the museum of antiquities. In assuming state power the Proletariat by that very act destroys the state as such. The first act of the state in which it really acts as a representative of the whole of society, namely the assumption of control over the means of production on behalf of society, is also its last independent act as a state. Under Socialism much of the primitive Democracy will inevitably be revued.
>
> * * *
>
> The bureaucracy and the standing army constitute a parasite on the body of the capitalistic society. In these words "to shatter the bureaucracy and military machinery of the state" is to be found tersely expressed the principal teachings of Marxism on the subject of the problems concerning the state, facing the Proletariat in a Revolution. All former Revolutions helped to perfect the machinery of government whereas now we must shatter it, break it to pieces.
>
> * * *
>
> The interference of the authority of the state with social relations will then become superfluous in one thing after another and finally will cease of itself.[15]

Nobody, not even the most enthusiastic admirer of the Soviet

Union will deny that the revolution evolved in the opposite direction. Stalin himself recognizes that there is

> contradiction in our treatment of the question of the state. We are in favor of the state dying out and at the same time we stand for the strengthening of the dictatorship of the Proletariat. The highest possible development of the power of the state, with the object of preparing the conditions for the dying out of the state: that is the Marxist formula.[16]

Stalin explains this apparent contradiction as a reflection of Marxist dialectics.

Justification of Oppression

It is possible then to describe the evolution of the Soviet Union as an accumulation of all those evils of oppression characteristic not merely of capitalistic society but of autocracy. The rationalization given for this development toward totalitarianism was the persistence of enemies within and abroad. The real psychological motives may be described briefly as a desire to perpetuate unlimited power and to suppress the anarchistic and rebellious impulses unleashed by the revolution with its shattering of the old ego ideal. The ruling group took over the ideology of proletarian violence in order to rationalize these desires, and it identified itself with the interest of the masses, so that every act of oppression came to be regarded as an act in the service and actual self-preservation of the Russian nation. In fighting the capitalistic oppressors the rulers extended their hostility to all opponents.

By a searching analysis of the Bolshevist justification of violence and of proletarian dictatorship in terms of the future, that is, the establishment of freedom and equality at some unspecified future date, we may arrive at the political realities that obtain in Russia. Instead of the former masters, we have, in the Soviet system, a new set of rulers who have acquired power. But in the last analysis are they the very same proletarians who up to the moment of the seizure of power had been wronged and oppressed? The entire course of the Russian Revolution shows just the opposite to be true. The actual masters are a bureaucracy, a small group of prominent party members. They seem to have put into practical operation Nietzsche's concept of the masters who must rule ruthlessly in order to dominate the masses. Indeed the duped masses have been so skillfully imposed on that they believe in many instances that they have exercised a choice in the selection of their rulers. That such freedom of choice was the merest illusion can be gleaned from Lenin's remark: "It is true that liberty is precious; it is so precious that it must be rationed." The subsequent course of the Russian Revolution proved convincingly that even the immediate goal of liberating the workers and peasants had been converted into an enslavement incomparably worse than in any modern capitalistic society. Gradually, the laboring public lost all the individual freedoms that their fellow workers in Western democracies had succeeded in achieving after long years of hard struggle. The story of the peasants and their exploitation by the state is no less tragic, fraught as it is with the terrors and sacrifices in the course of frantic resistance to complete extermination. As is well known, in the course of this struggle against the "kulaks," whole rural districts were completely depopulated either through famine caused by wholesale requisitions or by forced deportations. This, by the way, was the first application on a large scale of the principle of mass deportations, continued ruthlessly by the Soviets and emulated by the Nazis.

Thus, the proclaimed dictatorship of the proletariat turned into the dictatorship over the proletariat. In fact, the whole structure of ruthless despotism and submission to authority and, eventually, the submission of all to the almighty leader is really strikingly similar to fascism.

After his death, Lenin the leader and the idol of the masses, and at the same time Lenin the tyrant, responsible for immense suffering, was deified, embalmed, and deposed in the great mausoleum in the Red Square—a holy mummy imposed on the people to substitute for the icons worshipped before the advent of the revolution. From the remotest corners of Russia, worshippers arrived to do homage to the sacred figure. Ironically, the rulers feared that such homage might be mixed with aggression, for they took exceptional pains to examine each visitor scrupulously, to inspect the tiniest package with minute care. It seemed as if they expected an outrage against the holy shrine, as if sons mourning their dead father had projected their bad conscience, their own guilt, into the masses. It is necessary to dwell on this psychological aspect if one is to understand the succession of Stalin to power.

The Struggle for Succession

The struggle for succession, which began during Lenin's illness, was carried on by Stalin with great skill and utter ruthlessness. He removed all potential rivals and was always extremely careful to preserve his unique position as dictator of the Soviet republic. This struggle between the sons of the revolution for the succession of the beloved father went through all the drastic stages that, as we have learned, characterize primitive tribal societies, in which the sons are destroyed by the most cunning and powerful among them for fear of retaliation. Thus it was inevitable that the revolution itself foundered on the rocks of a Thermidorian or Bonapartist reaction. The events after the death of the father of a primal horde, as hypothetically described by Freud and developed and expounded on the basis of abundant ethnological evidence by Róheim, give some cue for the understanding of the vicissitudes of the revolution.[17]

After the dreaded, simultaneously hated and loved father had been killed and devoured by the rebellious sons, they began to identify themselves with the ideal hero. Some among them attempted to take over the lead, but were prevented from doing so by hatred and jealousy of their rival brothers. At last one succeeded and imposed his authority on all the others by eliminating his most important rivals, the potential successors.

The father murder resulted in deep feelings of guilt and fear of retaliation. The leading among the sons, that is, the successors to the father, feared revenge not only from the remaining brothers but also from the slain parent. Many of their reactions derive from these sources. Because the guilt was shared by the brothers, this common factor helped to strengthen the bond between them. Through the devouring of the slain father, they absorbed—so they felt—his secret powers, and thus established an identification with him and with one another. Totemistic feasts in primitive societies bear witness to these feelings and practices, which probably have laid the foundations of human society.[18]

This process of identification of the murderer with the victim is a phenomenon frequently observed in the mourning rites of the primitives and has been studied extensively by Róheim. It finds its clinical counterpart in the psychopathology of melancholia. This identification results finally in the murderers' establishing an internal image of their victim as a powerful ideal, worshipping and deifying him, thus trying to deny their guilt and to placate his vindictive wrath. In this way, their suppressed hostility becomes transformed into overgrown loyalty.

However, there is always the danger of a breakthrough of this hostility, which would this time be directed against the successor, the new father substitute. Therefore, the successful murderer and his group have to create powerful safeguards to hold in check the threatening hostility of the rival brothers, each of whom may aspire to the succession. This is accomplished by taboos, which are important in all primitive societies and which, in a period following a revolution, take the form of rigid rules, of reaction formations, characterized by absolute severity and terrible penalties.

The slain parent, who in the history of the primal horde became deified, was made the center of a cult. In a revolution, the original leader and his successors acquire similar mythological characteristics and become identified with the new ideology. Thus, in magnifying and protecting his personal power, the leader seemingly protects and exalts the ideals for which the revolutionaries shed blood.

Hostility of the rebellious sons, held in check by the powerful successor and suppressed by the idealized image of the slain parent breaks through in form of paranoid projection. The "sons" project the hatred on one another and especially on any groups that differentiate themselves from the original horde. In a revolution, this is easily rationalized by ideological divergencies behind which the ruling group suspects, sometimes correctly, the lust for power.

After the victorious group has become cemented by the common shedding of the blood of its enemies, the suppressed hostility of its members manifests itself in paranoid reactions that center around possible opposition as well as around foreign groups with different social and national structure. Thus, in the process of the final merging of internationally minded Bolshevism with pure Russian nationalism, we find a peculiar fusion of revolutionary ideology with the old nationalistic ideals breaking through, as it were, from repression. In all these processes, the cementing of the ruling group and of the revolutionary nation has its inevitable parallel in hatred and suspicion directed toward foreign countries. This suspicion is easily rationalized as differences of ideology and in terms of old historical conflicts.

Interestingly enough, the struggle of the son against the father had been a strong factor in forming the personality of Lenin's successor. Consequently, it might have proved of benefit to Stalin's bid for power when the same struggle was to take place in the political arena. What are the cornerstones of Stalin's personality as far as we can deduce them from the available data?

Stalin's Childhood

The only surviving son of a crude and tyrannical peasant shoemaker, Stalin, the boy, learned early how to hate and how to suppress hostility until the opportune moment. Despite the position assigned to the father in the traditional patriarchal structure of a Georgian family, the main responsibility of the family seemed to have fallen on the shoulders of the mother. She toiled hard but earned very little as a servant in the homes of the rich. Naturally, she had no way of protecting her son against the brutality of the father and helplessly watched as her husband mistreated him. Undeserved, frightful beatings made the boy as grim and heartless as his father. Indeed, his suppressed hatred against the father transferred itself to persons in power and to all authority. The death of the father occurred when Stalin was eleven years old, too late to change his character pattern. Probably the boy breathed with relief on the father's death, and felt and acted as the savior of the mother who had shown him so great a devotion. Stalin's mother was indeed ambitious to elevate her son. She determined to enter him into the priesthood, a career that for a boy in such poor circumstances seemed the only possible way of social elevation. Thus Greek Orthodox theology, with its rigid dogmatism, became the steppingstone to satisfying both his own and his mother's ambition.

Social humiliations naturally increased Stalin's general feeling of inferiority and his desire for revenge and compensation. In addition to social humiliations, there were mortifications caused by the domination of Russian officials over the Georgian population. It may be noted that there were also some elements of inferiority in Stalin's physical makeup: weakness of the left arm, pock-marked face, and other unprepossessing features. According to Alfred Adler, such organic inferiority plays an important part in distortion of personality through the mechanics of psychological overcompensation.[19] Indeed, young Stalin became hard and unsympathetic: "I never saw him weep," remarks his childhood friend Iremashvili—, "he had only a sarcastic sneer for the joys and sorrows of his fellows. As boy and youth he was a good friend to those who submitted to his domineering will."[20]

In the theological seminary where Stalin received his training for a future vocation, he went further in developing a personality in which dissimulating his hatred and biding his time, in anticipation of revenge in the future, became dominant features. The rigorous discipline of the seminary instilled in him a deeper hatred for authority. In this seminary, punishments were inflicted for such crimes as reading a "liberal" book. The inspectors and the monks were hostile and suspicious, maintaining a strict watch over the students, observing their movements, closely searching their rooms and their persons at the slightest pretext.

Forced to submit to his masters, Stalin found an outlet in asserting his despotism in the secret circle of his comrades.

> He deemed it something unnatural, Iremashvili writes, that any other fellow-student might be a leader and organizer of the group. Joseph knew how to persecute and how to avenge himself. He knew how to strike at weak spots. . . . In his struggle for mastery Koba [Stalin's nickname] with his supercilious and poisonous cynicism fomented many personal squabbles among his friends.[21]

Thus, the future revolutionary was serving an apprenticeship in the exercise of coldness, ruthlessness, and guile. In his student days, moreover, his fantasies of revenge became more pronounced.

When Joseph Stalin became familiar with the revolutionary movement, he broke with theology and substituted Marxism for Greek Orthodoxy. It was only natural for him to embrace it with the dogmatic fanaticism absorbed from his own theological preceptors. At a later period it became quite natural for him to vent his hatred on the theological institute, which had chastized him, by launching a ferocious campaign of atheism.

Once Stalin had embraced the hazardous career of a professional revolutionary, he found at last the opportunity to express his accumulated store of hatred and resentment. His life had prepared him well for conspiracy. He had learned to suspect everyone and with this attitude his slyness and shrewdness grew correspondingly.

His hatred and envy of established authority received further impetus from the persecution by tsarist secret police. Moreover, the young revolutionary absorbed the technique of his persecutors who resorted to the methods of inquisition in securing confessions. He learned, as it were, all there was to know about threats, physical violence, moral torture, falsifying the depositions of witnesses, the subornation of false witnesses, and other techniques of terror and oppression. These lessons he never failed to remember and, when in power, applied them with a thoroughness that would have shamed the tsarist persecutors.

His slyness and the insidious talent for inciting others to dangerous action while remaining safe and secure, are reported by an eyewitness who spent a year or so in various prisons with him.[22] His capacity for cunning, his adroit dodging of punishment, was such that it was impossible to upset his balance. As a result of his early experiences, he developed a strong armor of self-defenses that made him insensitive to suffering and unable to sympathize with the pain of others. During confinement in the Baku prison, Stalin's cell neighbor reported to him a dream about revolution. "Have you a craving for blood?" Stalin asked him unexpectedly. He took out a knife that he had hidden in the leg of his boot, raised high one of his trouser legs and, inflicting a deep gash on himself, he said: "There is blood for you!"[23] It would seem that the entire development of Stalin's personality is contained in the implications of this incident. His sadistic character had been formed beyond redemption, and the course of world history was to be deeply affected by a personality formed primarily through the repressive authorities of his youth.

Stalin's ruthlessness, which had its roots in the enforced submissiveness to his father, became complete at the death of his first wife, which desolated him. His biographer Iremashvili wrote:

> Beginning with the day he buried his wife, he lost the last vestige of human feelings. His heart filled with the inexpressibly malicious hatred his merciless father had already begun to engender in him when he was still a child. He crushed with sarcasm his less and less frequently recurring moral impulses. Ruthless with himself, he became ruthless with all people.[24]

Kamenev, one of the old guard who opposed Stalin and was liquidated in due course, remarked to Trotsky in 1925: "You imagine that Stalin is preoccupied with replying to your arguments. Nothing of the kind! He is figuring out how to liquidate you without being punished."[25] Not unlike Robespierre, Stalin felt that any opposition to him was disloyal and criminal. He rationalized his cruelty in dealing with mere differences of opinion by asserting the need for party harmony and Bolshevist unity and discipline.

If Stalin's irrational attitudes toward criticism are viewed not merely as a means of preserving power, we may arrive at broader aspects of his outlook. On closer scrutiny, it appears that both his and Robespierre's rationalizations expressed a megalomaniac strain to the effect that the highest purity of the ideas of the party were incarnated in their persons. Stalin not only identified himself completely with the leaders and theoreticians of communism but believed that he represented the purity of the absolute truth they had formulated. In the name of idealism, calling on the past to sanction his cruel, repressive measures, he unleashed terror on an unprecedented scale. Of course, there were not wanting professional apologists who would interpret the significance of Stalin's attitudes and justify them historically. Thus, a Professor Tarle, an official historian accredited by the regime, praised the French Terror and Robespierre who, in practicing it, was expressing the will of the people.[26]

Certain trends may be detected in the long course of Stalin's terroristic practices. It hardly needs mentioning that he exterminated all his actual and potential rivals and opponents in the service of his unique dictatorial position. Not satisfied with his simple and efficient system, however, he liquidated the entire old Bolshevist guard, as if he feared that they knew too much of his past and might function as witnesses in detriment to the legend formed about him.

> Stalin requires that in every circumstance he shall be the leading light; he destroys the last witnesses capable of producing one day a true testimony about him. He avenges himself now on these for not having known how to keep silent. And he shows the measure of his courage, as of his "humanism," when, secure from all risk, he insults the defeated, stamps on his prisoners, and rages over their dead bodies.[27]

Identification with the Enemy

Another outstanding and, from our point of view, most important tendency of a dictator is the identification with the enemy. It is typical of Stalin, who can hardly be esteemed as a thinker of any originality, that he was not averse to adopting as his own the ideas of opponents whom he had liquidated. Thus, he fought Trotsky, allegedly on the ground of Trotsky's policy toward the kulaks and collectivization, only later to proclaim the very ideas of his enemy. All the plans of General Tukhachevsky, liquidated during the mass purge of 1936, were subsequently adopted and carried out by Stalin. Among those plans was a pact of close cooperation with Hitler, which formed the basis of Tukhachevsky's indictment in treachery. However, the same pact promulgated by Stalin was hailed as an act of supreme wisdom.

A peculiar combination of shrewd cunning and merciless vindictiveness enabled Stalin to organize terror on a vast scale and to create a powerful apparatus in support of such terror. The Cheka, a secret police force, was formed in the first period of the revolution and then developed into the notorious G.P.U. and finally into the no less notorious N.K.V.D. These immense organizations were states within a state, endowed with the greatest privileges, unhampered by existing laws, and responsible only to Stalin himself. Some of its sinister mechanisms have been revealed to the astounded world during the famous purges of 1936. Other revelations were forthcoming when Kravchenko and others divulged its worldwide ramifications. These revelations, however, would not have been so overwhelming if the world had not been shocked by several internationally famous cases of murders and kidnappings by which the N.K.V.D. got rid of Stalin's enemies.

All opposition, even that of minor political significance was exterminated without qualms. What, one asks oneself, could have been sufficient motivation for the bloody purges in the navy? They seemed attributable only to the ideas of younger navy men who considered light units (submarines, torpedo boats, hydroplanes) preferable to large, costly, and vulnerable cruisers and dreadnoughts. They were charged with serving the enemies of the people by depriving the U.S.S.R. of a fleet of major proportions. Fortunately, "the glorious officials of the People's Commissariat of the Interior cut off the heads of these reptiles."[28]

Stalin's methods of systematic terror, his merciless annihilation of antagonists, remind one strongly of the long line of Russian despots, headed by Ivan Grozny ("the Terrible"). It was he who initiated the system of *opriczniki*, his faithful servants, notorious for their cruelty and freedom from legal restraint, who exercised the function of a modern secret police. Their chief, Skuratov, was infamous for his brutality and absolute, blind obedience to the tsar. The organization bore striking resemblance to the N.K.V.D., particularly in its exemption from all law. It is only natural that today Ivan Grozny is praised by the professional Soviet writers, who compose history and art, as a great constructive monarch who was compelled to use stringent measures because of the ignorance and lethargy of the Russian masses, in particular because of the opposition of the nobility.

In spite of the analogy between the methods of tsarist despotism and Stalinism, it must be recognized that Stalin has magnified terror and cruelty thousandfold since the days of his eminent predecessors. Stalin, the head of a modern organization and endowed with immense power, tortured and persecuted his victims on a scale undreamed of by the former tyrants. Moreover, the N.K.V.D., Stalin's secret police, was immeasurably more efficient than the tsarist *okhrana*. Deportations of criminal and political prisoners to Siberia had been instituted by the tsars, but their unfortunate victims numbered in the tens of thousands. It was left to the country of the proletariat to deport millions to the remotest corners of Siberia and Kazakstan. Forced labor was not invented by the country of the proletariat, but it reached its largest scope in Soviet Russia. The total numbers in the labor and concentration camps is estimated to be between 15 and 20 million. Great enterprises, which are the pride of Soviet industrialization and of the various five-year plans, as for example Dnieprostroy, the White Sea Canal, and many others, have been executed predominantly by these modern slaves of Stalin under the whip of the N.K.V.D.

It would seem that Stalin, a Georgian, himself a member of one of the national minorities oppressed by the tsars, had absorbed all of the latters' sadism and was revenging himself by giving it vent throughout the whole of Russia. In this process, however, he did not forget his native Georgia. The role he played in the Sovietization of this land was marked by most relentless cruelty. The Georgians, a proud and independent people with strong Social Democratic leanings, offered serious resistance to the Bolsheviks, which was crushed in the true Stalinist manner. Lenin himself felt quite indignant when informed of Stalin's brutal tactics, but his efforts to stop him were of no avail.

One may recall at this point the parallels with Hitler's attitude to the incorporation of Austria, his homeland, into the Reich. The mercilessness and bitterness displayed by these dictators toward their native lands becomes explicable when it is understood how deeply they had suffered as children at the hands of cruel and stern fathers. Apparently the conquests of the mother country had to the unconscious the symbolic significance of both redeeming their mothers and taking revenge on their hated fathers. The conquest rationalized by flaming ideology and supported by military power, served to free the mother and to compensate the conquerors for their early humiliations.

Stalin transferred all the pain and resentment of his miserable childhood from his native land to the vast area of the tsarist empire. He, representative of a minority persecuted by the tsarist regime, behaved as if he identified himself with the old aggressor and, once in power, carried out the old imperialistic policy. An analysis of his foreign policy shows that he realized not only all the imperialistic aspirations of the tsars but went far beyond them and would have gone even further had he not been halted by other powerful nations. It was impressive to witness the process of reincorporation of independent countries, which had been a part of the tsarist empire and had been freed during the revolution, only to be reabsorbed by a despotism incomparably stronger than that of the tsars. Soviet imperialism in action was much different from Lenin's eloquent appeals against annexations; it was justified by transparent fictions. Loud and pious statements rang out that Soviets had arrived to liberate a nation from its oppressors, a nation moreover whose allegedly evil government had participated in the capitalist encirclement. It is significant that the concept of encirclement arising from cynical utilitarian reasons ultimately became a singular delusion, paranoid in its scope and characteristic for the dictators.

Not satisfied with successful destruction of past and future antagonists, Stalin took great pains in erasing from the memory of the nation whatever could in any way prove detrimental to his mythological grandeur. In some analogy to the so-called retrospective unconscious falsifications of a paranoiac, Stalin, by a perfect and certainly conscious sytem, did everything in order to create an image of his incomparable greatness. In successive editions of the Soviet encyclopaedia, of textbooks of history, and above all of the Soviet Bible—the so-called Kratky Kurs, a short history of the Communist party—Stalin's role was exaggerated and fulsomely praised while his antagonists were vilified or simply remained unmentioned.

Thirst for Flattery

Almost every trite word uttered by the beloved leader was hailed by the official Pravda as the beginning of a new era in history. Stalin's thirst for flattery was particularly active in the domain of ideas. To be considered an original and powerful thinker remained his constant desire. It was not enough that Stalin was praised on every occasion as the greatest teacher and genius of the world proletariat; nor was it sufficient that the Russian press overflowed with adulation of his person and every meeting, every speech had to culminate in an ecstatic tribute to his genius. Even on utterly unexpected occasions, such as an anniversary of Spinoza, or in an article about Kepler, he was praised as an expert on Spinoza's philosophy or as a talented astronomer. One professor of philosophy wrote that the true meaning of Kantian philosophy was revealed by a letter of Comrade Stalin's. The periodical *Cultural Front* stated that "in reality certain pronouncements of Aristotle have only been fully interpreted and expressed by Stalin."[29] Another professor was happy to admit that the meaning of Cervantes had at last been realized through the illuminating pronouncement of Comrade Stalin, who had declared that "Don Quixote was a great satire."[30]

All these flowery eulogies were a proper form of overcompensation for the lack of education and intellectual training, which are important factors in Stalin's unconscious inferiority complex. Under favorable circumstances it was natural for Stalin to claim praise as a great and original thinker, philosopher, and as a brilliant theoretician. Ideas of grandeur are usually determined in their content by the specific elements in which originated the sense of inferiority. Thus the "sun of nations" and the "beloved leader" of workers and peasants became standard terms in the new Soviet mythology, Homeric in nature, in which a pantheon of heroes was endowed with semidivine, eternally fixed attributes. To be sure, we find precedents in Russian mythology itself. Some of the hymns and eulogies dedicated to Stalin remind one of the old Russian folk tales "Byliny, in which a hero of gigantic proportions and supernatural powers performs wonderful deeds in succoring the oppressed and wronged. Because the hero is of supernatural dimensions, all the common mortals dwindle in their significance. Similarly we are told that Stalin, "the great machinist of locomotive history" is such a powerful giant that all the other statesmen on the international scene seem "so tiny, so pitiable, such pygmies. . ."[31] Not only obscure poets of the Asiatic, the so-called autonomous republics, exalt Stalin beyond human limits. Even the poet Alexey Tolstoy, a writer of distinction and real talent, has written a hymn addressed to Stalin:

> Thou bright sun of the nations,
> The unsinking sun of our times
> And more than the sun, for the sun has no wisdom.[32]

Such incredible flattery reached its peak on the day of Stalin's sixtieth birthday. In *Pravda,* on December 21, 1939, only one column each was devoted to the Finnish-Russian war and World War II, whereas seventy-one columns were devoted to the leader. In the words of an American newspaper correspondent, "a world's record was established for newsless newspapers."[33]

This megalomania of the dictator was accompanied by other forms of idolatry; pictures and statues of Stalin, sometimes of immense size, can be encountered throughout all Russia, in all railroad stations and public buildings. The murdered tsar, Batiushka ("father"), became reincarnated on a tremendously magnified scale, much greater than in the past, because the reincarnation was supported not only by the megalomania of the leader but also by the cynical or naïve response of his followers.

This collective Soviet idolatry is sufficiently well known to require little further elaboration. However, some examples may be selected from the vast number at hand. For example, after an interview with Stalin regarding Trotskyist contraband in historical and artistic works, some Russian musicians declared: "In the light of Comrade Stalin's letter, new and great tasks arise on the musical front. Down with rotten liberalism, with its bourgeois resonances, inimical to class theories."[34] They undertook to revise the scoring of the composers of the past beginning with Beethoven and Moussorgsky. "Stalin's letter has to make of each Soviet orchestra a collective struggle for authentic Marxist-Leninism."[35]

At the congress of chess players in 1932, Krylenko declared:

> We must finish once and for all with the neutrality of chess. We must condemn once and for all the formula: "chess for the sake of chess," like art for art's sake. We must organize shock-brigades of chess-players and begin the immediate realization of the five-year chess plan.[36]

The full apotheosis of the leader required, as a preliminary, the complete vilification of his antagonists of any period. This was carried out by a harmonious chorus directed by the great man himself and consisting of faithful, obedient, frightened, or merely cynical followers. A perusal of the records of the trials, as far as they have been made accessible to the public, shows what an amount of obloquy it was necessary to heap on those who dared to oppose Stalin. "Traitors," "lackeys of fascism," "reptiles"—these were some of the epithets accorded to the unfortunate who dared provoke Stalin's wrath. In compulsive fashion he must besmirch the victim's memory. This was particularly true in cases where the victim was of any political significance and had some important deeds to his credit. It is of considerable psychological interest to analyze some of these accusations whose complete incredibility makes one speculate as to their deeper motives. For instance, in studying the real source of the indictment of Bukharin, one of the most prominent members of the old Bolshevist guard, whom Stalin charged for having prepared, in 1918, an attempt on Lenin's life, certain facts emerge. Bukharin was well known for his boundless love and admiration of Lenin. We may surmise that the accusation was a projection of the designs, or even plans, lurking in Stalin's mind.

Policy of Reprisals

In this process of moral destruction of his antagonists, Stalin was aided by his followers. Organizations and special meetings demanded the execution of the alleged traitors long before the court convened. One could read in the *Journal of Soviet Psychiatry and Neurology* violent condemnations of the "criminals," the "bloody fascist agents," "the vile reptiles." These tirades were signed by men outstanding in the Russian scientific world.

Because every means of education and every channel of expression is dominated by the regime, the process of molding public opinion in accordance with the party's own interests presents no difficulties. Generations have been brought up in blind obedience to the party and the beloved leader. Their ideas are shaped with sternest rigidity, and differences of opinion are not tolerated. Criticism of the "general line" is tantamount to heresy and meets with reprisals no less merciless than the Inquisition. Apparently, the fear experienced by the leader and the ruling clique is such that they have to maintain a constant system of physical and mental defenses. This explains the striking sensitivity of Soviet rulers to every criticism from abroad. It explains also the typical Soviet custom, so incomprehensible to the democratic mind, of branding writers and artists for "lack of ideology" and of expelling them from professional unions for "bourgeois deviation." Such an expulsion, especially if followed by banishment from the party, may mean loss of employment, imprisonment, or deportation. The dictatorship wields all the positive and negative instruments of coercion: positive—through the methods of incessant propaganda such as press and radio; negative—through constant vigilance of censorship and threat of merciless punishment. Fear and propaganda are powerful enough to achieve a monolithic public opinion, an ideal that was sought by Robespierre but could never be realized by him. A unanimous resolution at a Soviet meeting is as easily achieved as a standardized prison garb in a concentration camp.

Until recently, isolation from the dangerous West had been imposed so thoroughly that people were afraid to receive and to answer letters from relatives residing abroad. For an average Russian to know a foreigner, to be seen with him in Moscow, was dangerous. Constant repetition of such phrases as "capitalistic encirclement" created in the population a psychological preparedness for approving whatever defensive—in reality aggressive measures—the regime wished to undertake. Those measures have been recently topped by the decree, unique in modern history, forbidding Soviet citizens to marry a foreigner. This propaganda created a justification for all the deprivations imposed by the regime on the existence of an average citizen.

All these defensive measures, some of them petty, some terrible, indicate constant fear of either overt rebellion or dissidence. It is only natural that the greater the oppression and terror the Stalinist dictatorship applied to its citizens, the more it had to fear some retaliation. It tended to react with defensive measures on a grandiose scale.

The *pierietasowka* ("shuffling"), that is, deportation of an entire population of a "liberated," or otherwise ideologically uncertain, province to the farthest corners of the Soviet Union, and importation of some remote tribe into the province deprived of its native population, is one of the monstrously inflated methods of self-protection. It is evident that the populations of Kalmouks, resettled after 1945 in the annexed part of Poland, or of the Ukrainians, deported to remote parts of Siberia, are uprooted and so weakened in their possible political, national, and even physical resistance that they cannot be expected to start any irredenta. Besides, such procedures are an excellent safeguard against plebiscites in the future. Ideological purity of the country of proletariat is also better preserved if Spaniards, who had fought against Franco in the Civil War and had to flee from their country, are settled in the Uzbekistan; they had been given all sorts of promises by Moscow, only to find themselves deported and forced to lead a meager existence, toiling in the cotton fields, side by side with the Koreans transplanted sometime between 1934–1939, after the border skirmishes, constituting a sort of an unofficial war between the Soviets and Japan.

Such methods seem completely incredible and repulsive to the civilized mind. Obviously they are indicative of a profound contempt for human individuality. One infers from this attitude that a human being has no value in himself. The mission of the individual, according to these tenets, consists in utter abject abandonment to the will of the state and to the dictatorship. A mentality of this order excludes any possibility of creating an ethical structure. However, even Stalin and his henchmen were made uneasy at the prospect of appearing unprincipled. Accordingly, they constantly performed semantic distortions of democratic and liberal ideas. Such words as freedom and democracy are used as labels for Communist dictatorship in the U.S.S.R. and in satellite countries. They even use the term "election" to designate an obedient acceptance of one-list candidates, imposed by the regime on the submissive masses.

When one realizes that this system of oppression evolved from socialist theories, which contained some of the noblest ideas ever conceived by the human mind, one cannot but wonder at this tragic paradox of history. We may reach a better understanding of the Russian phenomena if we review the main points of our analysis. Though originating in socialism, the Bolshevist ideology culminated in hatred, lust for revenge, and violence. These impulses replaced rapidly the original ideals, and their main instrument—the dictatorship of the proletariat—became a goal in itself. Ideas growing in an atmosphere loaded with aggressiveness and hatred could not evolve a society based on ethical values. On the contrary, the Soviet ideas were fanatical, corrupt, and often tinged with paranoid delusions.

In the final crystallization of Russian autocracy, individuals of special mentality came to the fore. Stalin, who possessed all the essential characteristics of a fanatic dictator, gained the upper hand. He not only knew how to exterminate his rivals and possible successors, but also how to blend his personal hatreds and resentments with powerful collective emotions. It was natural to him to rationalize his individual cruelty by putting it into the service of collective ideals. Because he identified himself with the cause, he could impose his personal tyranny as a token of an ideological triumph. Through terror, coercion, and incessant propaganda and indoctrination, he and his followers have succeeded in imposing a new set of values and concepts on the masses, superseding the old collective ego ideal. They have blended their ideology with methods and goals originating with and represented by a long series of their tsarist predecessors. A new mythology has been created in which Stalin has become enthroned as supreme being endowed with attributes of an archaic barbaric father image. Thus, under the guise of liberation, dictatorship laid solid foundations for a system of political and psychological enslavement, and the revolution that was supposed to deliver a definite blow to the state as institution resulted in the creation of a superstate relentlessly exploiting the individual.

Unconscious Identification

As a result of a process of thorough identification, the new rulers have taken over the methods and ideals of the Russian tyrants of the old past, and under the disguise of sublime ideals made them acceptable not only to the vast masses of their own people but even to followers and sympathizers all over the world. Anxiety and frustration of the post-war world, superimposed on the inherent weaknesses of our social structure, have created in the masses a deep need for ideals backed by material power. This collective longing invests the Soviet system with an aura of salvation, which makes sympathizers overlook the suffering and depression on which it is based.

It is possible then to describe the evolution of the Soviet Union as an immense accumulation of all these evils of oppression, which were characteristic not merely of capitalist society, but of autocracy. The rationalization given for this development toward totalitarianism was the persistence of enemies within and abroad. The real psychological motive may be described as a desire to perpetuate unlimited power and to suppress the anarchistic and rebellious impulses unleashed by the revolution with its shattering of the old ego ideal. The ruling group took over the ideology of proletarian violence in order to rationalize these desires, and it identified itself with the interests of the masses, so that every act of oppression came to be regarded as an act in the service and actual self-preservation of the Russian people. In fighting the capitalist oppressors, the rulers extended their hostility to all opponents and dissidents. They identified themselves unconsciously with all the powers of despotic oppression that have existed in Russian history.

This set of unconscious identifications was supplemented by a system of identifications performed on a more conscious level. On this level, the rulers set themselves up as representatives of the masses of the formerly oppressed and now supposedly liberated Russian people. They even extended this identification to the oppressed proletariat or, if expedient, to the oppressed nationalities of the entire world. In short, they have been successful in promoting communist ideals to the point where they have formed the core of a new collective ego ideal that superseded the old one. Thus, the masses learned to surrender their desire for personal freedom and happiness, exchanging these goals for the new ideal of collective achievement in the present and universal communist felicity in some remote future.

Stalinism in its disruption of the collective superego, built through centuries of civilizing processes, necessarily involves a regression to the archaic unconscious. Hence, it should not at all be a matter of surprise that situations arising in Russia should present so marked a resemblance to processes described as typical of more primitive societies. We recall that the successful murderer of the primeval father and his group had to create powerful safeguards to hold in check the threatening hostility of the rival brothers, each of whom might aspire to the succession. This was accomplished by taboos, which are so important in all primitive societies and which, in a period following the revolution, take the form of rigid rules, reaction formations, characterized by absolute severity and terrible penalties.

In conclusion, we arrive at some understanding of the extremely complex processes that have transformed the powerful upsurge toward liberation into a system of relentless oppression. Here as in every other dictatorship we have studied, this result was possible by a cooperation of historical and sociological factors with the personality of a fanatic leader who had succeeded in imposing himself as an ideal on the suffering masses.

II

The historical events that occurred after 1948 call for some reflections and amplifications.

Dostoyevsky

Let me begin with a comment of a general order. One of the most striking features of the Stalinist era are the purges and the extraordinary trials accompanying them. We are rather well informed about the techniques of moral and physical torture that were a part of the so-called brainwashing, a technique that subsequently was used with such success by the Chinese Communists. Yet, all our knowledge notwithstanding, time and again one could not help marveling at the uniformly self-destructive character of the "confessions."[37]

A renewed study of Dostoyevsky, a most extraordinary writer, who in his novels prophetically anticipated many events in the development of Russian socialism and communism, proves most illuminating. It puts in a sharp focus certain basic trends in Russian mentality, which manifest themselves again and again throughout Russian history.

To put it as briefly as possible. In his study on Dostoyevsky Freud writes:

> He reminds one of the barbarians of the great migrations, who murder and do penance therefor, where penitence becomes a technique to enable murder to be done. Ivan the Terrible behaved in exactly this way—in fact this compromise with morality is a characteristic Russian trait.[38]

In *The Brothers Karamazov* the towering figure of the Great Inquisitor, drawn after the notorious reactionary minister of the interior and archenemy of all liberalism, Pobedonostzeff, could serve as a prototype of Stalin himself and some of his henchmen. Similarly, in *Biesy* (in English translation *The Possessed,* though in reality the word means the "evil spirits") Dostoyevsky presents us with the picture of mental degeneration of Russian revolutionaries, truly prophetic of the vicissitudes of communism. The main common trends in all this are as follows: the inherent belief, indeed the conviction that human beings, vicious and depraved as they are, have to be coerced into the acceptance of ideas for which they are not ready, but which, ultimately, will serve them well. To achieve this goal, no means should be shunned, no cruelty spared. In their abysmal ignorance and sinfulness they do not know themselves, poor innocents, what is good for them; therefore, freedom of choice, in fact any trace of liberty, is not for them: it would mean their undoing. They themselves are or can be so convinced of this that they are ready to renounce their sins, to confess and to repent, in submitting to the superior knowledge and power of those who are truly enlightened (the church, the party, or the government). Here then, by virtue of a perverse and cruel dialectic, freedom of thought and freedom of choice become the supreme evil, worthy of supreme punishment. In this context and from a broad perspective, it becomes really and truly irrelevant whether the sinner is a young liberal student who, like Dostoyevsky himself, kneels in abject submission before the tsar and the orthodox church and reneges on the ideals of his brief Sturm und Drang period; or whether he is a social revolutionary or some other heretic who beats his breast and submits to the authority of Stalin, that is, of the party reigning supreme and in the possession of absolute Truth. When one reflects on Dostoyevsky himself and the vicissitudes of his life and ideas, one cannot help being struck by the analogy between his spiritual fate and the fate of Russian socialism, as embodied by J. V. Stalin. I quote Freud:

> Nor was the ultimate result of Dostoevsky's moral struggles anything very glorious. After the most violent battles to reconcile the impulsive claims of the individual with the demands of the community, he ended up, retrograde fashion, with submission both to the temporal and the spiritual authorities, with veneration for the Tzar and the God of the Christians, and a narrow Russian nationalism, a position which lesser minds have reached with less effort. This is the weak-point of the great personality. Dostoevsky threw away the chance of becoming a teacher and liberator of humanity; instead, he appointed himself its jailer. The future of civilization will have little to thank him for.[39]

As to Stalin's personality, I am not aware of any new material that might significantly add to the understanding of its formation. However, to put things into a sharper focus, I cannot resist, at the risk of being repetitious, to quote again from Freud: "If the father was hard, violent, and cruel, the super-ego takes these characteristics from him, and in its relation to the ego, the passivity which was supposed to have been repressed, reestablishes itself."[40]

Some interesting new data relevant for the functioning of Stalin's mentality have reached us. I turn first to personal observations.

Close Observations

Achmed Amba was a young Turkish idealist who went to Russia in 1933, joined the ranks of the Red army and was distinguished by the dictator. Stalin took him into his personal guard in the Kremlin where the young convert could observe his hero for two years. Despite this distinction he, too, fell victim in the period of the great purges, was thrown into prison, and barely escaped execution. Amba speaks of the duality of Stalin, who could cajole him, play lovingly with his child, and show him warm and friendly understanding and yet let him be engulfed by the wave of incredible terror and cruelty that he himself unleashed. Amba draws an interesting comparison between this duality of his beloved hero and Russian mentality at large. "Diese unglaubliche Menschlichkeit der Männer, die ja am Ausbruch der unseligsten aller Kriege mitschuldig waren—das ist eben Russland, wie in einem Tropfen Wasser gespiegelt."[41]

Some of the most personal and lively impressions are those gathered by a man who at the time of his contact with Stalin was one of his most convinced admirers. Milovan Djilas, one of the closest friends and comrades of Marshal Tito (which did not prevent him in later years from falling from grace and languishing for many years behind prison walls), had between 1944 and 1948 three encounters with Stalin: he was a member of the official Yugoslav mission to the Soviet government.

As an old and trusted party member, he arrived full of admiration and idolization of Stalin, only to end in deep disillusionment. He was struck by Stalin's suspiciousness, and when he quotes Stalin's comments on his Western allies, one can almost hear the rumblings of the Cold War.

Because Stalin identified himself and his personal power with the power of the party and the state, his personal suspicions could be aroused as easily by opposition to his opinion as by anybody who, to his suspicious mind, might in some remote future become a threat to himself or to Soviet power and hegemony. "Everybody beyond the control of his police was a potential enemy."[42] It was for these reasons that Stalin was wary of revolutions in other countries and "helped (them) only up to a certain point—up to where he could control them—but he was always ready to leave them in the lurch whenever they slipped out of his grasp."[43]

Stalin's attitude toward violence, as disclosed in Djilas' observations, cannot surprise a student of the Russian dictator. He never forgave Djilas for allegedly insulting the Red army by accusing it of rape and violence in the liberated Yugoslav territory. "Can't Djilas understand it if a soldier who has crossed thousands of kilometers through blood and fire and death has fun with a woman or takes some trifle?"[44] Djilas made notice of Stalin's cynicism in avowing anti-Semitism and advocating most brazenly pure and simple imperialism. "We have no special interest in Albania. We agree to Yugoslavia swallowing Abania. . . . Yes, yes. Swallowing! But we agree with you: you ought to swallow Albania: the sooner the better."[45] Finally, Djilas makes subtle and most pertinent observations on Stalin's self-adulation and, correspondingly, his idolization by the Russians and Yugoslavs alike. The latter is, of course, best illustrated by his own example.

Stalin's Violence

And yet, after his personal encounters and his political disillusionment, Djilas reached quite a different image of the beloved leader. He considers him capable of every crime of violence.

> Every crime was possible to Stalin, for there was not one he had not committed. Whatever standards we use to take his measure, in any event—let us hope for all times to come—to him will fall the glory of being the greatest criminal in history. For in him was joined the criminal senselessness of a Caligula with the refinement of a Borgia and the brutality of Tzar Ivan the Terrible. . . . All in all, Stalin was a monster who, while adhering to abstract, absolute, and fundamentally utopian ideas, in practice recognized, and could recognize, only success–violence, physical and spiritual extermination.[46]

On the basis of his deep inside knowledge Djilas explains the role of Stalin in ruling the party.

> The ruling political bureaucracy of the Party found use for just such a man–one who was reckless in his determination and extremely practical in his fanaticism. The ruling party followed him doggedly and obediently and he truly led it from victory to victory, until carried away by power, he began to sin against it as well.[47]

We find valuable material in the study of that profound student of Soviet Russia, the former American ambassador to the Soviets, George F. Kennan. He confirms our opinion of the personality of the dictator by pointing out that Stalin was able "to see the world only through the prism of his own ambitions and his own fears. His fundamental motive was the protection of his position . . . and this is the key to his diplomacy."[48] Kennan, like many others, establishes the fundamental analogy between his attitude toward his real or potential enemies in personal as well as in political life. "His strategy was a simple one. It could be summed up in the single phrase 'divide and rule'".[49]

Stalin vented his immense hostility in his personal life where it led to the untimely death of his wife. It is characteristic of the man that the question remains unanswered whether she killed herself or whether it was Stalin who shot her. "That he drove her to her death seems inescapable."[50] His reactions of mourning offer a poignant illustration of a trend of Russian mind to which we alluded at the opening of this chapter. Kennan writes: "He showed afterward signs of remorse and sadness; gave her a curiously Christian sort of burial; followed the hearse on foot through the streets of Moscow; loved to talk about her with those who had known her well."[51]

It appears that Stalin did not hesitate to murder even such a universally beloved and venerated figure as the great Gorky, possibly because in his criticism of his strategy of terror he heard the voice of his own conscience, which he did his best to repress and deny.

Kennan's analysis of the great purges demonstrates once more the combination of incredible cunning and cruelty that went into the staging of this terror on a grandiose scale in the disguise of a mockery of justice. In an astute observation Kennan remarks that Stalin learned a great deal from his German counterpart: he was deeply impressed by Hitler's blood purge of June 30, 1934.

> This exhibition of ruthless brutality against Party Comrades evidently made a profound impression upon Stalin. Alone among his leading associates he is said to have insisted that this act would strengthen, not weaken, the Nazi regime. He was, I am sure, filled with admiration. From now on, there was no stopping him.[52]

However, already prior to his German model, Stalin used mock trials as a sure way of deflecting his own culpability. Three times, in the course of the years 1928 to 1933, great propaganda trials, involving foreign specialists and Russian technicians, served the objective of demonstrating to the suffering and constantly frustrated Russian people that their hardships were the result of sinister machinations of foreign saboteurs and Russian traitors rather than of bungling by their own government. Here, too, Stalin played cunningly on the old, inveterate Russian suspiciousness of the hostile

West. This strategy was resorted to by Stalin on many other occasions.

In a famous and often quoted article "Dizzy with Success," published in 1930, Stalin criticized the excesses of agricultural collectivization, which was inflicting terrible suffering on the farmers. In this way he was trying to disclaim his responsibility for this drama, because it was he, after all, who signed all the laws promulgated to that effect. Thus, the fault would lie not with him but with some inept officials.

A similar alibi was attempted by Stalin after the period of terror and purges in 1936. At first, no longer satisfied with his chief of secret police, Yagoda, he insisted on the appointment of one of his most sinister henchmen, N. T. Yezhov. From that moment on

> the purges took that fantastic course which defies the powers of description and nearly defies the imagination. Heads rolled by the thousands, the tens of thousands, probably even the hundreds of thousands. . . . In a vast conflagration of mock justice, torture and brutality at least two thirds of the governing class of Russia literally devoured and destroyed themselves.[53]

And yet, after this vast destruction of all possible, potential, and imaginary rivals and enemies was successfully carried out, Stalin destroyed the grand inquisitor Yezhov himself. He was doomed as one of "the witnesses" who had seen too much and knew too much, but also as a scapegoat on whom Stalin could conveniently blame the excesses of his cruel "justice."[54]

Apparent Pathology

Kennan notes that with increasing political terror, inspired and directed by Stalin, his mental abnormality became more and more apparent. This is confirmed by some personal observations recorded by a small number of observers. Even Djilas speaks of signs of senility by which he means increased vulgarity in speech and manners and primitive rudeness of behavior.

Much has been written about Stalin's megalomaniacal self-adulation supported by eager acolytes or—especially in earlier years—by true admirers. Yet, such was his cunning and astute forethought, such was his duplicity that even here he tried to disclaim his part in this process of deification of the living Caesar of the communist world. In one of his articles he protested against the personality cult long before the twenty-second congress of the party. Not content with this, in his short biography written and corrected by himself, he praised himself for his lack of vanity![55]

Political analysis by such men as Kennan, Basseches, and Uralov demonstrates the intricate connection between Stalin's paranoid personality and his political machinations. It is, for instance, apparent how, in complete analogy with his German counterpart, he created or rather remodeled the secret police as the extended arm of his vicious cruelty and vindictiveness. It is also quite apparent that his paranoia took advantage of the political scene inside Russia as well as abroad, to raise political adversaries to the rank of personal mortal enemies (for instance, the struggle against Trotsky); and, vice versa, he rationalized personal hostility by presenting its objects as traitors and counterrevolutionaries, and thus justifying their ruthless liquidation. We know that no lie, no defamation was beyond him in this process, which hit the living and the dead alike.[56]

In this way we gain a better understanding of some of Stalin's more sinister political maneuvers, which otherwise would be difficult to comprehend. Here belongs, for instance, his handling of the Spanish Loyalists or his love affair with Adolf Hitler.

In conclusion, our review of new material illustrates how, with his personal psychological background, and given the social and historical events and configurations, the Russian dictator, from his start as a leader, became a ruthless dictator, a criminal paranoiac of the type described by the French classic school of psychiatry as the *persécuteur persécuté* ("the persecuted persecutor").

In studying the collective processes that had made this development possible, we have pointed out how the collective ego through love and admiration but also through dread and terror had incorporated the image of the leader and ended in his deification. The events of the post-Stalin era provide a unique illustration of the process of dethronement of the dead leader. His successors, in their desperate attempt to disclaim their own culpability and complicity in his crimes, set out to abolish the so-called cult of personality. However, they went much further: they did everything within their power to eradicate the holy image from the collective mind of his faithful subjects and mourning sons. The holy mummy was taken out of the mausoleum, the names of the cities were changed, and, first, the faithful comrades, then, the rest of the people were shown the hideous face of the cruel, demented paranoiac emerging behind the façade of the universal genius, the Father of the Russian masses, and the oppressed proletarians throughout the world.

In his secret speech to the twenty-second congress Khrushchev described Stalin's cruelty as unmatched in the bloody chronicle of history. He pointed to his delusions of grandeur which made him lose completely the sense of reality.[57] Thus, even before the corpse was cold, or his memory had begun to dim, the orphaned sons began to wrestle with the Father's ghost."[58] Indeed, one of the authors analyzing the speech of Premier Khrushchev and comparing his interpretation to historical events with the official Soviet version in Stalin's time, chose for his book the appropriate title *Autopsie du Stalinisme.*[59]

Unfortunately, we lack sufficient data to analyze the effects of this autopsy of the dictator on the Russian masses. Therefore, I shall terminate with this brief glimpse of the tragic postscript to the great tragedy of our times.

NOTES

1. Vladimir I. Lenin, *State and Revolution* (New York, 1932).
2. *Ibid.*
3. D. Spearman, *Modern Dictators* (New York, 1939).
4. Georges Sorel, *Reflections on Violence* (New York, 1941).
5. Lenin, *State and Revolution.*
6. Leon Trotsky, *Terrorismus und Kommunismus* (Hamburg, 1920).
7. D. Spearman, *Modern Dictators.*
8. Karl Marx and Friedrich Engels, *Communist Manifesto* (New York, 1934).
9. K. Marx, quoted in Vladimir I. Lenin, *The Deception of the People by the Slogans of Equality and Freedom* (London, 1934).
10. Vladimir I. Lenin, "Democracy and Dictatorship" (1919), in *Collected Works,* vol. 23.
11. Vladimir I. Lenin, *Letter to American Workingmen from the Social Soviet Republic of Russia* (New York, 1918).
12. Friedrich Engels, quoted in Vladimir I. Lenin, "Prophetic Words," (1918), in *Collected Works,* vol. 23.
13. K. Zetkin, *Reminiscences of Lenin* (London, 1929).
14. Sigmund Freud, *Civilization and Its Discontents* (London, 1930).

15. Lenin, *State and Revolution.*
16. Josef V. Stalin, *Problems of Leninism* (Moscow, 1933), vol. 2.
17. Sigmund Freud, *Totem and Taboo* (New York, 1931).
18. Geza Róheim, "Nach dem Tode des Urvaters," Imago 9 (1923).
19. A. Adler, *Studien über die Minderwertigkeit der Organe* (Berlin, 1907).
20. L. Trotsky, *Stalin* (New York, 1941).
21. *Ibid.*
22. *Ibid.*
23. *Ibid.*
24. *Ibid.*
25. *Ibid.*
26. E. Tarle, *Textbook of Modern History* (Moscow).
27. B. Souvarine, *Stalin, A Critical Survey of Bolshevism* (New York, 1939).
28. *Ibid.*
29. E. Lyons, *Stalin, Czar of All Russians* (Philadelphia, 1940).
30. *Ibid.*
31. *Stalin, A Collective Volume Published on the Occasion of His Sixtieth Birthday.*
32. *Ibid.*
33. Lyons, *Stalin.*
34. *Ibid.*
35. *Ibid.*
36. Souvarine, *Stalin.*
37. Compare this with the historical anti-Stalinist speech by Premier Khrushchev: "and how is it possible that a person confesses to crimes which he has not committed? Only in one way: because of the applying of physical pressure, torture, bringing him to a state of unconsciousness, deprivation of his judgment, taking away his human dignity." Quoted in Wolfe, *Khrushchev and Stalin's Ghost* (New York, 1957).
38. S. Freud, "Dostoevsky and Parricide" (1928), in *Collected Papers* (New York, 1959), 5: p. 222.
39. *Ibid.*, p. 223.
40. *Ibid.*, p. 231.
41. A. Amba, *Ein Mensch Sieht Stalin* (Hamburg, 1957). The translation reads: "This incredible humaneness of men who were guilty collaborators in unleashing the most terrible of wars—this is Russia as though mirrored in one drop of water."
42. M. Djilas, *Conversations with Stalin* (New York, 1962).
43. *Ibid.*
44. *Ibid.*
45. *Ibid.*
46. *Ibid.*
47. *Ibid.*
48. G. F. Kennan, *Russia and the West under Lenin and Stalin* (Boston, 1960).
49. *Ibid.*
50. *Ibid.*

51. *Ibid.*
52. *Ibid.*
53. *Ibid.*
54. This mechanism is pointed out with great clarity in N. Basseches, *Stalin* (New York, 1952).
55. *Ibid.*
56. One of innumerable examples is the execution of Alter and Ehrlich, the two famous Polish Jewish socialist leaders, as Hitler's spies.
57. For instance, speaking to Tito, Stalin said: "I will shake my little finger and there will be no more Tito." Quoted in Wolfe, *Khrushchev and Stalin's Ghost.*
58. *Ibid.*
59. *Autopsie du Stalinisme,* Angelo Rossi (Pierre Moray, Paris 1959).

6

THEODOR HERZL: A PSYCHOANALYTIC STUDY IN CHARISMATIC POLITICAL LEADERSHIP

Peter Loewenberg

The founder of modern political Zionism, Theodor Herzl, presents an excellent case of the charismatic personality whose psychopolitical fantasies influenced history and were acted out in reality. The true subject matter of history is human consciousness. As a man who has left a startling record of his conciousness at work in all its levels, Herzl is a particularly attractive subject for a psychoanalytical historical case study. In him we confront many problems rarely bound together in one historical figure. We trace the entire unfolding of a program of political action from the painful regression to narcissism out of which fantasy brought a frustrated man. We may derive insight into the nature of the charismatic political mass leader and the dynamics of ideology formation as we see personal fantasies as a prelude to action, these fantasies then being acted out in the social world. Herzl is one of the rare political leaders who was a *littérateur*. He has left us a rich body of creative writings from both his nonpolitical and his Zionist periods. By correlating his plays, stories, essays, and novels with his political fantasies, we may observe the interaction of the literary creativity with the psyche of the author. Herzl also gives the historian a fascinating demonstration of the value of perceiving the psychic response of historical figures to organic disease. Biographical and medical data are often abundant in the case of famous figures. The unconscious fantasies induced by disease, whether infectious or degenerative, are of value to historical interpretation.

A further fact that makes Herzl exceptional as an historical subject is the rare quality of total candor in his *Diaries*.[1] He confessed his private feelings and his most grandiose fantasies to his notebooks because no one in his world took him seriously. Even his best friend thought him mad.

Herzl was born in Budapest in 1860, the second child of a highly assimilated Jewish middle-class family. His father was a bank director and timber merchant. Theodor was almost exclusively raised by his mother, his father being involved in business affairs and often away from home. The boy worshipped his mother and sought her counsel; the man remained very close to her until the end of his life. Herzl's father had a managing nature, which he tried to exercise on his son. The Herzl home was noted for its formality and its attention to externals. Theodor was always elegantly clothed and well mannered.[2]

His paternal grandfather, an orthodox Jew who died when Theodor was twenty, was a follower of the Sephardic rabbi, Alkalai of Semlin (1792–1878), who preached the ideal of the return of the Jews to Palestine. It is doubtful whether the young Herzl could have avoided hearing his grandfather talk of Alkalai and his dream of returning to the homeland. It is a matter of speculation as to what impact this may have had on him.[3]

In 1878, following the death of Theodor's elder sister, Pauline, the family moved to Vienna. There is now an emerging body of scholarship on the social, political, and aesthetic culture of late nineteenth-century Vienna.[4] Bearing in mind the social and cultural milieu that is Herzl's scene of action, we will focus on the depth interpretation of his biography.

Zionist hagiography would have it that Herzl came to his Jewish nationalism by firsthand observation of the Dreyfus case as a correspondent in Paris. I suggest that Herzl's Zionist calling was determined by a personal need to be a messiah—savior—political leader.

At about age twelve, the period when a Jewish boy is thinking of his forthcoming bar-mitzvah, Herzl had a dream, which he later recounted as an adult. In the dreamer's own words:

> "The King-Messiah came, a glorious and majestic old man, took me in his arms, and swept off with me on the wings of the wind. On one of the iridescent clouds we encountered the figure of Moses. The features were those familiar to me out of my childhood in the Statue by Michelangelo. The Messiah called to Moses: It is for this child that I have prayed. But to me he said: Go, declare to the Jews that I shall

come soon and perform great wonders and great deeds for my people and for the whole world.[5]

The fact that this youthful dream was remembered all his life is an indication of its profound unconscious significance. We note in this dream Herzl's passivity.[6] He was carried up by a man. Twenty-four years later he experienced his great Zionist conception in the same passive manner, writing: "Am I working it out? No, it is working through me!"[7] This is the passivity experienced when the unconscious is in control of mental activity, and this close contact with the unconscious is the wellspring of all mental creativity.

Herzl's mental associations of himself with the messiah and with Moses are already in evidence in this dream. He has a mission to become a powerful charismatic leader and, like Freud, he has chosen to identify with the greatest leader of his people.

As Herzl grows up, it becomes evident that his emotional life is split into two currents of feeling. The tender, affectionate feelings springing from the earliest years of childhood and attached to the members of his family and the sensual erotic elements that became powerful at the age of puberty were never fused, as is essential for a normal attitude in love. Thus Herzl's tender feelings remained attached to unconscious fantasies of his mother and sister, whereas his sensual feelings were aroused by a "lower" type of sexual object, the woman of the street, to whom he had no tender romantic feelings, but with whom he could find physical gratification.[8]

From documentary evidence it appears that Herzl had an infection (possibly gonorrhea) when he was twenty. The evidence appears in a letter to his closest youthful friend and confidant, Heinrich Kana. Kana, who shot himself in 1891, is the man whom Herzl later wished to make the central figure of his novel. The letter was written in the friendly spirit of cameraderie of young single men during late nineteenth-century Vienna. Herzl tells his friend that he has laid his syringe aside, that he hopes that his next attack of "xxx" will be cured by zinc sulphate. He has commissioned a custom-made linen sheath for his penis in a prominent ladies' fashion shop. He notes that fortunately the seamstress was a young girl of seventeen years who therefore would not yet know what consequences unhappy love (unplatonic of course) could have. Though she tried her best to please him, the sheath was too narrow for his penis, but how was she to know this with her mere seventeen years? The penis is only placed in its sheath when he behaves himself quietly as a peaceful dweller in trousers. A second sheath commissioned at the same shop had the shortcoming that either his "young candidate for knighthood" felt cramped, or he slipped out. Herzl complains of being plagued by an erection dilemma. Perhaps, he asks, he should take off the hair shirt? But, much dripping water flows down into the valley; and what would his laundress think? She might despise him. Dare he risk it?[9]

The significance of the disease for the historian is less in its pathology than in the impact it had on Herzl. How did he respond to the knowledge that he had contracted venereal disease? What were his psychological defenses and accommodations, and what may we learn from them? We see in this letter an attempt to cover a depression with frivolity. The surface tone of the letter is gay and joking. But beneath the light-heartedness are the indications of worry over the unhappy consequences of "unplatonic love." Herzl must have been full of anxiety over his penis drip and threatened loss of potency. Social disapproval of the disease indicated by Herzl's concern over the possible reaction of his washerwoman compounded his fear of injury. We also find a boastfulness on the subject of his manly prowess. Herzl makes a point of recounting to his friend the size of his organ, its erective power, the wide experience of his "young knight" in the pursuit of women.

The other side of the emotional split between sensuality and tenderness apparent in Herzl in his twenties was a penchant for deep infatuations with young pubescent girls. When he was twenty-one he fell passionately in love with his sixteen-year-old cousin. "She is a beautiful girl such as one only sees in a dream," he wrote Kana. If he were four years older, he would marry her immediately. "I tell you, my dear friend, I am in ecstasy ['schwarme'] for this sweet child, as in the time of my full blown versifying and love-making . . . she is a lyric poem, and I could conceive of no finer life task than to read this prize forever." He visits her parents as often as possible without arousing their suspicion and then he feasts on the sight of her. Herzl thought of asking for her hand. His heart pounded when he suddenly met her on the street. "If I ever do marry," he says "my wife must be like my lovely cousin."[10]

Four years later Herzl confides to his diary that he is in love—with a thirteen-year-old child. He sought her out at a children's ball.

> I wished to kiss her. She merely turned her blond little head away. I did not kiss her. Then she climbed up onto my arm, like a little queen . . . I could not see enough of this proud fine little person . . . she ruled me from the first moment. I was sad when she withdrew from me, the premature coquette; I was jealous of the boys with whom she danced . . . A true princess? I looked at nothing but her, the sweet, sweet, sweet! The little dress was still short, the darling body undeveloped . . . but the fine, aristocratic, lovely face! . . . Later, as she was frazzled [zerzaust] and stood in front of a lamp, I saw a halo around that sweet little head.

When Herzl danced with her and she winked at him slyly, he was beside himself. He had to restrain himself from professing his love to her as to an adult. He tried to rouse her jealousy by flirting with the most beautiful of the "big" ladies. "In short," he says, "I behaved madly." He would rather let himself be torn to pieces than not have a dance with her. He thought of her in the night and dreamed of her. It was all he could do to avoid going down to the ice skating rink where she would be. "Dear God, Dear God!" he moans as he closes the diary entry of his passion for a little girl half his age.[11]

Throughout these two infatuations of his twenties Herzl's emotions are highly romanticized projections. His objects are virginal maids, pure and sentimentalized. They are women to be adored and worshipped, not to whom he could relate sensually or from whom he would catch a disease. From such a split between the sensual and tender emotions toward women we expect to find an inadequate or differential potency and a strengthening of homoerotic currents in the personality. Because a mature level of genitality has not been reached, libidinal satisfaction must be derived from a source other than women. In the case of a charismatic leader, this source is the adoration given him by the masses. Herzl, already having established the pattern of his great creative phase of the mid-1890's, succeeds in defending against his underlying depression with megalomanic fantasies.

Moods of melancholy alternating with periods of elation pervaded Herzl's personal life. At age nineteen, shortly after a serious illness of his mother, he wrote: "I have much to complain about the changes in my moods: to exult to heaven, to be deathly depressed [*Himmelhoch jauchzend, zu Tode betrübt*],—soon to delude myself with hope, far like the billowing sea, again to die, to be rejected unto death [*zu Tode, zum Sterben versagt*]." In contrast with the countless hopes and plans with which he had commenced his trip two months previously, he has brought home nothing real and positive, "and this arouses a sneering rage against myself in me," he says. His pessimism of the moment is expressed in an aphorism, undoubtedly inspired by Schopenhauer: "Pain is the substance of life and joy consists only of the temporary absence of pain."[12]

At the beginning of his twenty-third year, Herzl chastises himself because he has to date achieved nothing in life. He is filled with doubts about his capacity; he has no great achievement in him. He derogates his journal notes as literary onanism. His dreams, hopes and desires are unachieved. His inability to fulfill is an impediment to matrimony with the muse of creativity. "But this is an impotence that one hopes may be healed, even if in fact it cannot be; one always hopes for means to lift this sterile failure."[13] The etiology of Herzl's melancholia is suggested by his closely related imagery of masturbation, inability to marry, and creative impotence.

The year 1883 was a year of many crises for Herzl. Two years earlier he had joined the Burschenschaft Albia, a dueling fraternity where he dueled for four hours each day. In March 1883 he resigned from Albia because its members had participated in an anti-Semitic commemoration of the death of Richard Wagner. Herzl's decision was made on a point of honor. It was a move that caused deep feelings of isolation and rejection. People do not know how much "pain, suffering and disappointment" he carried with him hidden beneath his vest, he confided to his diary.[14] This was a decisive encounter with social anti-Semitism which was to leave a lasting impression on him. He referred to his depressions as "an evil guest who calls himself Mr. Uncertainty [*Herr von Zweifel*]" and who was related to the devil. His mood of happiness or misery depended on whether he was potent or impotent in his work.[15]

Further defeats that year were experienced in Herzl's quest for love and in the rejection of his literary efforts. He had a mild flirtation with a young girl and was slapped for it.[16] His diary notes of the same week are desperate and inconsolable. "Powerless, inactive, luckless time!" he dejectedly writes. "Death and pestilence, will this never cease? he asks. "Success refuses to come. And I need success, I thrive only on it," he cries. His finished work containing his aspirations, hopes, the blood and striving of the years of his youth lies in the drawer. He has no desire to submit it, certain that it will be sent back with a printed rejection note. "No love in the heart, no longing in the soul, no hope, no joy . . ." is the refrain with which Herzl closes his melancholy entry.[17]

Some of Herzl's most depressed entries were on the New Year's Eves of his early twenties. He usually spent them alone, writing his diary and retiring early without waiting for midnight, thus closing what he felt was an empty day in an empty life. "All is empty! The heart is empty of hope, the head is empty of ideas, the pocket is empty of money, and life is empty of poetry." He is unable to study for his forthcoming examination in Roman law. He doubts his fitness for love. He is already useless, even for that! He has a piece of work in his desk that embodies his best efforts, but it is not fit for success.[18]

When he was completing his studies at the university, Herzl journeyed at his parents' expense to southwest Germany.[19] In a letter dated "The month of distress," Herzl terms himself an "old gambler" who cannot restrain himself from risking his money at the green table.[20] Herzl's episode of unrestrained gambling is psychodynamically related to his later political career and thus deserves our notice. The gambler dares fate, forcing it to decide for or against him. He believes it his right to ask for special favor from fate. Good luck is the delivery of protection and the promise of continued blessings for future acts. Gambling is an attempt to force fate to do right by the gambler. In any casino gambling the odds of losing are slightly larger than the chance of winning. The gambler dares the gods to make a decision about him, hoping for their beneficence. If winning means the getting of needed supplies, loss is interpreted as ingratiation with the gods for the same purpose.

Gambling begins as play. The omnipotent god is asked how he would decide in an actual situation. The earnest cycle of anxiety, need for reassurance, and heightened anxiety over the violent need for comfort overwhelms the ego, and the playful character of "gaming" is lost. It has become a serious matter in which the gambler must in the end be ruined.[21]

For Herzl in Baden, at age twenty-three, gambling was what politics was to become for him later—a trial with fate to prove his destiny. Herzl fought fate at the casino and as a Zionist. He rebelled against her and sought to compel her to let him win.

There is also a deeper psychoanalytical meaning to gambling which bears confirmation from Herzl's references to masturbation. The passion for gambling is an expression of conflicts centering on infantile sexuality, particularly masturbation. The excitement of "gaming" is analogous to sexual excitation. Both gambling and masturbation are "play." Masturbation among children is playing at sexual excitement. Gambling also begins as play. The unconscious masturbatory fantasies of gambling are patricidal. Winning corresponds to orgasm and killing the father; losing has the emotional meaning of castration and of being killed.[22]

Herzl idealized his parents all his life. To him they were the "best" parents in the world, to be honored and adored.[23] According to his biographer, the bond with his father "had never been strained."[24] The oedipal struggle with his father was repressed. It never was externalized in conflict between father and son. The processes of love and hate were separated, affording relief from the guilt of hostility. Only the "good" father was admitted to consciousness. The feelings of rivalry and hatred for his father, undoubtedly caused the punishment Herzl experienced in his depressive periods.

Herzl on one occasion relished posing as a nobleman, "Baron Rittershausen," in a social setting. If he ever should become something more than a talentless scribbler, which his doubting self, "Mr. Uncertainty," convinced him was decidedly unlikely, then he would do as the *Arabian Nights* hero, Harun al Raschid, the caliph of Bagdad, who went among his people in disguise to hear what they were truly thinking.[25] Herzl enjoyed the role of the Prussian nobleman at home in the world of letters. He easily pictured himself the romantic *Arabian Nights* ruler who puts on the mask of a new identity to help his people. At a later date he was to say: "[I]f there is one thing I should like to be, it is a member of the old Prussian nobility."[26]

Herzl fell in love with Julie Naschauer, the daughter of a wealthy businessman, in the spring of 1886. His diaries show a powerful, highly romanticized infatuation. He records his first kiss from her as they stood on a balcony at a party.[27] Three weeks later he received two more kisses.[28] The romance had its vacillations until the couple were married on July 25, 1889. On March 29, 1890, their first child, a daughter named after Herzl's dead sister Pauline, was born. There is no record of this child having been premature. If she was a full-term baby, we may say from all the evidence that she was a child of love. Herzl was attached to his three children and loved them dearly.

Herzl was faced with frustration and rejection personally, professionally, and socially in the period 1891 to 1895. His marriage was marked by discord "almost from the start."[29] His biographers attribute the breakup of Herzl's marriage to "a mother-in-law problem" and his wife's lack of sympathy as a helpmeet to the struggling journalist-playwright.[30]

Herzl remained attached to his powerful and possessive mother.[31] He would often have dinner with his parents to escape domestic scenes.[32] Julie was spoiled and immature. Plans for a divorce did not materialize, apparently for the sake of the children. In 1891 the family separated with Herzl settling in Paris after he was appointed correspondent for the prestigious *Neue Freie Presse.* In 1892 his wife and children came to Paris, but the attempted reconciliation was to no avail. Herzl was not to have a lasting relationship with a woman, other than his mother, for the rest of his life. She remained the primary "spiritual" love object in his life to be recreated in the mother figures of his stories and his novel *Altneuland.* As far as we know, physical sexual gratification was not a factor in his life between the time of his separation from his wife and his death in 1904.

The significant emotional fact for us is that in August 1891 Herzl separated from his wife and children. From this time on his emotions were detached from close libidinal ties to others. He was a loner—masterful, narcissistic, independent.[33] Max Weber[34] suggests that the holders of charisma often live in celibacy or at least renounce family life and in fact are single as stated in the call to asceticism of Jesus: "If any man come to me and hates not his father, and mother, and wife, and children, and brethren, and sisters, yea, and his own life also, he cannot be my disciple."[35] According to W. W. Tarn, Alexander the Great "apparently never cared for any woman; he apparently never had a mistress, and his two marriages were mere affairs of policy."[36] Hitler has been considered asexual by Trevor-Roper.[37] Herzl's case would confirm Weber's ideal typology in that the breakup of his marriage coincided with his emergence as a prophet. Weber does not explain the dynamics of such libidinal displacement by charismatic leaders. He recognizes, defines, and evaluates the phenomenon of charisma itself without offering any personality theory to explain it. Psychoanalysis, though confirming Weber's observations on charisma, also presents a dynamic personality theory that interprets it. We may see the depth dynamics of charisma operate in their full manifestations in Herzl's evolution to celibacy, isolation, and charismatic political leadership.

A record of Herzl's unhappy marriage and of his melancholia exists in memoirs of his friends and colleagues. It is apparent that Julie Herzl had little insight into what her husband was truly about. There is no indication of empathy with his fantasies, understanding of his emotional needs, or interest in his political ideas on the part of his wife. A striking characterization is that of Mrs. Herzl's reaction to the Zionist writer Israel Zangwill, one of her husband's most vital English supporters, when he was a guest in her home. His small unaristocratic stature "visibly disappointed" Julie. Zangwill relaxed after a long journey; he let his hair down. He did not know how to properly eat the crab she served. His natural folksy demeanor was all that she could see. She interpreted it as vulgarity and retired from the table as soon as she could, "distressed by his peculiarities."[38]

The Nobel prize-winning author Maria E. Delle Grazie records the change perceivable in Herzl when he was with his wife. From a man gripped by the obsession of a personal mission who tells the writer: "I have staked all my life and all my will on a single hope. Palestine! . . . I too can no longer help myself; for the vision burns in the night when my eyes are closed and I cannot hide from it," he changes in the presence of his wife to nothing more than a sauve Viennese wit. The authoress recalls:

> I saw him once again, once only, in his home, beside his beautiful blond wife who—it became clear to me in a moment—found only torment in that which was life and fate to him. For that one hour, in her presence, he was . . . the witty feuilletonist–that and nothing more. It was only then that I understood the full tragedy of his life.[39]

Herzl's first attempts at a solution to the Jewish problem were romantic dreams with himself in the role of fantasy hero. To combat anti-Semitism he would use the classic aristocratic mode of dealing with opposition—the duel. He wrote: "Half a dozen duels will do a great deal to improve the position of the Jews in society."[40] He contemplated challenging the leading Austrian anti-Semites, Prince Alois Lichtenstein, George von Schönerer, and Karl Leuger, to duels. If he were killed, a posthumous letter would announce to the world that he had been a victim of "the most unjust movement in the world." He continued,

> If however, it had been my lot to kill my opponent and be brought to trial, then I would have delivered a brilliant speech which would have begun with my regrets for the death of a man of honor . . . Then I would have turned to the Jewish question and delivered an oration worthy of Lassalle. I would have sent a shudder of admiration through the jury. I would have compelled the respect of the judges, and the case against me would have been dismissed. Thereupon the Jews would have made me one of their representatives and I would have declined because I would refuse to achieve such a position by the killing of a man.[41]

His next fantasy has moved from a personal to a social solution—he will lead the Jews of Austria in a mass conversion to Catholicism: "We must submerge in the people."[42] But, again, the solution is one embodying Herzl's strictest conceptions of chivalric honor. The baptism would be for the children and the masses only;

> the leaders of this movement—above all myself—would remain Jews and as Jews would propagate conversion to the religion of the majority. In broad daylight, at noon on Sunday, the conversion should take place at St. Stefan's Cathedral in solemn procession with the pealing of bells. Not in shame, as individuals have done it up to now, but with a proud gesture. And because the leaders would remain Jewish, escorting the people only to the threshold of the church and themselves staying outside, the whole procedure would have a feature of great uprightness . . . [W]e would have made Christians of our young sons before they came into the age of independent decision, after which conversion looks like cowardice or social climbing.[43]

Herzl's last nonpolitical attempt to overcome anti-Semitism was through culture. He would persuade by writing a play of such force that it would forge a new mutual understanding between Jews and Gentiles. Herzl wrote *The New Ghetto* in seventeen days in the fall of 1894. Its hero, a young Jewish lawyer, Dr. Jacob Samuel, is transparently Herzl himself. He is married to the spoiled and willful daughter of a rich businessman, thus a replica of his wife Julie as described by his biographers.[44] The Jewish hero of the play has learned gentlemanly conduct and bearing from his Christian friend to whom he says: "I have learned from you how to honor a man without crawling at his feet, how to be proud without being arrogant." He professes to have "taken a number of steps out of the Jewish street."[45] Having learned honor Dr. Samuel is killed in a duel, but not before he can make a dying statement to the "Jews, my brothers, there will come a time when they will let you live again—when you know how to die."[46] It was in vain that Arthur Schnitzler pointed out to Herzl that Jews had known how to die for centuries and had done so by the thousands; this, said Schnitzler is why they were not permitted to live.[47] Herzl has presented here a solution embodying his future formula—the "new" Jew, the man who has a sense of aristocratic honor and virtue—and knows how to die like a cavalier; but he has done so in the idiom of the old Herzl, the frustrated playwright and author. He is not yet Herzl the political man, the charismatic leader; he is still the bourgeois writer using the aesthetic culture to persuade.

At this time of personal desperation, Herzl tried to gain the friendship of Schnitzler, a man whom he admired, by taking the well-known playwright into a compact of secrecy in trying to get his play *The New Ghetto* produced. Schnitzler faithfully carried out his commitment to act as broker for the anonymous Herzl, but the latter wished a greater degree of intimacy:

> Why don't you send me your play? Have I not come close enough to you in our secret conspiracy of the last months? I have a great need for a good friendship. I almost feel like advertising in the newspapers: "Man in prime of life seeks friend to whom he can confide without fear all his weaknesses and foolishness." . . . I really don't know, am I too shy, or am I seeing too well: I don't find any such friend among my acquaintances here.[48]

Rather than growing closer, the two men grew apart with Herzl's dedication to Zionism.

Herzl was already writing *The New Ghetto* when the Dreyfus case broke in Paris. The case made no particular impression on him that has been recorded in his contemporary letters or diaries, thus suggesting that it was not the Dreyfus case, but antecedent fantasies that provided the primary impulse for his political development.[49]

In Herzl's *Diaries* we have one of the most candid and historically unique sources available in the literature for the investigation of charismatic leadership formation. To them he disclosed his most intimate thoughts and candid doubts. We may trace his day-by-day regression to narcissism, his increasing feelings of estrangement and depersonalization. For him everything has changed. He has the ecstatic experience of a grand and pleasant inflation of the self and a withdrawal of interest in the external world of people and things.

The *Diaries* open in the spring of 1895 with the modest statement: "I have been laboring for some time on a work of infinite magnitude." The line between illusion and reality is blurred: "Even now I don't know whether I will be able to carry it through. It appears like a mighty dream." But it is so powerful he cannot resist—it is an obsession: "For days and weeks it has possessed me to the limits of my consciousness; it accompanies me wherever I go; hangs suspended over my everyday conversations; looks over my shoulder at my comical little journalistic work, disturbs me and intoxicates me."[50] We note the self-depreciation concerning his vocational role in life. Herzl's narcissistic ego ideal is not satisfied with being a prominent journalist, he must be much more—a world shaper and leader of men. His description of the ever-present idea that hovers over his conversation and daily affairs indicates a perception of his narcissistic regression and his libidinal displacement, though he is perplexed by it: "How I move from the ideas for a novel to a practical program is already a puzzle to me, although it occurred in the last weeks. That lies in the Unconscious."[51]

Herzl now compensates for the loss of love in the external world by increased self-love. There is a marked eroticization of his inner world of ideas. He describes his feelings toward his fantasy in the only suitable metaphor—that of a lover to his beloved: "So sehr füllt mich das jetzt aus, dass ich alles auf die Sache beziehe, wie ein Liebender auf die Person."[52]

This self-absorbed proposition is the psychological equivalent of the proposition: "I love only myself."[53] It is the narcissistic expression of the overestimation of the love object, which Freud described as a "[diminished judgment] concerning the psychic attainments and perfections of the sexual object, and . . . a credulous yielding to the judgments emanating from the latter. The absolute faith inspired by love thus becomes an important, if not primordial, source of authority."[54] Thus, Herzl's megalomania is an overestimation of the self. The love of external objects is replaced by self-love, and the overestimation usually directed to a loved person is now directed to his own ego and its fantasies.

Herzl's megalomania is visible in the ego ideals he has formed of conspicuous leaders. He draws comparisons between himself and Moses,[55] Bismarck,[56] Napoleon,[57] and Moltke.[58] When he walks in the Tuileries and views the statue of Gambetta, he says: "I hope the Jews put up a more artistic one to me."[59]

Herzl tells us that he is a passive agent of his inspiration. His mission to redeem the Jews is an inspiration from God: "Am I working it out? No! It is working me. It would be a compulsion if it were not so rational from beginning to end. This is what was formerly called 'inspiration.' . . . But if it comes about, what a gift of God to the Jews!"[60] He describes his sensation as like a volcanic eruption shooting up within him.[61] It promises to be a process of internal purification. His work will consist of a life full of manly acts that will dissolve and lift up everything base, barren, and confused within him and reconcile him with all, just as he has reconciled himself to all through his labor.[62]

Herzl was in a hypomanic period which was a defense against depression. He found release from tension through living in the world of his ideas. Writing them down became a relief for him. He was in the grip of unconscious creative forces not of his own volition. His expression is consistently passive, that of natural forces: "I am writing myself free of ideas which rise like bubbles in a retort and which would burst it to pieces if they found no outlet."[63] Or the imagery may be of labor and delivery: "For three hours I have been tramping about the Bois to dispel the pangs of new trains of thought."[64] He is overexcited by his fantasies. He goes to the gardens of the Tuileries and recovers by looking at the statues.[65] He lives in his own world, an inner realm apart from his friends: "Today I dined at a brasserie near the Châtelet. I avoid all my acquaintances.

They hurt me because they fail to realize the world I come from; this makes everyday life terribly wounding."[66] Herzl felt an identity with artists and poets because he lived in the realm of his fantasies:

> Much in these notes will seem laughable, exaggerated, crazy. But if I had exercised self-criticism, as I do in my literary work, my ideas would have been stunted. What is colossal serves the purpose better than what is dwarfed, for anyone can do the trimming easily enough.
>
> Artists will understand why I, who otherwise reason clearly, have allowed extravagances and dreams to grow wildly among my practical, political, and legislative ideas—as green grass sprouts between the paving stones. I could not permit myself to be tied down purely to sober fact. This light intoxication was necessary.
>
> Yes, artists will understand this fully. But there are so few artists.[67]

At times Herzl feared that he was going insane. His ego carefully observed his actions and commented: "According to these frank notes, some people will think me a megalomaniac. Others will say or believe that I want to do some business or engage in self advertisment. But my peers, the artists and philosophers, will understand how genuine all this is, and they will defend me."[68] Or: "Lombroso will perhaps think me mad. And my good friend Nordau will muffle in silence the anxiety I cause him. But they are wrong: I know that two and two is four."[69]

At other times he was unsure of his ability to discriminate between reality and fantasy:

> During these days I have often been afraid of going insane. So shatteringly did the streams of thought race through my soul. A lifetime will not suffice to realize all of it.
>
> But I am leaving behind a spiritual legacy. To whom? To all men.
>
> I believe I shall be named among the greatest benefactors of mankind.
>
> Or is this belief already megalomania?[70]

There were occasions when Herzl sounded like a man who is undergoing a psychotic break: "I believe that for me life has ended and world history has begun."[71] He sees himself as a savior and messiah: "They will pray for me in the synagogues. But also in the churches."[72] He believed in his own total omnipotence: "If I point with my finger at a spot: Here shall be a city, then a city shall rise there."[73]

In early June 1895 Herzl was in a high state of excitation while writing *Der Judenstaat.* He compared his sensation to Heine's description of eagle's wings above his head when he was poetically inspired. Herzl writes:

> I worked at it daily, until I was completely exhausted. My one recreation was on the evenings when I could go to hear Wagner's music, and particularly *Tannhäuser,* an opera which I go to hear as often as it is produced. And only on those evenings when there was no opera did I have any doubts as to the truth of my ideas.[74]

On the day on which he was so cathected to his idea that he wrote: "I am so filled with it that I relate everything to it, like a lover to his beloved," he sought relief from his excitement by attending Wagnerian opera and fantasized incorporating the opulent staging of medieval chivalric opera into his political program:

> In the evening, *Tannhäuser* at the Opera.
>
> We too shall have such splendid lobbies, the men in formal dress, the women as luxurious as possible. Yes, I will exploit the Jewish love of luxury, as everything else.
>
> Again, I think of the phenomenon of the crowd.
>
> There they sat for hours, tightly packed, motionless, in bodily torture! and for what? For an imponderable, which Hirsch does not comprehend: for sounds! for music, and pictures!
>
> I shall also encourage stately processional marches for great occasions.[75]

Herzl tells us that he understands what the old style of philanthropic leadership such as the Barons Rothschild and Hirsch do not, that the modern mass crowds demand operatic spectacle and a politics of emotional manipulation.

He carefully notes the theatrical decor of the setting of the First Zionist Congress in the concert hall in Basel.[76] He compliments Wolffsohn's cleverness in making the new Zionist banner on the format of the *talit,* the traditional Jewish prayer shawl—a white field with two blue stripes and the star of David. Herzl, the playwright, was always supremely conscious of his political costumes and staging. A visitor to the congress recorded his impression of the leader as stage manager:

> The first time I saw Herzl was in Basle in 1897 when, dressed in evening clothes at ten o'clock in the morning, he appeared on the

> tribune and opened the First Zionist Congress. The evening dress was characteristic of the man. He had given strict orders that all delegates were to appear at this First Congress in festive attire.[77]

At the opening of the congress Herzl made an issue of dress with Nordau, who refused flatly to go home and change to a full dress suit.

> I drew him aside and begged him to do it as a special favor to me. I told him: Today, the presidium of the Zionist Congress is as yet nothing, we must establish everything. People must grow accustomed to seeing only the finest and most elegant at this Congress. He allowed himself to be persuaded, for which I embraced him in gratitude. In a quarter of an hour he returned in formal dress.[78]

When Herzl prepared to meet the German Kaiser in Istanbul, he noted: "Careful *toilette*. Namely the color of my gloves was a success: a delicate gray."[79] In Jerusalem he inspected the clothes, linen, ties, gloves, shoes, and hats of his entourage to see that all was in order.[80] He gave his party instructions for the reception, the order in which they were to stand and their deportment.[81] In the last minute the cuffs of one of his party did not pass inspection and had to be replaced.[82]

Herzl was a man of the theater who brought the theater into politics, making drama of politics. He had the capacity to pass from the unreal to the real, to mix the spheres of dream and politics, to transfer the enchantment of make-believe staging to the world of diplomacy and political power.

Viennese politics during the 1890's witnessed the decline of rational moralistic bourgeois liberalism and the ascendency of a new style of politics marked by the demagogic manipulation of masses in an emotional movement dedicated to the personality of a leader. The anti-Semitic lower middle-class Christian Social party of small tradesmen and independent craftsmen had as its popular and effective leader Karl Lueger. Lueger was to perfect the new style of charismatic Wagnerian mass politics. He was an important politician from 1885 on. In the two years from May 1895 to the end of April 1897 Lueger was elected to the mayoralty of Vienna on five different occasions. The government refused to confirm his election four times. By 1897 the Christian Social tide could not be stopped, and Lueger was proclaimed the lord-mayor of Vienna. He served until his death in 1910.[83]

It was against this background of political events that Herzl conceived his style. He observed Lueger's electoral campaigns and the response of the crowd to the public image the anti-Semitic leader projected. He describes an election evening in Vienna's third district, a partly proletarian quarter: "Before the polling place, a silent tense crowd. Suddenly Dr. Lueger came out to the square. Wild cheering; women waved white handkerchiefs from the windows. The police held the crowd back. A man next to me said with tender warmth but in a quiet tone: 'That is our Leader [Führer]'."[84] A year later Herzl noted that Lueger's wishes were the same as his own: fostering Jewish colonization.[85] He firmly believed that the failure to confirm Lueger was a mistake, for it would only stimulate mass anti-Semitism.[86]

Herzl viewed politics as the craft of effectively creating an uproar: "Yes, noise is everything, . . . in truth noise is a great deal. A sustained noise is in itself a noteworthy fact. All of world history is nothing but noise. Noise of arms, noise of progressing ideas. One must put noise to one's service—and still dispise it."[87] "With nations," he said, "one must speak in a childish language: a house, a flag, a song are the symbols of communication."[88] Recently "much of the form and poltical style" of Herzl's Zionism has been attributed to "his direct experience with the German nationalist student movement in Vienna."[89] An examination of the influence of Herzl's thespian experience and the personality needs it failed to fulfill, which were the same narcissistic needs that charismatic politics succeeded in supplying for him, may be more directly relevant to explaining Herzl's "aesthetic symbolic" politics.

Herzl, who failed in the theater, turned politics into theater. He became the director, stage manager, and reserved for himself the leading rôle. The play was the poignant salvation of a people, the plot was one man's vision and sacrifice, which would overcome all odds, the supporting cast was the rulers of the world's nations, and the backdrop was the grim tale of anti-Semitism and racial persecution in European history. Herzl's genius was that he was simultaneously a man of the theater and a man of action. His familiarity with the theater where magic and make-believe create stage reality enabled him to write a scenario for politics that also shaped reality.

Herzl had a "constructive" personality, that of a builder rather than a destroyer. As a boy Herzl's hero was Ferdinand de Lesseps. He would become an engineer and duplicate de Lesseps' work. He was going to cut a canal through the Isthmus of Panama. His parents enrolled him in the Pester Technical School where he took an engineering course.[90] Though Theodor was academically unsuccessful as a technician,[91] he was captivated by technology all his life. He wished to erect a Jewish house in Basel in a "neo-Jewish style." He wrote: "The art which is now most meaningful to me is architecture. Unhappily I have not mastered its techniques of expression. If I had learned anything, I would now be an architect."[92]

When he visited Palestine in 1898 Herzl was filled with visions for the rebuilding of cities, the draining of swamps, and remodeling the countryside.[93] As he first saw Jerusalem he invoked the converse of an ancient Jewish prayer: "When I remember thee in days to come, O Jerusalem, it will not be with pleasure. The musty deposits of two thousands years of inhumanity, intolerance, and filth be in your foul smelling alleys.[94] But he was going to rebuild it:

> If Jerusalem becomes ours, and I can still do something at that time, the first thing I would do is clean it up.
>
> I would remove everything that was not holy, set up worker's housing outside the city, clear out the filth nests, and tear them down, burn the non holy rubble, and move the bazaars elsewhere. Then, while keeping the old style of architecture where possible, build a comfortable, airy, sewered, new city around the holy places.[95]

It was typical of Herzl that he was much more impressed by the Suez Canal than by the Acropolis.[96] To him the modern engineering feat represented the triumph of one man's will over nature. When this will grew senile in the case of Panama, the project could not be carried through. Herzl saw the canal as an example of what sheer vision and strength of will can do to overcome obstacles of man and nature. To be a man whose powerful will would transform reality and transcend adversity was Herzl's ego ideal.

The twentieth century has witnessed a dramatic change in the Jewish character. Such a change is unique in history, and of particular interest to historians because the very concept of national character is a highly controversial one that they handle gingerly and with misgiving. When in one generation in modern times we see such a decisive change, it is one that bears close study.

The Jewish people in this generation have been through two crises whose magnitude is so great as to defy ordinary language. Only a term from the realm of geology, a word that connotes a change in substance itself, such as "metamorphosis," will suffice for the process of psychic transformation with which we are concerned. The two shattering experiences that have altered the Jewish character have been the holocaust of Nazi Germany that cost them a third of their number and the return of the Jewish people to organic life in the land of their origin. The metamorphosis they have undergone is a transformation of values and behavior in response to aggression. The traditional Jewish values had taught passivity and the internalization of guilt in the face of aggression.[97] It was divine punishment for disobedience to the word of God to be accepted stoically in the hope of living for a better day. This traditional pattern of palliation and accommodation tragically failed the Jews of Europe when they had to deal with psychotics having the modern technology of a police state at their disposal.

A new ethos of militant resistance was adopted out of the holocaust. This was the value system and set of emotional responses to anti-Semitism first codified in modern times by Theodor Herzl. It is as a maker of new Jewish values that he can be appreciated as a creative shaper of ideology. The idea of the return of the Jews to Jerusalem is as old as the expulsion. Herzl's contribution was a new behavioral ethos that first sprang from the needs of his own social position and psyche and was in the end to determine the character of a new people—the new Jew of his fantasied old-new land. Herzl postulated values in direct conscious contradiction to the ghetto way of life. He intended to, and did, found a new nation peopled by new men. It is Herzl as the formulator and institutionalizer of this psychological change whom we will investigate.

Herzl propagated a noble ideal of a new Jew, a man living by the myth of chivalry. For Herzl, Zionism implied a radical transvaluation of Jewish concepts of honor. The traditional virtues of restraint, passivity, and intellection, of the social isolation of the ghetto community were no longer adequate in an assimilated nineteenth-century Viennese milieu where social interaction with a dominant Gentile culture demanded new psychic defenses. The courtier and noble gentleman became Herzl's ego ideal, his model of conduct. His behavioral code was that of feudal aristocratic honor. The motive of honor was important to Herzl throughout his life and was to be eventually cast as the emotional foundation of the Jewish state.

As a man, Herzl remembered shifting schools in boyhood because of indignation at a teacher's anti-Semitism.[98] As a university student he belonged to a dueling fraternity. When anti-Semitism was on the rise in the university, he withdrew from his fraternity on grounds of Jewish honor.[99] His pre-Zionist solutions to the Jewish question included a fantasy of challenging the leading Austrian anti-Semites—Prince Alois Lichtenstein, Schönerer, Lueger—to duels.[100] "Half a dozen duels would do much to raise the social position of the Jews," he commented at the time.[101] His plan for the mass conversion of all Austrian Jews in St. Stephen's Cathedral would be a solution of pride and integrity because he and the other leaders would remain outside the church doors, "to insure uprightness, and so that the group baptism does not appear as cowardice or opportunism."[102] In Herzl's play *The New Ghetto,* the ghetto Jew acquires a new knightly chivalric conception of honor, and the hero, a transparent projection of Herzl himself, is killed in a duel defending Jewish honor.[103]

In the early days of his movement, indeed while he was conceiving the movement, Herzl noted in his diary, "Jewish honor begins . . ."[104] "And it will be the beginning of our respect in the eyes of the world."[105] At this time he wrote of some middle-class Viennese Jewish friends with whom he has dined: "They do not suspect it, but they are Ghetto creatures, quiet, good, fearful. Most of our people are like that. Will they understand the call to freedom and manliness?"[106] "If they have not yet emigrated at the time of the next European war, Jews must fight for their present fatherlands, on account of Jewish honor."[107]

In his initial interview of 1895 with Baron de Hirsch, Herzl posed the first task of Zionism as improvement of the race, to make it strong for war (*Kriegsstark*), love labor (*Arbeitsfroh*), and virtue (*Tugendhaft*). He even proposed that Hirsch offer prizes for *actions d'éclat,* for acts of great moral beauty, courage, self-sacrifice, ethical conduct.[108] He planned to "educate all to be free, strong men . . . by means of patriotic songs, sports clubs, religion, heroic theater, honor, etc."[109] Could anything have been a more complete rejection of traditional Jewish values of the ghetto?

Herzl consciously intended to smash stereotypes. He noted in his diaries: "Everyone who comes in contact with me must receive the opposite of the proverbial opinion of the Jew."[110] The images that dominated Herzl's thought and motivated him appear with full clarity when he and his party saw Jewish horsemen singing Hebrew songs during his visit to Palestine in 1898: "We had tears in our eyes as we saw the agile, courageous riders, into which our pants-peddling boys could be transformed."[111] He compared them to cowboys of the American West he had seen in Paris.

This expressed a deliberate effort to forge a new heroic national character (or to recapture a mythical Biblical racial character), create a flag and accessory symbols that would be honored and would win "respect in the eyes of the world." This fantasy of a nation peopled by proud militant "new men" is, in Herzl's case, what Anna Freud has defined as "identification with the aggressor.[112] He shares with anti-Semites a negative stereotype of the Jew. Herzl's contempt for "pants-peddling boys" is an admission of hatred of the Jews of the ghetto—and of the self. He hates but also identifies with this image that he wishes to alter. He hates it because it fails to live up to the derived standards of honor he imposes on it. He loves it and hates it because it is himself—what he was and is, but does not wish to be. In this sense Herzl was a Jewish anti-Semite. He depised the defenseless subjugated Jew of the pale. Herzl's idea was the self-reliant pioneer. For the learned, humiliated, sensitive Jew of the ghetto, he would substitute the rigorous, heroic, healthy farmer in his own land. Yiddish, the language of suffering, would be replaced by any cultured language.[113] The exclusive nationalism of Europe which rejects Jews would be replaced by a chauvinistic nationalism of Zion. The values of the dominant majority are internalized and via reaction-formation would become the ego ideal of the persecuted minority.

Historians should avail themselves of the tools of modern literary criticism in considering the psychological significance of the language used, the imagery employed, the creation and utilization of symbols by their subjects. Images, symbols and words were formed in the consciousness of Herzl. In seeking the inner emotional content of a novel or story, we should remember that the work is Herzl's and no one else's. It is not an impersonal thing. The character and nature of these fantasies have issued from his consciousness. Their contents are thus always relevant and not fortuitous. The old and rather naïve notion of artistic inspiration that spontaneously appears in the poet's mind no longer suffices. These contents are tissued out of images from his life and fantasies that have become emotionally charged. The work itself may yield what the state of mind and the emotion of that consciousness was. Henry James wrote of the novelist that he "is present in every page of every book from which he sought to eliminate himself." And Henry David Thoreau told us that poetry "is a piece of very private history, which unostentatiously lets us into the secret of man's life."[114]

Among those who seriously imagine private worlds of their own in which they rearrange actuality and create a new order that suits them better are creative artists and writers. They invest fantasies with a great deal of affect, nevertheless separating their fantasy sharply from reality.[115] By the successful objectification of his private illusion, the writer releases his mental tension and gives us the pleasure of sharing highly charged emotional experiences. But when we leave the artist, we go back from the world of imagination to the firm ground of reality.

In the case of a political leader such as Herzl, the form he gives his fiction, its historical and geographical setting, even the words he uses, his choice of phrase and emotional tone, and above all the characters and their interaction, are all, in the last analysis, biographical self-revelation, signatures of his inner being. The historian is particularly well advised to consider Herzl's creative writings most carefully, subjecting them to every possible analytic technique, for the return will be manifold insights into the fantasies of a great leader as he emerges.

We have three products of Herzl's fantasy from the period of the end of his depression in 1896. There is a short fable that bears the imprint of a broken marriage and thoughts of suicide. But its interest for us is special because it also contains the theme of resolution of despair in affirmative creation. From the discarded and worthless material of life, Herzl will mold a new and valued essence. The story concerns a professor of philosophy who has a nagging wife. In bitterness and desperation he goes to the river determined on suicide. There he sees a man with a pipe sitting on a tree stump who identifies himself as a "fisherman of men" and invites him into his Inn of the Anilin. The inn reeks with the odor of tar from the laboratory in which the innkeeper experiments with making synthetic food for the world's hungering millions. Just as beautiful gay colors are made to bloom from dyes that are mere factory waste, so men can be kneaded and shaped into something constructive out of their deepest despair. So says the innkeeper to his moribund guest,

> For despair is a precious substance, from which the most wonderful things may be generated: courage, self-denial, resolution, sacrifice. . . . To the stubbornest I recommended self realization in a great task, and they have achieved the most. . . . As I look back at the past, it seems to me that all of the great men of history were once at the river's edge and turned back so that their despair bore fruit. All discoverers, prophets, heroes, statesmen, artists—yes, all philosophers also, for one never philosophizes better than when staring death in the face.[117]

With this coda we have Herzl's affirmation from the extremity of despair and his self-dedication to a world historical role. Having once contemplated death and having decided not to forsake the world, he would remake it. It is noteworthy that in this story the central figure was bound on suicide by drowning, that this urge to self-destruction was brought on by the perfidy of a woman, and that he was saved by a fatherly older man.

In the same year Herzl wrote another story with the themes of marital unhappiness and self-destruction. Here too, the means of suicide are by drowning. This time the subject is a young girl, Sarah Holzman, and the inciting cause, the marital infidelity of her mother.[118] The third published story of the year 1896, "Das Lenk bare Luftschiff," concerns an inventor with a great idea—a flying machine. People think he is crazy and he is locked up in an insane asylum. Even the woman he loves makes fun of him. He protests: "Men resent him who plans great things."[119] He gives up the flying machine and turns to the invention of functional appliances: a railway brake, an unpuncturable bicycle tire, and a gas lamp. He earns millions of gulden with which he buys off the woman who has now become loving and admiring toward him. He tells her to bother him no more. In his own story Herzl becomes the hero and vindicates his dream, and thus he evens the score with his materialistic wife. Once again the woman is a cold, selfish, pleasure-seeking creature, but Herzl wreaks vengeance in fantasy.

Taken together with the fact of his depression during 1891–1896, these three stories suggest that he was preconcerned with creative loneliness, carping women, marital disharmony, and suicide in these years. I am not necessarily asserting that he ever seriously considered taking his life, though he may have done so. But it is to say that the subject of suicide, women who drive men to it and men who resolve their conflicts through great historical achievements, were in his fantasy life. Otherwise he could not have built them into his plots so consistently.

One of the most personal and revealing fantasies of Herzl is his literary creation *Altneuland*. In this novel he places himself and persons close to him, both living and dead, in constructed relationships that, because they are creations of psychic reality, deserve to be taken seriously as self-revelation. As literature, it is a poor novel. The figures are wooden, the exposition is labored, and the plot sentimental. But as a re-creation of the real and emotional world of Herzl, it offers rich material to those who would wish to know its author.

Herzl himself is the central figure, the young Viennese Jewish lawyer Friedrich Loewenberg. As the novel opens, he is heartsick with unrequited love for a rich Viennese Jewish girl who, unlike Herzl's wife, married a prosperous merchant instead of the struggling journalist. So he rejects the world of women and turns to that of men. He sails to the South Pacific idyll as the devoted companion of a Prussian excavalry officer with the evocative name Koenigshoff ("king's court"). He is pledged to the Junker aristocrat for life[120] in terms of the Book of Ruth: "I belong to you, and go with you wherever and whenever you choose."[121] The two men spent "twenty beautiful years" alone in the paradise of an island archipelago "hunting, fishing, eating, drinking, sleeping, playing chess . . ."[122] En route to their island idyll, the two men visited Palestine and found it as did Herzl in his visit of 1898: a malaria-ridden, decadent backwater of the decaying Turkish empire. "The once royal city of Jerusalem could have sunk no lower," muses Friedrich as he and Kingscourt walk through the Holy City arm in arm.[123]

Twenty years later, the year is 1923, the Prussian nobleman and his faithful liege return to a transformed Palestine. The Jewish emigration has transpired and rebuilt ancient cities and constructed new ports, water and power projects, and rail networks. Swamps have been drained, deserts irrigated, and agriculture flourishes in cooperative settlements. Socially the "new society" as he called it, is an equalitarian welfare state with all the *accoutrements* of advanced early twentieth-century social theory: rights for women, free schools and universities, model penal farms, medical, accident, old age, and life insurance. Jews, Arabs, and European Christians live together in harmony. There is no military service because international relations are governed by world law. Amid this cosmopolitanism, it is clear that the more cultured people, even the Arabs, speak a literary high German, "with a slight northern accent."[124]

When he arrives in Palestine, Herzl-Loewenberg finds again the family of a poor beggar boy whom he had saved from starvation in Vienna. They are now prosperous leaders of the new community. The son David is about to be elected president of the new society. This family greets him as "our benefactor, our savior" ("Unser Wohlthäter, unser Retter")—a self-accorded accolade for a man who has dreamed of being a messiah.[125]

The women portrayed in Herzl's novel are divided into two types, the coarse, vulgar, and emotionally destructive (dangerous) woman and the delicate desensualized virginal maiden. In Palestine Herzl-Loewenberg meets the wealthy girl who had broken his heart in Vienna and sent him on a twenty-year voyage with another man. She has become a gaudy "faded, would-be arch coquette (gefallsüchtige, verblühte Frauenzimmer)".[126] Indeed, he stoutly defends a sweet young schoolteacher, Miriam, for her dedication to her vocational duties and social responsibilities against the carping criticism of the bejeweled, overdressed woman. Miriam was serious about her duties, unlike Herzl's wife. Such was his revenge on his wife Julie!

Herzl suddenly lost his only sister, Pauline, in 1878 when he was eighteen. She was a year older than he and "the image of her mother."[127] She had been his "earliest and nearest playmate" to a point where "she made other playmates almost superfluous." After the shock of her death, he "guarded every keepsake of hers like a sacred relic."[128] Pauline was to play a major role in his novel. The book was dedicated to her, and she figures in the plot as Miriam, a shy and devoted schoolteacher whom he, Herzl in the person of Friedrich Loewenberg, marries.

The device by which this courtship is consummated tells us a great deal about Herzl's desensualized view of women. Friedrich and Miriam are scarcely aware that their love is mutual. There have been no declaration of intentions. Miriam's mother, a representation of Herzl's own, brings them together on her deathbed. She expires moments after the young couple confirms their engagement to her and to each other. They become engaged *to please the mother.* Only in this way is the fulfillment of an incest fantasy possible for Herzl. Any quality of emotional intensity or passion toward the would-be sexual object is absent.

Herzl's attitude toward men of power is a significant reflection of his relation to father figures and an index of father transferences in his unconscious.[129] His stance toward the great of the world was worshipful. He feared being so overawed that he would be ineffective. His defense against the threat of being overawed was to intellectually reduce great men to small size. When he felt impressed, he reduced potent father figures to managable dimensions by concentrating on their most mundane features or weaknesses. When he for the first time visits the Grand Duke of Baden, we see him fighting against the effects of awe: "It was my first drive up in front of a princely castle. I tried not to be overimpressed by the soldiers on guard."[130] When he has entered the castle and seen the antechamber, it takes his breath away. His response was "to divert myself from becoming overawed by taking inventory like a reporter." He noted the green furniture, the brown wood of the chair legs, and the photographs of the three German emperors.[131]

The pattern of defense against low self-esteem by focusing on the weakness of the powerful man with whom he was dealing is most striking in Herzl's response to a personal encounter with Kaiser Wilhelm II. He found it was essential to study:

> the small side of great people. And this is necessary if one is not to be confused by their flashy exterior glitter and if one wishes to associate with them naturally. That is why, when I saw the German Kaiser so frequently during the past week, I sharply observed his deformity. . . . It brings him closer to me as a human being. It proves

> that underneath his many uniforms of the regiments he commands, he is only a helpless man. As I saw the display of his might, the brilliance of his court, the warlike prowess of his legions on the parade field, I always merely kept observing his crippled arm, in order not to let my spirit be overwhelmed in case I should speak with him personally.[132]

Whereas Herzl's defense against men of power was to reduce their stature so he could cope with them, his attitude toward his subordinates and followers was fatherly. He shows warm affection for "my good Wolffsohn,"[133] who stood the test of disappointment "as always and bore with me through thick and thin."[134]

When he felt betrayed or frustrated by members of the Zionist movement Herzl committed his anger to his diaries. He referred to the congress opposition as "rascals" and "bastards."[135] At the second congress he was furious with "the successful dirty trick of the Galician bastards . . . Landau was the noisiest and stupidest."[136]

We have here a definite character style of leadership that differs from ordinary people primarily in its object relationships.[137] The leader of Herzl's type does not develop object relations to persons. After the death of Heinrich Kana he did not have what one could call an intimate friend. After the estrangement of his marriage Herzl had an object cathexis exclusively with his own ideas. His ability to control his aggression, even when sorely tried and when it would have been fully justified, is an indication of the powerful synthetic function of Herzl's ego. His object relations were not primarily to people; they were to his idea, his cause. For this goal he was able to subvert all impulses and other personal relations. His object realm was ideational. He demanded and received support from others for his ideas. Opposition was fought in the name of the cause. Aggression was rationalized by the injury that opponents were doing to the movement. Herzl thought nothing of sinking his own and his family's personal fortunes into his movement. He was able to convince others of the grandeur of his idea and to persuade them to serve his vision.[138]

Success did not come quickly or easily to Theodor Herzl. He faced storms of criticism and derision. He was jeered at as the "Jewish Jules Verne."[139] The editors of his newspaper asked him to desist from publication of *Der Judenstaat,* threatening his position as *feuilleton* editor by telling him he could easily be replaced.[140] *Neue Freie Presse* was never to mention Zionism during Herzl's lifetime. But surely the most poignant case of his attempt at reality testing is best related by Herzl himself:

> When I had completed the book I asked my oldest and best friend to read the manuscript. In the midst of the reading he suddenly burst into tears. I found this natural enough, since he was a Jew; I too had wept at times during the writing of it. But I was staggered when he gave me an entirely different reason for his tears. He thought that I had gone off my head, and since he was my friend he was touched to tears by my misfortune.[147]

Yet Herzl persevered. He was able to discipline his fantasy and adapt it to the service of the ego. He converts all his hostility into partnerships. He is inclusive. There is room for everybody in his fantasies. "Not everyone embarks on the ship at the starting point," he says, "some find it more convenient to travel overland, and join her farther on." To the Jewish communities he said: "We welcome you. There is room and work for all."[142]

In contrast to Herzl's earlier fury toward anti-Semites, for example, Dühring, whom he called "this rascal, who should have his teeth knocked out,"[143] he now incorporates all oppositional tendencies into his plan. There is a place for the tsar, the Vatican, liberalism, Turkey, the Rothschilds, both orthodox and reform Jewry, the tiny group of settlers already in Palestine and even the anti-Semites. He graphically described his difficulties as those of doing a dance on invisible eggs. We may subscribe to his appraisal that this was a "labor of Hercules—without exaggeration," and may sympathize with him when he complains that he has "lost his zest for it."[144]

For Herzl there was no choice—he had to continue being a messiah. He could not have stopped laboring for his cause if his life depended on it—and evidently it did. Within less than a year of commencing his Zionist work the family physician diagnosed a heart injured by excitement and warned him against wearing himself out in the Jewish cause.[145] Two years later he wrote: "I am tired, the heart is not in order."[146]

Meanwhile Herzl had in fact become a messiah. He found his following where he least expected it, not among the assimilated bourgeois Jews of Western Europe, but among the impoverished masses of the East. In Sofia he was "hailed as 'Führer,' as the heart of Israel."[147] He was greeted by great crowds and told "you are holier than the Torah."[148]

Herzl derives his libidinal rewards from the crowd; he is loved by them, and receives his emotional fulfillment from his audience, from the mass response to his public utterances. This is sublimated oral gratification. His vital organ is his mouth. Words flow from him like warm milk. And from the group he obtains generous supplies of esteem and affection.

Herzl wished to be a messiah, and messiahs must die as martyrs. Herzl willed it so and he died for his cause. His reply to a warning not to work so hard was: "I *will* work, until I kill myself."[149] By 1904, at age forty-four, he was deathly ill. He frightened his friends by his appearance. His doctors found a disturbingly heavy alteration of the heart muscle. He said, "I have become a tired man in these months."[150] A planned trip to London in April was cancelled owing to his poor health. In May Herzl went to Franzensbad for a heart cure. He had heavy attacks of loss of breath and weakness.

A Zionist emissary to Russia came through in May. Despite his illness Herzl stayed up all night to complete a memorandum for St. Petersburg. When his friend Katzenelsohn reprimanded him saying: "So this is how you wish to get well? This is supposed to be your cure?" Herzl replied: "Yes my friend, as you saw yesterday, we have no time to lose. These are the last weeks or days . . . we must hurry!" On July 1 he had a lung inflammation and said to a friend: "Greet Palestine for me, I have given my blood for my people."[151] Herzl died on July 3, 1904.

At the time of his death Herzl had established the institutions that would result in the realization of his fantasy—a Jewish state. He had appealed to a mass following in dire need and had invited them to share his vision. The World Zionist Organization was created as the central organ of Jewish national policy. A bank and the Jewish Colonial Trust had been founded. The newspaper he founded, *Die Welt*, became the mass-media organ of the movement. Herzl's most significant personal contribution was the building of diplomatic affiliations with powers and influential public figures, especially in England, that were to eventuate in the Balfour Declaration of 1917.

Fantasy may be defined as patterns of thought about actions or desired objects that are unavailable in existing social reality. Fantasies may be conscious or unconscious. When unconscious, they are usually thoughts that have been repressed because they are morally unsanctionable in the adult world. When conscious, they are unsatisfied wishes that are fulfilled in thought and thus improve on an unsatisfactory reality. Fantasies are the universal property of mankind; we sometimes call them daydreams.[152] They usually consist of erotic wishes or dreams of ambition serving to exalt the dreamer.[153] In either case, "His Majesty the Ego" is the hero of all fantasies.[154]

The initial trigger for a fantasy is some immediate dissatisfaction with present reality, some unsatisfied wish. Fantasy improves on this painful reality by bringing two other time dimensions into play. In the intensity of present desire, the mind calls on its memories of an earlier time when things were ideal, when the wish was fulfilled. This realm, often that of early infancy, is recalled, not as it was, but as transmuted into symbols and images of the world as it appeared to the consciousness of an infant. The fantasy then takes the idyllic satisfaction of the past, and transcending immediate experience by illusion, projects it into the future when the wish will again be fulfilled in reality. Paradise lost is recalled by desire present to merge through fantasy with paradise future.[155] Obviously there are neurotic and nonneurotic fantasies. These fantasies may include the idea of an equalitarian world or schemes for the rebuilding of a city, as well as fairy tales and improbable personal triumphs.

Though fantasy always implies an initial turning away from reality, it can also be a preparation for the alteration of reality. Fantasy can be fruitful, not only in art and creative literary realms, and even in that most rational of realms, scientific thinking, but also in politics. There is an epistemological fallacy in the common dualism that opposes spiritual and poetic imagination to scientific and empirical rationality. From the technical fantasies of Leonardo to the spatial images of Einstein, the two antagonistic faculties are interdependent and complementary. The imagination plays with technical possibilities and assumes a rational character when it comes to their realization.[156]

The psychic life of "normal" adults is never free of some denial of reality. The denied reality is replaced by fantasy formations.

These may fulfill a constructive synthetic function by ideationally connecting the needs and goals of a man faced with mental and spiritual collapse with possibilities of their realization, thus enabling him to emerge from his subjective world of omnipotent illusion to increased mastery of the external world.[157] The positive value of fantasy for Herzl was that it enabled him to retreat from the onslaught of pressures of the immediate setting and search for a new role and environment that would offer him and the people he would lead a more fulfilling and congenial existence.

As a *fin de siècle* Viennese liberal, Herzl was typical of his class in its retreat to an internal world of consciousness. In art, literature, psychology, theater, and philosophy this class turned to inner worlds to discover new realities following their defeat in the social and political realm of Austrian politics.[158] Thus, when Herzl said: "No one has thought of seeking the 'Promised Land' where it truly is—and yet it lies so near. Here it is: within ourselves,"[159] he was expressing in Zionist terms the search of his class for truth within man's mind rather than as an external datum to be discovered. In dreaming of a better world which he then labors to bring about, the late nineteenth-century Central European utopian intellectual found it in the psyche. For Herzl the promised land had no specific geographical location. It could have been anywhere. It initially found its home in the consciousness of its adherents.

In spring 1895 Herzl was disturbed almost to the point of a psychotic break. He was abandoning reality and withdrawing his libido from object ties to his environment. Personal, vocational, and social frustration released redeemer and passive feminine fantasies in him. He took as his fantasy objects Prussian Junker prototypes such as Kingscourt and Kaiser Wilhelm II. His homoerotic fantasies had their root in a longing for his father, which was intensified by heterosexual frustration and professional disappointment.[160]

He withdrew interest from the external world, substituting fantasy for reality. His overestimation of the power of his own wishes and mental processes, his belief in the omnipotence of thoughts was close to a faith in the magical power of his words: "If you will it, it is no fantasy."[161] Herzl's libido was withdrawn from external objects and returned to his ego. He substituted for actual human relationships (family, journalism, theater) imaginary objects founded on infantile fantasy. The internalization of libido in the ego aggrandized the ego to the level of megalomania. He regressed to the stage of narcissism in which his only sexual object was his own ego and its fantasies.[162]

Herzl's idea usurped his libido and his aggression. He derived little gratification from relationships to individuals because of the affect intrinsic in the relationship. The finding of a distant delibidinized object is a defense against internal conflict. Objects that are too close may be dangerous, they are too laden with ambivalence. To select a remote ideational object is a defense of avoidance. Herzl was able to sublimate many of his passive ambivalences toward his father in political work.

Herzl's latent homosexuality was strengthened by his denial of the need for the love of a woman and of sex. This appears in his literary fantasies where he is for twenty years the loyal companion of a Prussian officer and of the values he projected for his "new man."

Herzl's ascetic self-denial strengthened his dedication to his messianic vocation as father to his people. He was committed to his task with the celibate devotion of one who is religiously "called" to his historic role. Without such single-minded self-abnegation, Herzl would have been just another dreamer. Instead he found a new identity. His sexual ambivalences were harnessed in the personal role of charismatic leader of a political mass movement. Now his craving for immortality, his desire for a political role, and most important, his conflict riven Jewish identifications were resolved in an affirmative and productive program that provided for Herzl personal generativity and integrity.[163]

There is sufficient surface material from Herzl himself to permit specific depth interpretation of his idea structure. Reference here is not to the instincts but to instinctual derivatives that come to the fore during ego regressions in times of emotional stress when the ego defenses are weakened. The libidinal excitement of Herzl's creative period, his state of euphoria during which he relates "to his idea as to a lover," is the state of elation accompanying the trespass over established boundaries into realms that are forbidden and dangerous, areas of megalomanic, incestuous, and homoerotic fantasies. The process of his fantasies becoming conscious is experienced by Herzl as an action on him, thus activity of the unconscious is turned into passivity.[164]

The dreams of being carried by a man and literary fantasies of being saved by men or faithfully serving men suggest a homosexual passivity to the father. A passive attitude toward the father implies a feminine identification. Herzl's imagery of birth and conception when writing of his ideas is the masculine creative analogue to women's capacity for biological creation.

According to Freud's libido model of genetic psychosexual development, when the defenses of the phallic genital phase have been overwhelmed, the subject regresses to the anal phase of tension and relaxation. We note Herzl's imagery of retention and release when speaking of his ideas. They "would burst it [the container] to pieces if they found no outlet."[165] The idiom is of the gratification that accompanies expulsion: "For me these notes are not work, but a relief."[166] Creation itself signifies anal production. When he writes: "Goethe! Goethe!" he is saying: "I produce!, I am creating too!"

Behind the imagery of anal activity lies a level of oral activity in talking and verbal manipulation. A further psychogenetic derivative is a deeper oral passivity in which Herzl's activity is experienced as passivity. His experience is: "something is happening to me!" The driving of his unconscious toward consciousness is encountered as an action upon him rather than by him: "Am I working it out? No! it is working me." Herzl's personal life has ended; world history has taken over.

The absence of normal sexual gratification reinforced regression to forms of oral gratification such as speaking and deriving emotional rewards from the adulation of the crowd. He achieved this love from the masses by fantasizing about the world of the oral mother—a "promised land" bountifully "flowing with milk and honey." We see evidence of ambivalence toward his mother not only in Herzl's portrayal of mother figures in his creative writing where women consistently drive their children or menfolk to destruction, but also in the reparative fantasies evident in his ideas regarding the promised land.

Deeper than any attitudes toward the father are ambivalent feelings toward the oral mother of early infancy. Together with the receptive position there is oral aggression: there are violent fantasies of devouring a grudging mother, of attacking her breast. The derivatives of such infantile fantasies are dreams of forcibly extracting wealth from the soil, of cutting great canals, rebuilding cities, and transforming the land. Such aggressive and destructive fantasies give rise to strong guilt feelings and the need to make reparation to rebuild fantasy damage. By seeking to return to the mother land, to preserve and restore it, to make it "flow with milk and honey," Herzl is repairing fantasy damage to his infantile mother. He is making restitution in his unconscious by re-creating the promised land, making it rich as a productive, fertile, haven of peace. The motherland will be cared for and cultivated, will be made to bloom and to bear fruit.[167]

What distinguishes Herzl from an ordinary dreamer is his unique ability to act on his vision. He permitted his unconscious omnipotent fantasies to register on his consciousness in political terms. He adapted his operational plans, but never his dream, to the demands of immediate rational "reality." In truly creative ways he adjusted to the demands of a powerless position in a scornful world. He had the insight to appeal to the self-interest of the powers of Europe. Where possible, as in England, he also appealed to the idealism of leaders. His own Jewish following gave him the greatest measure of distress. It is testimony to Herzl's ego strength that he was able, despite repeated crises when all seemed in dissolution, to hold his following together in a movement that he institutionalized for action toward his fantasy goal.

Herzl escaped the injured feeling of nothingness by molding himself in fantasy into a messianic leader. His psychic reality became a substitute for his undermined self-esteem. By creating a fantasy world of his own in which he was the hero, he consoled himself for not being loved and appreciated. Herzl's inner fantasies were to him far more than substitute satisfactions for rejections in the outer world; they saved him from being crushed entirely. They may have literally, but certainly they spiritually, saved his life.[168]

Herzl's Zionist period may be divided into two phases. The primary experience of inspiration was characterized by ego regression. He took little notice of his environment. His consciousness received id impulses and closer derivatives from his preconscious with relative facility and without censorship. We may see a secondary elaborational phase during which his ego functions of reality testing, formulation, and communication with his public, were recathected.

His inspiration was the thoughts produced by his unconscious, which were permitted to reach consciousness in a world-shaping politico-messianic guise. But the regression was only a partial and temporary ego regression, one most of the time under the control of Herzl's ego, which in the last analysis retained the function of communication. Herzl strove to establish contact with an audience. His fantasies were not for himself alone as in the case of a psychotic.[169]

He identified himself with his public in order to invite their participation in his fantasy, a participation postulating their identification with him as leader.[170] This was regression in the service of the ego, a regression that made his inspiration possible and that made him a prophet, a leader, and a man of action. Herzl's instinctual processes were dominated by his ego and put to its own purposes. His fantasies and regressions were sublimated in creative activity that changed history.

Herzl's recovery from his depression took place as his narcissistic ego ideal was fulfilled. His infantile narcissism and omnipotence was confirmed as he appealed to the urgent needs of masses of people and became identified with their ancient messianic dream. Herzl became a secular messiah and functioned effectively in the role that corroborated his omnipotence.

Changes in reality are often achieved by regressive adaptation of the ego as in the case of Herzl. His alterations in reality were made by detours over irrational elements, by regressions to megalomania and narcissism. Such regressive detours were the prerequisites to achievement that created a new reality. By withdrawing to an inner world of self-absorbed fantasy, Herzl was able to emerge with a certainty and strength of conviction that transformed the world.

Herzl underwent a renunciation in his personal life that enabled him to act as a chosen one in carrying the responsibility for a people on the stage of history. His sense of mission was so strong that it carried him through ridicule and isolation, detours and blind alleys, rejection and disillusionment, until he found a responsive public in the poor Jews of Eastern Europe and they found a charismatic leader in him. Herzl as a leader, gifted in evoking images from his audience, and motivated by the need to be a modern savior of his people, used the great crisis of a people under social and political pressure to resolve personal ambivalence and conflict by creating a program of action that was to shape history. His people consecrated him as a prophet and validated his historical vision.

NOTES

NOTE: I am indebted to the members of the Los Angeles Interdisciplinary Psychoanalytic Study Group for discussions and stimulation on this topic and the psychodynamics of political leadership in general. A grant from the Ford Foundation administered through the Chancellor's Committee for Comparative and International Studies, U.C.L.A., aided the completion of this study. Research was facilitated by the generous cooperation of Dr. Alex Bein, Dr. Michael Heymann, and the staff of the Central Zionist Archives, Jerusalem.

1. The original diaries reside in the Central Zionist Archives. The first edition, *Theodor Herzls Tagebücher*, 3 vols. (Berlin, 1922–1923), edited by a group led by Martin Buber and Leon Kellner, has numerous excisions on grounds of political expedience or what was interpreted as good taste. It will be cited as *Tagebücher*. I have used this basic German edition wherever possible. Unless otherwise indicated, the translations are my own. I have relied on *The Complete Diaries of Theodor Herzl*, ed. Raphael Patai, trans. Harry Zohn, 5 vols. (New York, 1960) to supply the excised material. It is hereafter cited as *Complete Diaries*. The translations, however, are superior in Marvin Lowenthal's abridged one-volume edition, *The Diaries of Theodor Herzl* (New York, 1962), hereafter cited as *Diaries*. For the reader's benefit I have explicitly indicated where portions deleted from the German edition are used.

A complete Hebrew edition of Herzl works, including the diaries, is now in preparation in Jerusalem.

2. Leon Kellner, *Theodor Herzl's Lehrjahre (1860–1895)* (Berlin, 1920), pp. 9–12.

3. Alex Bein, *Theodor Herzl: A biography* (Philadelphia, 1962), p. 15.

4. See Carl E. Schorske, "Politics and the Psyche in *fin de siècle* Vienna: Schnitzler and Hofmannsthal," *American Historical Review* 66, no. 4 (July 1961): 930–946, and "The Transformation of the Garden: Ideal and Society in Austrian Literature," *American Historical Review* 720, no. 4 (July 1967): 1283–1320; and William J. McGrath, "Student Radicalism in Vienna," *Journal of Contemporary History* 2, no. 3 (July 1967): 183–201.

5. Bein, *Theodor Herzl*, pp. 13–14.

6. For a Jungian interpretation of this dream, see Grete Mahrer, "Herzl's Return to Judaism," in Raphael Patai, ed., *Herzl Year Book* (New York, 1959), 2:28–33.

7. June 12, 1895, *Tagebücher* 1:106.

8. Sigmund Freud, "The Most Prevalent Form of Degradation in Erotic Life (1912), in *Collected Papers* (New York, 1959), 4:204–207.

9. Herzl to Heinrich Kana, June 8, 1880, Herzl-Kana Correspondence, Central Zionist Archives, Jerusalem. I am indebted to Ernst Lewy for his suggestive discussion of this material.

10. Herzl to Kana, March 5, 1882, Herzl-Kana Correspondence.

11. January 10, 1886, "Jugendtagebuch," in *Theodor Herzl Jahrbuch*, Tulo Nussenblatt, ed. (Wien, 1937), p. 47.

12. Herzl to Kana, September 4, 1879, Herzl-Kana Correspondence.

13. May 2, 1882, "Jugendtagebuch," p. 40.

14. April 13, 1883, *ibid.*, p. 42.

15. Herzl to Kana, November 22, 1883, Herzl-Kana Correspondence.

16. Herzl to Ludassy, November 22, 1883, Herzl Papers, Central Zionist Archives, Jerusalem.

17. "Jugendtagebuch," November 27, 1883, p. 43.

18. New Year's Eve, 1883–1884, *Ibid.*, pp. 43–44.

19. Bein, *Theodor Herzl*, pp. 43–44.

20. Herzl to Kana, Herzl-Kana Correspondence, Month of Distress (August?) 26, 1883.

21. Otto Fenichel, *The Psychoanalytic Theory of Neurosis* (New York, 1945), pp. 372–373.

22. Sigmund Freud, "Dostoevsky and Parricide" (1928), in *C.P.*, 5:222–242.

23. Bein, *Theodor Herzl*, p. 48.

24. *Ibid*, p. 385.

25. Herzl to Kana Herzl-Kana Correspondence, August 30, 1883.

26. July 5, 1895, *Tagebücher*, 1:223.

27. February 28, 1886, "Jugendtagebuch," p. 49.

28. March 21, 1886, *ibid.*

29. Marvin Lowenthal, "Introduction: The Diaries and the Man," *Diaries*, p. xiv.

30. *Ibid.*, pp. xiv–xv; and Bein, *Theodor Herzl*, pp. 68–69.

31. Bein, *Theodor Herzl*, p. 64.

32. Arthur Stern, "The Genetic Tragedy of the Family of Theodor Herzl," *Israel Annals of Psychiatry and Related Disciplines* 3, no. 1 (April 1965): 100.

33. Sigmund Freud, "Group Psychology and the Analysis of the Ego" (1921), in J. Strachey, ed., *Standard Edition* (London, 1955), 18:123–124.

34. Max Weber, "The Sociology of Charismatic Authority," in *From Max Weber: Essays in Sociology*, H. H. Gerth and C. Wright Mills, trans. and eds., (New York, 1958), pp. 245–248, and *The Theory of Social and Economic Organization*, A. Henderson and Talcott Parsons, trans. (New York, 1964), pp. 358–363.

35. Luke 14:26.

36. W. W. Tarn, *Alexander the Great* (Boston, 1956), p. 123.

37. H. R. Trevor-Roper, *The Last Days of Hitler* (New York, 1962), pp. 155–158.

38. Leon Kellner, "Herzl and Zangwill in Vienna: A Contrast in Per-

sonalities and Types," in *Theodor Herzl: A Memorial* (City, 1929), pp. 73–74.

39. Maria E. Delle Grazie, "Father and King: A Remembrance of Herzl's Views on Jewish Destiny," in *Herzl: A Memorial*, p. 40, Grazia Deledda (1875–1936) received the Nobel Prize for Literature in 1926.

40. Bein, *Theodor Herzl*, p. 89.

41. *Ibid.*, pp. 87–88.

42. *Ibid.*, p. 91.

43. *Tagebücher*, 1:8.

44. Lowenthal, *Diaries*, pp. xiv–xv; and Bein, *Theodor Herzl*, pp. 64–65.

45. Bein, *Theodor Herzl*, p. 105.

46. *Ibid.*, p. 106.

47. Arthur Schnitzler to Herzl, November 17, 1894, in Olga Schnitzler, *Spiegelbild der Freundschaft* (Salzburg, 1962), p. 88.

48. Herzl to Schnitzler, February 15, 1895, *ibid.*, p. 92.

49. See Bein, *Theodor Herzl*, p. 117.

50. *Tagebücher*, 1:3.

51. *Ibid.*, 1:15.

52. June 5, 1895, *ibid.*, 1:38.

53. Sigmund Freud, "Psycho-Analytic Notes Upon on Autobiographical Account of a Case of Paranoia" (1911), *C.P.*, 3:451.

54. Freud, "Three Contributions to the Theory of Sex," in A. A. Brill, ed. and trans., *The Basic Writings of Sigmund Freud* (New York, 1938), p. 564.

55. June 3, and July 23, 1895, *Tagebücher* 1:32, 240.

56. June 3, 1895, *ibid.*, 1:33.

57. June 3, 1895, *ibid.*, 1:32.

58. June 7, 1895, *ibid.*, 1:42.

59. June 7, 1895, *Diaries*, p. 36. Omitted from *Tagebücher*.

60. June 12, 1895, *Tagebücher*, 1:106–107.

61. Herzl to Schnitzler, June 23, 1895, in Schnitzler, *Spiegelbild*, p. 94.

62. *Ibid.*, p. 95.

63. June 12, 1895, *Tagebücher*, 1:104.

64. June 16, 1895, *ibid.*, 1:117.

65. June 18, 1895, *ibid.*, 1:127.

66. June 11, 1895, *ibid.*, 1:82.

67. *Ibid.*, 1:84–85.

68. June 12, 1895, *ibid.*, 1:105.

69. June 12, 1895, *Diaries*, p. 44. *Omitted from Tagebücher.*

70. June 16, 1895, *Tagebücher*, 1:115–116.

71. *Ibid.*, 1:116.

72. June 16, 1895, *Diaries*, p. 49. Omitted from *Tagebücher*.

73. September 30, 1898, *Tagebücher*, 2:129.

74. Theodor Herzl, "Experiences and Moods: An Autobiographic Sketch" (1897), in *Herzl: A Memorial*, p. 184.

75. June 5, 1895, *Tagebücher*, 1:39.

76. August 27, 1897, *ibid.*, 2:22; and September 3, 1897, *ibid.*, 2:27.

77. Joseph Cowen, "My Conversion to Zionism: Reminiscences of First

Meetings (sic!) with Herzl in England and elsewhere," in *Herzl: A Memorial*, p. 104.

78. September 3, 1897, *Tagebücher*, 2:24–25.

79. October 19, 1898, *ibid.*, 2:168.

80. October 31, 1898, *ibid.*, 2:216.

81. *Ibid.*, 2:215.

82. November 2, 1898, *ibid.*, 2:223.

83. For a satirical description of Lueger see Mark Twain (Samuel L. Clemens), "Stirring Times in Austria," in *How To Tell a Story and Other Essays* (New York, 1904). Most of the historical treatments are uncritical apologies for Lueger regardless of whether they are pre- or postwar. See Rudolf Kuppe, *Karl Lueger und seine Zeit* (Wien, 1933); Kurt Skalnik, *Dr. Karl Lueger: Der Mann zwischen den Zeiten* (Wien, 1954); Heinrich Schnee, *Karl Lueger: Lieben und Wirken eines grossen Sozial und Kommunalpolitikers* (Berlin, 1960).

84. September 20, 1895, *Tagebücher*, 1:279.

85. September 24, 1896, *ibid.*, 1:540.

86. November 3, 1895, *ibid.*, 1:298–299, and November 10, 1895, *ibid.*, 1:308–309.

87. May 12, 1898, *Tagebücher*, 2:81–82.

88. July 10, 1898, *ibid.*, 2:95.

89. McGrath, "Student Radicalism," pp. 195–201.

90. Bein, *Theodor Herzl*, p. 13.

91. *Ibid.*, p. 19.

92. July 10, 1898, *Tagebücher*, 2:95–96.

93. October 27, 1898, *ibid.*, 2:207.

94. October 31, 1898, *ibid.*, 2:212.

95. *Ibid.*, 2:212–213.

96. October 27, 1898, *ibid.*, 2:204.

97. Mark Zborowski and Elizabeth Herzog, *Life Is with People: The Culture of the Shtetl* (New York, 1962), pp. 341, 343, 424; Bruno Bettelheim, *The Informed Heart: Autonomy in a Mass Age* (Glencoe, Ill., 1960), pp. 248–265; Kurt Lewin, "Time Perspective and Morale," *Resolving Social Conflicts* (New York, 1948), pp. 104–105; Rudolph M. Loewenstein, *Christians and Jews: A Psychoanalytic Study* (New York, 1952), pp. 107–147; Erik H. Erikson, *Childhood and Society*, 2d. ed. (New York, 1963), pp. 353–357.

98. Bein, *Theodor Herzl*, p. 19.

99. Kellner, *Herzl's Lehrjahre*, p. 30.

100. Bein, *Theodor Herzl*, pp. 87–88.

101. *Ibid.*, p. 89.

102. *Tagebücher*, 1:8.

103. Bein, *Theodor Herzl*, p. 104.

104. June 5, 1895, *Tagebücher*, 1:38, and June 8, 1895, *ibid.*, 1:48.

105. June 5, 1895, *ibid.*, 1:37.

106. June 8, 1895, *ibid.*, 1:52.

107. June 10, 1895, *ibid.*, 1:73. and June 11, 1895, *ibid.*, 181.

108. Spring 1895, *ibid.*, 1:25.

109. *Ibid.*, 1:44.

110. October 8, 1898, *ibid.*, 2:151.

111. October 29, 1898, *ibid.*, 2:208.

112. Anna Freud, *The Ego and the Mechanisms of Defence* (New York, 1946), pp. 117–131.

113. Schnitzler, *Spiegelbild*, p. 96.

114. As quoted by Leon Edel, "The Biographer and Psychoanalysis," *International Journal of Psycho-Analysis* 42, pts. 4–5 (July–October 1961): 462.

115. Sigmund Freud, "The Relation of the Poet to Day-Dreaming" (1908), in *C.P.*, 4:174.

116. See Lionel Trilling, "Art and Neurosis," *The Liberal Imagination: Essays on Literature and Society* (Garden City, N.Y., 1954), pp. 159–178.

117. Theodor Herzl, "Das Wirtshaus zum Anilin" (1896), in *Philosophische Erzählungen* (Berlin, 1919), pp. 264–265.

118. Theodor Herzl, "Sarah Holzmann" (1896), *ibid.*, pp. 41–58.

119. Herzl, "Das Lenkbare Luftschiff" (1896), *ibid.*, p. 33.

120. Theodor Herzl, *Altneuland* (Leipzig, 1902), pp. 176–177.

121. *Ibid.*, p. 207.

122. *Ibid.*, p. 95.

123. *Ibid.*, p. 48.

124. *Ibid.*, p. 77.

125. *Ibid.*, p. 80.

126. *Ibid.*, p. 206.

127. Bein, Theodor Herzl, p. 8.

128. *Ibid.*, p. 22.

129. I am indebted to Robert M. Dorn for conceptual suggestions concerning Herzl's relations to male figures.

130. April 23, 1896, *Tagebücher*, 1:378.

131. *Ibid.*, 1:379.

132. September 9, 1896, *ibid.*, 1:531–532.

133. November 5, 1898, *ibid.*, 2:232.

134. *Ibid.*, 2:231.

135. September 3, 1897, *Complete Diaries*, 2:585. Omitted in *Tagebücher.*

136. September 2, 1898, *ibid.*, 2:653. Omitted in *Tagebücher*.

137. I am indebted to Alfred Goldberg for conceptual suggestions concerning Herzl's object relations.

138. For the psychodynamics of the prophet who emotionally impoverishes his human relationships while obtaining social participation in his vision, see Jacob A. Arlow, "The Consecration of the Prophet," *Psychoanalytic Quarterly*, 20, no. 3 (1951): 374–397.

139. February 1, 1896, *Tagebücher*, 1:330.

140. February 4, 1896, *ibid.*, 1:335–338.

141. Theodor Herzl, "Experiences and Moods: An Autobiographical Sketch," in *Herzl Memorial*, p. 184.

142. Theodor Herzl, *Die Welt* (Vienna, 1900); Vol. I, no. 1, as quoted

in Leonard Stein, "Arbeit fur Alle,: Herzl's Views on Capturing the Jewish Communities," in *Herzl Memorial*, p. 107.

143. Kellner, *Herzl's Lehrjahre*, p. 133.

144. August 24, 1897, *Tagebücher*, 2:21–22.

145. March 17, 1896, *ibid.*, 1:362.

146. March 12, 1898, *ibid.*, 2:64.

147. June 17, 1896, *ibid.*, 1:421.

148. June 30, 1896, *ibid.*, 1:463.

149. G. Sil-Vara, "At Herzl's Grave: The Burial of the Leader—and Other Memories," in *Herzl Memorial*, p. 21.

150. May 2, 1904, *Tagebücher*, 3:578.

151. Adolf Friedemann, *Das Leben Theodor Herzls* (Berlin, 1919), pp. 88–90.

152. Hans Sachs, "The Community of Daydreams," in *The Creative Unconscious* (Cambridge, Mass., 1942), pp. 11–54.

153. Freud, "Relation of the Poet to Day-Dreaming," p. 176.

154. *Ibid.*, p. 180.

155. Ernst Kris, *Psychoanalytic Explorations in Art* (New York, 1964), p. 293.

156. Heinz Hartmann, "Ego Psychology and the Problem of Adaptation," in David Rapaport, commentator and trans., *Organization and Pathology of Thought* (New York, 1951), pp. 372–373.

157. Heinz Hartmann, "On Rational and Irrational Action," Geza Róheim, ed., in *Psychoanalysis and the Social Sciences* (New York, 1947), 1:383.

158. I am indebted to Carl E. Schorske for this interpretation of *fin de siècle* Viennese culture.

159. June 16, 1895, *Tagebücher*, 1:116.

160. For the classic discussion of the elements of regression of libido, narcissism, megalomania, professional failure, and homoerotism in paranoia, see Freud, "Psycho-Analytic Notes," pp. 387–470.

161. Herzl, *Altneuland*, frontispiece.

162. Freud, "On Narcissism: An Introduction" (1914), *C.P.*, 4:30–59.

163. I have fused Erikson's two final ages of man, see Erikson, *Childhood and Society*, pp. 266–274.

164. Ernst Kris, "On Inspiration: Preliminary Notes on Emotional Conditions in Creative States," *International Journal of Psycho-Analysis*, 20, nos. 3–4 (July–October 1939): 380.

165. June 12, 1895, *Tagebücher*, 1:104.

166. *Ibid.*

167. Melanie Klein, "Love, Guilt and Reparation," in Melanie Klein and Joan Riviere, *Love, Hate and Reparation* (New York, 1964), p. 104.

168. Karen Horney, *New Ways in Psychoanalysis* (New York, 1939), p. 93.

169. Ernst Kris, "On Preconscious Mental Processes," in Rapaport, ed. and trans., *Organization and Pathology of Thought*, pp. 489–490.

170. Freud, "Group Psychology," p. 108.

7

ADOLF HITLER'S ANTI-SEMITISM: A STUDY IN HISTORY AND PSYCHOANALYSIS

Robert G. L. Waite

Any historian trained in traditional methods of historical inquiry must view with diffidence the prospects of applying psychoanalytic techniques to his research and writing. He feels uneasy because psychiatry, useful as it may be for understanding the living, seems somehow inappropriate—if not downright indecent—when applied to the dead. He has also been put off by seeing well-meaning colleagues use abnormal psychology to show the complexities of historical causation, but he has smiled ironically as they proceed to demonstrate in their writings not the complexity of history, but its apparent simplicity. For so seductive is psychoanalysis—at least to the newly converted amateur— that the intricacies of the historical past become reduced to simplistic psychological analysis. In short, any historian knows how much bad history has been written by those who are long on psychological theory and short on historical evidence, and whose works often remind him of one of Voltaire's more trenchant definitions: "History is that pack of tricks we play on the dead."

Yet, in dealing with such pathological personalities as Hitler, historians must inevitably feel a sense of professional embarrassment, for they soon encounter literally hundreds of facts that they are simply not trained *qua* historians to interpret. The problem is well stated by Alan Bullock, the distinguished biographer of Hitler, who admits with refreshing candor that the personality of his subject baffles him and that he finds Hitler's strange career "offensive" both to his reason and to his historical training:

> For my part, the more I learn about Adolf Hitler, the harder I find it to explain and accept what followed. Somehow the causes are inadequate to account for the size of the effects. It is offensive to our reason and to our experience to be asked to believe that [the youthful Hitler] was the stuff of which . . . the Caesars and Bonapartes were made. Yet the record is there to prove us wrong. It is here in the gap

> between the explanation and the event, that the fascination of Hitler's career remains.[1]

There is indeed a gap between the explanation and the event—and it certainly will not be filled by one essay addressing itself only to one aspect of Hitler's incredible complex personality: his personal anti-Semitism.[2] This foray into psychoanalysis and history will not provide conclusive answers. But the effort is made with the hope that the attempt will at least provide new departures for other investigators of the life of the bizarre little man who for a decade bestrode Europe like a colossus and decided the fate of nations.

The belief that the effort is worth making is reinforced in reading Percy Ernst Schramm's generally useful essay on Hitler's personality with which he introduces his excellent new edition of Picker's *Tischgespräche*—those interminable soliloques that Hitler inflicted on his captive audiences. Schramm quite rightly notices that throughout Hitler's monologues the theme of anti-Semitism runs "like a red thread." But he is unable to explain Hitler's monumental hatred for Jews and concludes despairingly, "We must be satisfied with the realization that there is about Hitler's . . . anti-Semitism an unknown factor." Though he has not consulted abnormal psychology in the matter, the distinguished German authority on Hitler is nonetheless positive "that psychology and psychiatry, in spite of all their refinements, must . . . also confess that they are confronted by an 'X'."[3] Mr. Schramm himself finally reaches the intriguing conclusion that Hitler's anti-Semitism resulted from certain nameless "demons" that plagued him.[4] Of course, in a larger sense, he may be right: historians may never know why Hitler became such a violent hater of the Jews. But we are not likely to find out if we continue to ignore the insights that abnormal psychology might be able to give us. At any rate it behooves us to try, for historians profess to follow Ranke's categorical imperative: to seek the full truth about the past.

ANTI-SEMITISM

The problem, then, is to interpret Hitler's anti-Semitism. It is not necessary here to belabor its importance. With him anti-Semitism assumed the proportions of a historic force. It was the undergirding principle of a society. It determined the law, the art, and the medicine of the Third Reich. It dictated that physics be studied without Einstein and psychology without Freud. It decided a man's profession; it chose his wife and his place of burial. It was the justification given for the murder of millions.

And anti-Semitism was the single most striking feature of Adolf Hitler's personality. The man was obsessed with hatred for the Jewish people. It is both symbolically and actually true that his political career began and ended with a warning against the "Jewish peril," which, he was convinced, threatened all civilization. In a letter dated September, 1919, which Ernst Deuerlein considers "the first piece of writing of Hitler's political career," Hitler states his goal as "ruthless intervention" against the Jews and their "removal" from Europe.[5] His last official act took place at 4:00 A.M., April 29, 1945 when he dictated his political testament. Notice the last word of the last sentence of this final entreaty to his successors: "Above all else, I charge the leaders of the nation . . . to a scrupulous maintenance of the racial laws and to the merciless opposition to the universal poisoner of all nations, international Jewry."[6] Hitler had spent his wedding night composing this last "testament." The next afternoon at about 3:30 P.M. he bit through an ampule of cyanide compounds. His bride then delivered the *coup de grâce* by shooting him through the left temple with her Walther 6.35 pistol before taking poison herself.[7]

Hitler's suspicions and beliefs about a vast international Jewish conspiracy were too ridiculous not to be taken seriously. He told a private meeting of his *Gauleiter* at the end of 1939, "The Jews may deceive the world . . . but they cannot deceive me. I know that they are guilty of starting this war—they alone and nobody else."[8] He found Jews lurking in the most unlikely places. He was sure, for example, that a small but highly influential minority of Jews really controlled Sweden, that Franklin Delano Roosevelt was a Jew, as were most of the British nobility. Jesus, on the other hand, could not have been Jewish and "if Genghis Khan was really as great a man as history says, then he was an Aryan and no Mongol."[9]

Because Hitler's hatred of the Jewish people was so intense, it is all the more unexpected that at crucial times in his life he was heavily indebted to Jews who befriended him or rendered him important services. The kindly family doctor who treated him and his mother and to whom Hitler said he was "eternally grateful" was a Jew. His landlady in Vienna who charged him minimum rent and obligingly moved out of her own room to accommodate him and his friend was said to be a Jew.[10] Antonescu, the Rumanian dictator who suffered from stomach trouble, as did Hitler, sent him his Jewish cook, Fräulein Kunde. When Himmler raised questions about the propriety of having a Jew prepare the Führer's food, Hitler turned furiously to Bormann and said, "Aryanize the Kunde family!"[11] When the youthful Hitler was really up against it in Vienna, he turned to Jewish art dealers who befriended him and paid generously for his mediocre watercolors.[12]

The most important honor Hitler ever received was the unusual distinction of earning the Iron Cross First Class as a corporal in World War I. The medal was the one decoration he wore constantly for it substantiated his claim of being the unknown hero of the war and was of enormous political value to him. He would not have received the cross if it had not been for the persistent efforts of his regimental adjutant, Hugo Gutmann, a Jew.[13]

In the issue of anti-Semitism as on many others involving Hitler, historians have tended to ignore psychological approaches to the problem and concentrated on narrative or descriptive history. Their books trace the development of anti-Semitism in Germany from Luther through Treitschke to Frau General Ludendorff and Dietrich Eckhart;[14] they describe in detail the persecution and murder of Jews in Nazi Germany;[15] they show how Hitler profited politically from his anti-Semitism;[16] and they explain how Hitler translated his own prejudices into public policy.[17]

It must be emphasized that these are all valuable books, which make important contributions to the study of the Jewish problem in German history. But it is also legitimate for an historian to ask a different kind of question about Nazi anti-Semitism: why did Hitler himself become an anti-Semite? At the moment this question is asked, the historian is probing the complex and subtle realm of human motivation. And at that point—whether he likes it or not—he has become some sort of psychologist. At least he is dealing with the kinds of questions about people that psychologists and psychiatrists are best equipped to handle.[18]

INTELLECTUAL INFLUENCES

Why then did Hitler become an anti-Semite, the most vicious and historically important anti-Semite in the history of the world? In part he became a hater of the Jews for intellectual reasons. During 1908, while he was an adolescent in Vienna, he became impressed with the arguments of certain anti-Semites. It was from racist pamphleteers and politicians, rather than from great figures in German intellectual history, that Hitler drew the ideas that were so important to his life and work. He was influenced by the mayor of Vienna, Karl Lueger, whom he considered the greatest mayor in history, and who reached the height of his popularity as the young Hitler arrived from Linz. Lueger's anti-Semitism is most clearly expressed in a speech that Hitler was to echo and reecho throughout his life:

> I know only one noxious thing in this country and that is the Jewish-Liberal press. That is the dragon . . . which has put the Germans in chains and held them imprisoned. I am proud that I have already given this dragon a couple of serious wounds. I'll see to it that these wounds remain open. This dragon must be crushed so that our dear German *Volk* can be freed from its prison.[19]

Hitler was also heavily and directly influenced by two racist pamphlet writers, Guido von List and Lanz von Liebenfels, men who reached the height of their influence during his Vienna period, 1908–1913. They are the people Hitler alluded to in his memoirs when he wrote that after having met a strange figure wearing a caftan he asked himself if this was a Jew and sought to find the answer, when, "For the first time in my life, I bought some anti-Semitic pamphlets for a few pennies."[20]

That List and Liebenfels wrote these pamphlets seems likely for a number of reasons. First, the mystical pseudoscientific nonsense contained in their writings was exactly the type of "scientific knowledge of race" that appealed to Hitler throughout his life. Second, the pamphlets were cheap and easily obtainable in Vienna —indeed there is strong evidence that Hitler bought them and went directly to Liebenfels in 1909 to ask for and to receive, free of charge, some back copies.[21] Third, the pamphlets were brief and dramatic and Hitler lacked the intellectual patience and discipline to read long books. Fourth, a book in his personal library—now in the rare books division of the Library of Congress—bears the following inscription dated 1921: "*An Adolf Hitler, meinem lieben Armanenbruder.*" It's a strange inscription, made comprehensible only when one knows that during 1908 to 1912 List had called for the establishment of a racially elite group called the Armanenschaft. Hitler's personal library also contains a copy of von Liebenfels' *Das Buch der Psalmen teutsch: Das Gebetbuch der Ariosophen Rassenmystiker und Antisemiten.*[22] Finally and most importantly, both in broad outline and in details the ideas of Liebenfels and List parallel Hitler's too closely to be accidental. Liebenfels, for example, in his *Ostara* pamphlets of 1907–1910, called for a "new order" of the racially elite; he used the swastika as the symbol of racial purity; and he promised that when his new order came, stringent laws would be passed against the "mongrelization" of the Aryan race. Hitler used the same expression in promulgating his Nuremberg racial laws in 1935. Liebenfels announced that all men are divided into two groups: creative Aryans and what he called ape-men—most notably the Jews. The function of the lower race was to be slave to the Aryans. In an issue of *Ostara* of 1913 he talked about "the Holy Grail of the German blood," which must be defended by a new elite bodyguard of the racially pure. Hitler apparently liked and remembered the phrase for he told Hermann Rauschning in the 1930's that "The problem is this: how can we arrest racial decay? . . . Shall we form . . . a select company of the really initiated? An Order, the brotherhood of Templars round *the holy grail of pure blood?*"[23] In another pamphlet of 1908, *Das Gesetzbuch der Manu und die Rassenpflege,* Liebenfels announced that the whole "mongrelized breed" of Jews and lesser men must be wiped off the face of the earth. In other pamphlets he urged the formation of breeding colonies and the sterilization of the weak and racially inferior. Twenty-five years later, Hitler put those ideas into practice.

The Führer also took seriously the advice of Liebenfels' racist colleague and fellow anti-Semite, Guido von List. In his pamphlets of the period 1908–1914, List called for the destruction of "the hydra-headed international Jewish conspiracy"—a phrase Hitler later adopted as his own. List also argued that two things were necessary to combat the Jewish conspiracy: the establishment of a racially pure state and a global war against the international Jews who sought to destroy civilization. He devoted many pamphlets to the racially pure Reich of his dreams. The new Reich would come only when a great leader—whom List called Araharl—made his appearance. The Reich would be divided in *Gaue* and each *Gau* would have a *Gauleiter*. Only Aryans would have citizenship rights. In a pamphlet dated 1908 List assured his readers that Aryans were superior people because the molecular structure of their blood was unique, but mainly because they had inherited certain powerful and secret Aryan symbols. These included the swastika and the runic letters, . List gives a long and loving disquistion on both. The origins of the letters, S.S., are runic, he says, and stood for "*Strick Stein*" which meant—if one may condense three chapters of spurious etymology—"secret law." He urged that the guardians of the racial purity of the new Reich should wear as their insignia the racial symbol.[24]

Clearly Hitler was influenced by other racists—no one man gave him his ideas. Dietrich Eckhart and the people of the *Thule Gesellschaft*, for example, were certainly important to Hitler after World War I, but they simply reinforced ideas that he got initially in Vienna during 1908–1913.[25] Hitler must be believed when he said of his years in Vienna, "In that city I received the basis of my view of life in general and a political way of looking at things in particular which later on I had only to supplement in single instances, but which never deserted me."[26]

There were other reasons why Hitler became an anti-Semite. As a consummately able political opportunist he saw, quite rightly, that it was smart politics in postwar Germany to be a Jew baiter. Indeed Hitler's establishment of the Jewish scapegoat was his greatest single political asset. He proved to those who desperately wanted to believe it that the Jews and not the Germans were responsible for all the ills that befell Germany from 1918–1933: Jews were to blame for the defeat in World War I, they were responsible for the Versailles "Treaty of Shame" and for capitalistic Western exploitation, for communism, and for the devastating inflation of 1923, and the crash of 1930, and for immorality in arts and public life. It was an effective political line.

PERSONALITY DETERMINANTS

The question of Hitler's personal anti-Semitism is, however, more subtle than these answers suggest. Why, *as a personality,* was Hitler attracted to anti-Semitism? Why did he make it the very cornerstone of his life and work? Because the question involves issues of human motivation, irrationality, and pathology, it directs us to the work of those psychiatrists and psychologists who have treated anti-Semitic patients and have concluded that anti-Semitism displays a variety of recognizable clinical syndromes. A fuller understanding of Hitler's personality can be gained by comparing him with hundreds of American patients who have been described as anti-Semitic personalities.[27]

First, anti-Semites display a confused definition of themselves—or, to use Erik Erikson's phrase, they are unable satisfactorily to solve their "identity crises."[28] They swing violently between the extremes of gnawing self-doubt on one end of the emotional arc to swaggering self-assurance on the other. So did Hitler. He often looked into the mirror and asked his valet anxiously, "I really do look like the Führer, don't I?"[29] But he announced roundly that, like the Pope, he was infallible, he compared himself favorably with Jesus and was convinced that he was the personal agent of God saying, "I go the way that providence dictates with all the assurance of a sleepwalker."[30]

Anti-Semites often have unsatisfactory interpersonal relations. Their friendships are notably precarious, constantly endangered by fear and mistrust. Hitler abused and abandoned Kubizek, his one childhood friend; the one adult, Röhm, who customarily called him by his first name, was murdered on Hitler's orders.

Without exception, the family background of anti-Semites treated by psychiatrists shows a conflict between father and mother. Typically the father dominates the home and the son clings to his indulgent mother. Hitler's stern and domineering father, Alois, was twenty-three years older than his placid, long-suffering wife, Klara. Whether or not he was justified in doing so,[31] Hitler certainly considered his father to be a drunken oaf and a sadistic brute who whipped him and raped his mother. Indeed at the age of three, Adolf may well have witnessed such a sexual attack. The evidence here is certainly not conclusive, but it is worth the conjecture. It comes from *Mein Kampf*, which is often more revealingly autobiographical than Hitler intended. In one highly interesting passage, where he ostensibly describes a "worker's" family, it is probable that he is bringing to the surface a searing memory of his own childhood. "Let us imagine the following: in a basement of two stuffy rooms lives a worker's family . . . Among the children . . . there is a boy, let us say of three. This is the age at which a child becomes conscious of his first impressions." Hitler then describes the contant arguments and fights "almost daily" of the parents and concludes: "Their brutality leaves nothing to the imagination . . . especially . . . in the form of brutal attacks on the part of the father toward the mother or to assaults due to drunkeness. The poor little boy, at the age of six senses things which would make even a grown-up shudder. Morally infected . . . the young citizen wanders off to elementary school."[32] At any rate, as will be shown in more detail later, Hitler hated and feared his father and loved his rather pretty young mother with unusual intensity. Let it be noted that Hitler's favorite opera was *Lohengrin*. He attended at least ten performances of it during his stay in Vienna alone, and he committed the entire libretto to memory.[33] Why this remarkable interest? The music is of course magnificent early Wagner, but Hitler was also fascinated by the plot. The story involves a blonde girl who is menaced by her lecherous guardian, Frederick of Telramund. The girl is rescued by Lohengrin, the pure-souled and silver-armored knight who possesses the redemptive power of the Holy Grail. It remains speculative, but perhaps Hitler was so intrigued with the story because he saw himself as the immaculate knight of "the Holy Grail of the German blood" who rescued his mother from the lusting advances of a contaminating father—who had been, in point of fact, the legal guardian of Klara before he married her. Indeed, in 1937 Hitler approved of a portrait of himself as Sir Adolf, a knight in shining armor astride a mighty stallion.

Next, the anti-Semite has an orientation toward the powerful and against the weak. Hitler endorsed Himmler's idea of organizing S.S. breeding settlements and gave orders to kill or sterilize the physically and mentally handicapped. The patients studied by psychiatrists characteristically reverted to primitive destruction. Hitler gave orders to burn Paris to the ground and planned to destroy Germany in the greatest *Götterdämmerung* in history.

Anti-Semites typically tend to be infantile personalities who show marked immaturity in their cultural tastes and political convictions. There is abundant evidence that Hitler did not outgrow the pleasures and prejudices of his boyhood. As Führer and Chancellor of Germany he loved to stay up late at night, read about cowboys and Indians, eat an enormous amount of candy and sweets, look at pornographic pictures, go on picnics, and play guessing games.[34] He liked to see at least one movie every night, and his favorite was probably *King Kong*. He was infatuated with this story of the great ape who loved a little blonde girl no larger than his hand. The political convictions of the chancellor were those of the adolescent in Vienna. The ideas are the same and so are the peculiar words and phrases he used to express them. In moments of tension, the Führer of the "Thousand Year Reich" sucked his little finger.[35]

According to psychiatrists, anti-Semites often seek a resolution to their Oedipus complex through sadomasochism. Part of their aggressiveness is absorbed and turned into masochism and another part is left over as sadism, which seeks an outlet against those who are blamed for the patient's difficulties. It does not seem necessary to document here Hitler's sadism. What needs emphasis—and will be discussed later—is his pronounced masochistic tendencies, which were manifested in feelings of guilt and in an extreme form of masochistic sexual perversion.

Personalities warped by anti-Semitism characteristically have unsatisfactory relationships with the opposite sex and are often prone to abnormal sexual practices. Hitler's relations with women were not notably happy. As an adolescent he fell in love with a pretty blonde girl in Linz. But he loved from afar and could never summon the courage to introduce himself to her. Stefanie never knew that Adolf existed.[36] All the other affairs took place with young women who were between twenty and twenty-five years younger than he.[37] Which is to say he chose women who were as much younger than he as his mother was younger than his father. The one true love of his life, he later said, was his niece "Geli" Raubal. She shot herself through the roof of her mouth with Hitler's pistol. Eva Braun became his mistress and wife, but the day after their marriage they both committed suicide. Indeed every woman intimately associated with Hitler either committed suicide or attempted to. The obvious question is *why?* And as usual, in history as in psychiatry, it is a question difficult to answer. Eva Braun, of course, was involved in the suicide pact, but she had attempted suicide long before 1945. It may be that in at least one or two of the other cases, women sought death in part because of a particularly abhorrent sexual perversion that had beset Hitler.[39]

Psychiatrists report that anti-Semites are adroit in their use of defense mechanisms, among which are projection and introjection. They project onto others the qualities they cannot admit are their own; they attribute to themselves qualities that appear highly desirable. The weaker or the more confused they feel, the stronger is their effort to find "compensatory identity." Typically, an anti-Semite insists that he is a person of tremendous willpower and that he belongs to a particularly elite and exclusive social group. Adolf Hitler's arsenal of defense weapons was impressive,[40] but he relied chiefly on projection and introjection. He insisted that "the Jew"—he spoke of Jews collectively as if they were all one—was the cause of literally all of Germany's misfortunes and belonged to a filthy, degenerate, perverted people; Hitler, of course, incorporated in his own person all the virtues of history's most elite and creative race.

It seems clear, then, that Hitler displayed symptoms that characterize the type of emotional disorder that uses anti-Semitism as its chief defense. But he was not merely an anti-Semitic type. There are thousands of such types in the world. Anti-Semitism was for Hitler the very ground of his being and the essence of his Reich. Hatred and fear of the Jews dominated his life, and the Jewish peril haunted him in his hour of death—to the last word of his last public statement. Never in history has there been such an anti-Semite. He sought, in the end, to kill all the Jews of Europe. Is there any possible way for the historian to explain that historical fact? Maybe not. There are some historical facts that defy explanation, and this may be one of them. But inasmuch as it is not possible to explain his anti-Semitism by relying solely on traditional tools of historic analysis, let us with due recognition of the difficulties, attempt to apply psychoanalytical techniques in a discussion of the reasons why Hitler hated Jews.

PROJECTIONS

We have said that he projected his own problems onto the Jews. Psychologically the use of a scapegoat often proves to be a way of covering up deep-seated feelings of inadequacy, self-hatred, and self-loathing. If, for example, a person has feelings of guilt about incest or sexual perversion, he can make these feelings more bearable by shifting the finger of guilt away from himself and pointing it at Jews. As Gordon Allport has pointed out, a kind of vicious circle is created by "projection": "The hated scapegoat is merely a disguise for persistent and unrecognized self-hatred. A vicious circle is established. The more the sufferer hates himself the more he hates the scapegoat, the less sure he is of his innocence; hence, the more guilt he has to project."[41]

Thus projection is a consequence of guilt and self-hatred. Because Hitler's hatred of the Jews was monumental, his feelings of guilt and self-loathing must have been very great indeed. Certainly the words "conscience" and "guilt" were often on his mind. Over and over again, in phrases more revealing than he realized, Hitler showed his concern about conscience and the need for rendering it inactive:

> Only when the time comes when the race is no longer overshadowed by the *consciousness of its own guilt,* then it will find eternal peace . . . .
>
> *Conscience* is like a Jewish invention. It is a blemish, like circumcision.
>
> I am freeing men from the restraints of intelligence . . . and from the dirty and degrading modifications of a chimera called *conscience and morality* . . . .
>
> We must distrust the intelligence and the *conscience* and must place our faith in our instincts.
>
> Only when the time comes when the race is no longer overshadowed by the *consciousness of its own guilt, then it will find internal peace* and external energy to cut down regardlessly and brutally the wild shoots, and to pull up the weeds.

> We must be ruthless . . . We must *regain our clear conscience* as to ruthlessness . . . Only thus shall we purge our people . . .[42]

He felt personal guilt about something. But what? Well, what did he talk about particularly with respect to the Jews, what accusations did he most often make against them? Above all he was fascinated with sex and incest. Time after time in public speeches and documents, in private conversations and letters, he showed that he was really worried about the dark evil sexual practices, which he insisted are typically Jewish practices. As Dr. Gertrud Kurth has noticed, Hitler made Jews responsible for many crimes, but "never did he become so emotional, so arbitrary, and so absurd" as when he fulminated about Jewish sexual aberrations and sexual crimes.[43]

Hitler tells us that he really began to hate the Jews with a vengeance when he made the monstrous discovery that they alone were responsible for the white-slave traffic and prostitution in Vienna. And that an "icy shudder" ran down his spine when he made the discovery about this "shocking vice."[44] But it was a vice that absolutely enthralled him. His friend Kubizek wrote in a private letter that Hitler studied the origins and development of prostitution "in all times and among all peoples" and talked about it by the hour.[45]

The Jews, Hitler never tired of saying, sought to pollute the blood of the German people through a calculated campaign of sexual subversion. He dwells in his memoirs on "the black-haired Jew boy" who with "diabolic joy in his face" waits in ambush for the unsuspecting girl whom he defiles with his blood.[46] And he accuses the Jews of turning other people into "sexless bastards."[47] He had recognized the threat during his Vienna days when he told Kubizek, "they are trying to infect the entire German people and to poison them in order to . . . dominate them."[48]

Hitler's preoccupation with the sexual threat of Jews is manifest in one of his most important state papers, the so-called Nuremberg Racial Laws of 1935, which he called *Blutschutzgesetz* "The Law for the Protection of the Blood." It is important to notice that Hitler personally dictated the wording of these laws and gave strict orders that not one word should be changed.[49] For reasons that will be discussed later, paragraph three is especially interesting: "Jews cannot employ female household servants of German or related blood who are under 45 years of age."[50]

PREOCCUPATION WITH INCEST

Hitler was particularly concerned about incest and associated it with the Jews. In 1919 he announced that the Jews had maintained themselves historically only by "thousands of years of incest."[51] And in a particularly revealing passage in *Mein Kampf* he wrote that Vienna was the city of the Jews and "the personification of *incest*."[52] It is an unusual use of the word. Hitler had good reason to be anxious about incest. His own mother and father were so closely related, according to baptismal records, that special Papal dispensation was needed before they could be married.[53] And he seems to have suspected that "incestuous poisoning of the blood"—to use one of his favorite expressions in condemning the Jews—was responsible for certain striking peculiarities about his own family. Of the children born to Alois and Klara Hitler, four of the seven died prematurely; one sister was kept hidden as an idiot child; and another, Paula, was a high-grade moron. His Aunt Johanna was considered "crazy" by the neighbors.[54] During a closed speech to his *Gauleiter* in 1937, Hitler showed his continuing concern about tainted blood when he remarked that in his family people always died young.[55]

Hitler's excessive attachment for women in his own family must also have been an important reason for his preoccupation with incest. The family doctor noted that he had never, in a long practice, seen a boy who showed such extreme devotion to his mother.[56] When Hitler heard that she was dying, he returned from Vienna to nurse her. He did the household chores, supervised the cooking of her favorite foods, read aloud to her from the maudlin love stories and novels she loved so much, held her tightly to him when her pain was great, and when she died he sat alone in the room with her body and sketched it "so that he would always remember."[57] Throughout his life, his mother's picture was in his pocket wallet and her portrait hung over his bed in all his bedrooms, whether in his Munich apartment, in the chancellory, or in the Berlin bunker.[58]

In addition to his mother, Hitler was very fond indeed of his stepsister, Angela, who had taken care of him at the age of five when his mother gave birth to a brother, Edmund. Indeed this mothering sister of eleven might easily have become for Adolf a replacement for the mother who neglected him while she nursed his baby brother.[59] Later he transferred his love for his half-sister to her daughter—and his own niece—Angela, or Geli Raubal. Geli was the one person, he often said, whom he could ever think of marrying. It does not seem to be merely coincidental that he longed to marry a person whose relation to him in age was similar to that between his father and his mother. Geli was twenty-three years old when she came to live in Hitler's apartment; his mother was twenty-five when she married Hitler's father. Geli habitually called Hitler "Uncle Adolf" or "Uncle Alf"; his mother had called her own husband "Uncle Alois." In his bedroom, there was one other picture besides that of his mother; it was of Geli.[60]

The evidence indicates that in both word and deed Hitler displayed a pattern of unusually intense concern about sexuality and particularly about incestous relationships, that he felt guilty about them, and that he projected his feelings of guilt onto the Jews.

SEXUAL PERVERSION

He was also concerned about sexual perversion and associated it with Jews. Ever since childhood he liked to look at pornography and as Führer of Germany he eagerly awaited each issue of Streicher's blatantly pornographic anti-Semitic magazine, *Der Stürmer*. "It was the one periodical that he always read with pleasure from the first page to the last."[61] The direct projection of sexual perversion onto the Jews is shown in an incident of 1938 involving the dismissal of General Blomberg as Minister of Defense, after he married a former prostitute. Hitler was outraged at this disclosure and used it as an excuse for dismissing an uncooperative general. Hitler had the Gestapo collect incriminating evidence against Frau Blomberg. They supplied him with photographs showing her plying her profession by participating in various forms of sexual perversion. A person who has seen the photographs says they were of the "most shocking depravity." But what concerns us here is Hitler's instinctive reaction on first examining the pictures. He said at once that the male partner in these photos "*must have been* of Jewish extraction." He then became "absolutely convulsed by the wildest anti-Semitic outpourings he had ever given vent to in his entire life."[62]

This extreme kind of projection suggests that Hitler himself had a sexual perversion so extreme that it produced in him intense feelings of guilt and self-loathing. There is reason to believe that Hitler's perversion took the form of acute masochism. He liked to watch a young woman as she squatted over his head and urinated or defecated on his face. Apparently only in this way could he get full sexual satisfaction.[63]

There seems to be enough evidence with respect to Hitler's curious and continuing concern about incest and sexual perversion to risk a tentative hypothesis about his anti-Semitism: one of the reasons why he hated the Jews with such incandescent fury and sought to destroy them was because he himself felt an enormous burden of guilt and self-hatred because of his own aberrant sexual desires. He therefore insisted that the Jews, and not he, were guilty of the very things he personally felt guilty about: incest—it is not important psychologically whether the incest was a fact or a fantasy—and a monstrous sexual perversion. To repeat, if psychoanalytic theory is correct, such massive hatred of the Jews must have been caused in part by a truly massive amount of self-hatred and self-loathing which he projected onto the Jews.

DISPLACED OEDIPUS COMPLEX

Hitler's anti-Semitism was intensified by both the timing and the circumstances of his mother's death. Klara Hitler died just before Christmas 1907—when Adolf was experiencing one of the most shattering personal experiences of his life. During the months before her death his cherished ambition of becoming an artist had been smashed when he was rejected by the Viennese Academy of Fine Arts. Then his application for the school of architecture was turned down because he lacked a diploma from Realschule. He had not graduated from school because, as he put it, he had wanted to "sabotage" his father's plans for him to become a government official.[64] The realization that his efforts to punish his father had now resulted in the frustration of his own ambition did nothing to diminish the antagonism he felt for his father. At this low point in his life, his beloved mother died.

The chronology is important; so too is the cause of death. Klara Hitler died in Linz after a mastectomy for breast cancer. The physician who attended her both before and after the operation was the family doctor, Edmund Bloch, a Jew.[65] Shortly after the funeral, which was held on the dark and miserable day before Christmas Eve, Adolf returned alone to Vienna. It is at this time, early in 1908, that Hitler became a fanatic anti-Semite. Other writers have set different dates for the genesis of his racist doctrine, but there seems to be no reason to dispute Hitler's own testimony. It is given in a rambling and ungrammatical letter now in the so-called *Gestapoberichte* of the former Party archives. In it Hitler wrote that "within less than a year" after the death of his mother he became a violent anti-Semite.[66] As we have seen, it was during this year that he devoured the racist pamphlets of Liebenfels and List.

It is very difficult indeed to exaggerate the importance to Hitler of what he later called his "Copernican discovery" of anti-Semitism. It unlocked all the secrets of history and seemed to solve all his own personal problems. His conversion to anti-Semitism was a veritable identity crisis and the turning point of his life. Years later he looked back on this year in Vienna and wrote: "This was the time in which the greatest change I was ever to experience took place in me. From a feeble cosmopolite I had turned into a fanatical anti-Semite . . . Therefore, I believe today that I am acting in the sense of the Almighty Creator: by warding off the Jews I am fighting for the Lord's work."[67]

The close association between the onset of Hitler's fanatical anti-Semitism and the death of his mother seems clear. It is of course entirely possible that the connection is purely coincidental. But it is also possible that there may have been a casual connection between his mother's death and the beginning of his extreme hatred of the Jews "within less than a year." Let us hazard an interpretation based on Freudian analysis.[68]

According to this view, Hitler had a pronounced "Oedipus complex" with a deeply felt conflict about his father. Consciously and publicly he always spoke well of "The Old Gentleman"; but "unconsciously" he hated and feared him as the rival for his young mother's love. His incestous feelings awakened an acute sense of guilt. The father had died, but now the Jewish family doctor, Edmund Bloch, arrived and reawakened the basic conflict he had had with his father. Indeed, according to this interpretation, Dr. Bloch became the "displacement" for Hitler's own father. Toward Dr. Bloch Hitler was as ambivalent as he was to his real father: he was at once deeply appreciative and bitterly resentful. His gratitude is attested by two hand-painted postcards he sent to Dr. Bloch from Vienna with the inscription, "From your ever grateful patient, Adolf Hitler."[69] But unconsciously he feared him as a new rival who took the place of his hated father.[70] For this Jewish doctor had done many of the things young Adolf had seen his father do: he too had often entered his mother's bedroom; he had seen her undressed; he had examined her breasts. Other medical intimacies became associated in Hitler's mind with his image of his father as the lecherous attacker of his mother. Brutality and multilation were now represented by the ablation of the breast. The incest and the poisoning of the blood, which Hitler feared so much and for which—as we shall see—he blamed his father, was now represented by the doctor's almost daily hypodermic injections of morphine, given to alleviate the woman's suffering. Thus, though Hitler consciously expressed his gratitude to Dr. Bloch, unconsciously the doctor had become the brutal attacker who had finally mutilated and killed his beloved mother.

This interpretation suggests the possibility of a further and more important displacement. The individual Jew, Dr. Bloch, was not only the "incestuous, blood-poisoning murderer" of his mother; by projection and the expansion of imagery to the Motherland—and it is worth emphasizing that Hitler often used this term rather than the more usual Fatherland—[71] Jews in general became the attackers of the German Motherland and the blood poisoners of "the Holy Grail of German Blood." They all had to be destroyed.

COMPENSATORY MECHANISMS

Hitler's actual annihilation of the Jews must also be associated with his feelings of self-doubt and weakness combined with military defeats. It is of course difficult to set any precise moment when Hitler realized that he could not win the war—and certainly he kept proclaiming the inevitability of victory long after he stopped believing in it—but Professor Schramm is probably correct in saying that Hitler realized during the first month of 1942 after the Russian defeats and the catastrophic winter of 1941–1942 that the kind of victory he had hoped to win was no longer obtainable.[72] It is no chronological accident that the final decision to kill the Jews of Europe was made at the Wannsee Conference during the same month, January 20, 1942. By thus "defeating" the Jews, Hitler was attempting to prove his own victorious strength and to quiet growing feelings that he was a weakling and a failure.

All his life he had been plagued by self-doubts about his masculinity and physical power—doubts that were made manifest every time he insisted so often and so vehemently that he really was not weak at all, he was really "hard as steel," "ice-cold," and "brutal." Of these, his favorite word was "brutal" and his eyes would flash fire as he rolled the "r" and hit the second syllable.[73] He used the word in the most incongrous places. In talking about chickens that "robbed" a man's garden, for example, Hitler concluded that in such cases "one could not be brutal enough."[74] To Hitler the word had a positive and complimentary meaning. Thus the reason he favored an alliance with England in the 1920's was because the English would always fight "with brutality";[75] he paid tribute to his friendship with Mussolini by calling it "our brutal friendship";[76] and he was impressed with Gottfried Feder because "he outlined, with ruthless brutality, the character of the stock exchange . . . ."[77]

He also felt the continuing necessity of insisting that he was a man of hardness with nerves of steel. Thus in a public speech in 1940 he proclaimed, "I am one of the hardest men Germany has had for decades, perhaps for centuries!"[78] In a strikingly revealing interview with the great scientist Max Planck, Hitler must have felt his own inadequacy acutely for he suddenly felt compelled to say, "People say I sometimes suffer from weak nerves. That is a libel. I have nerves of steel." Planck remembered that when Hitler said that "he pounded his knee, spoke even faster and worked himself into such a fury that there was nothing for me to do but to remain silent and excuse myself."[79] Thus did this Führer protest too much.

Hitler's ideal for German youth expressed his own self-idealization: "they must be lithe and taut, swift as greyhounds, tough as leather and hard as Krupp steel."[80] But now, during the period after 1942, it was increasingly evident that the soft-muscled, slightly paunchy man with the trembling and effeminate hands did not at all fit his own picture of the indominable, brutal, and all-conquering Führer. Indeed each military defeat unnerved him further and required more and more proof that he was the ice-cold, steel-hard, and ruthless victor of his fantasies. He could not play that role by conquering Russia or the Western Allies; he therefore manufactured ruthless and brutal "victories" over the Jews. Walter C. Langer, a distinguished psychiatrist who helped draw up a remarkably prescient analysis of Hitler for the American Office of Strategic Services during the war, recognized this fear of weakness in Hitler's personality and foresaw the consequences. Long before he had knowledge of Hitler's death camps and the massacre of the Jews, Dr. Langer predicted that Hitler would compensate for self-doubt and defeat by increasingly ruthless acts of destruction and brutality:

> Each defeat will shake his confidence still further and limit his opportunities for proving his own greatness to himself . . . He will probably try to compensate for his vulnerability . . . by continually stressing his brutality and ruthlessness . . . for only in this way [can] he prove to himself that he is not a weakling . . . but made of the stuff becoming his conception of what a Victor should be.[81]

THE QUESTION OF JEWISH ANCESTORS

Thus, compensatory reaction may help to explain Hitler's massacre of the Jews. But there may be a further reason why he launched the genocide. He may have done so because he suspected that he himself might have had a Jewish grandfather. Such a suspicion was, of course, for him absolutely unbearable. Psychologically he had based his very identity on the projection of his own feelings of guilt, inadequacy, and failure onto Jews. Politically, he had staked his entire career on the principle of the superiority of the Aryans, the inferiority of the "sub-human Jews", and the terrible threat of the Jewish peril. He simply had to do something about his suspicion. First—as we shall see—he had his personal lawyer and then his secret police investigate his ancestry in order to prove positively that he could not possibly have any Jewish blood. But they could not prove it because they could not establish the identity of his paternal grandfather. Hitler therefore felt compelled to prove it to himself, by himself. It was partly in order to convince himself that he could not conceivably be part Jewish that he became history's greatest persecutor and murderer of the Jews.

This arresting theory, first suggested by G. M. Gilbert, a prison psychologist at the Nuremberg trials,[82] is worth looking at rather closely. Is there any historical evidence to support it? Two questions are involved here. First, was Adolf Hitler's own father, who was illegitimate, the son of a Jew? This is the questions that German historians and journalists have belabored through dozens of heavily argued pages.[83] Their efforts might have been spared, for the question cannot be answered and it really is not very important. The crucial question is rather: did Hitler harbor the suspicion that he himself might have Jewish blood? The answer to this question is yes, he did so believe.

At this point we need to be reminded that the historian's job is not only to discover with Ranke what actually happened. Often in history it is at least as important to discover what men believed happened. For men act on their beliefs—whether they are objectively true or not matters little. It is not true, for example, that following 1774 English statesmen organized a nefarious plot designed to enslave the American colonists. But Jefferson, Dickinson, Samuel Adams, and Washington, along with thousands of other Americans, believed that there was a "settled, fixed plan for enslaving the colonies." The consequences of this unfounded belief helped to produce the Declaration of Independence and the American Revolution.[84] Nor is it true that Marie Antoinette was a "*putain autrichienne*." But when Frenchmen called her that and believed—quite wrongly—in her promiscuity, their beliefs served to undermine the French monarchy. It is not true that the German armies were undefeated until "stabbed in the back" in November 1918 by the traitorous republican plotters and Jews. Belief in the false "*Dolchstoss* Legend," however, helped mightily to condemn the Weimar Republic in the eyes of thousands of German patriots. In the case of Hitler's ancestry, it would be interesting to establish the objective truth about his father's lineage. But it is important to affirm a different kind of objective fact: Hitler believed that he had Jewish blood. The results of that fact are writ large in historical consequences.

Back to the first question: was Hitler's own grandfather a Jew? He might have been. But the evidence is not very convincing. First there is little negative evidence. The original birth certificate of Hitler's father, which still exists in the village baptismal registry, left the father's name blank. A name was added later, but much later and in a different handwriting and with a different ink.[85]

There is also some positive evidence in support of the theory. Before he was hanged as a war criminal, Hitler's personal lawyer, Hans Frank, recorded the following story in his memoirs: One day toward the end of 1930 Hitler sent for him because he was about to be blackmailed by a relative who claimed to have special information about Hitler's family. A letter hinted darkly of a Jewish ancestor. Hitler was so thoroughly shaken by the threat of such a disclosure that he ordered his lawyer to investigate. Frank did so and discovered that Hitler's father had been the illegitimate son of a certain Maria Anna Schicklgruber who had worked as a domestic in Graz, Austria "in the home of a Jewish family by the name of Frankenberger." From the day her baby—Hitler's father, Alois—was born until the the boy was fourteen Frankenberger paid money to the mother for support of the child. According to Frank, when Hitler was confronted with this evidence he said that the story of the Graz Jew being his own grandfather was an absolute lie. He knew it was because his grandmother had told him so. She had accepted the money from the Jew only because she was so poor.[86]

When Frank wrote this memoir he had been condemned to death and had converted to Catholicism. He wrote, in part, to expiate his sins. There seems no reason, as he stood "in the face of the gallows" to misrepresent Hitler in this matter or to misquote him. The interesting part of the story is not that Hitler lied when he said his grandmother assured him that his grandfather was not a Jew—Hitler's grandmother had died more than forty years before he was born. The key point is that Hitler made no attempt to deny that his grandmother had received money over the many years from a Jew. Certainly the evidence Hans Frank produced must have been pretty impressive. It was good enough to force Hitler to admit the possibility that a Jew had been very much involved with his own grandmother. Clearly such a suspicion would have served to intensify the already pathological hatred and fear of the Jewish evil and its blood-poisoning threat to civilization. The great threat lurked everywhere —and might even have infected the bloodstream of his own family.

That Hitler believed in the possibility of a Jewish grandfather who might have "contaminated" his blood is suggested not only by the preoccupation we have already noted he had with the general problem of incest and blood poisoning but by other evidence. Hitler was terribly concerned about his own blood. Apparently he thought there was something wrong with it for he sought to get rid of his blood. He often put leeches on his skin and watched as they sucked. Later he had his quack doctor, Morell, draw his blood and save it so that he could gaze at it. He also talked of making blood sausage of his own blood and feeding it to his secretaries.[87] Nor could he rid his mind of the possibility that his grandmother, the servant Maria Anna Schicklgruber, might have been seduced by a Jew. It will be recalled that in the Nuremberg racial laws of 1935, which Hitler personally dictated, he made a very special point of decreeing that henceforth no German woman under the age of forty-five could work as a servant in a Jewish household. His own grandmother was forty-one when she gave birth to Hitler's father. And he projected the fear that haunted him onto Matthias Erzberger, the deputy of the Center party whom Hitler accused of betraying Germany by accepting the Versailles treaty. In a revealing passage in his second book Hitler wrote: "Fate had chosen a man who was one of those principally guilty for the collapse of our people. Matthias Erzberger, . . . the *illegitimate son of a servant girl and a Jewish employer*, was the German negotiator who set his name to the document which had the deliberate intention of bringing about the destruction of Germany."[88] The servant girl was still on his mind years later. In one of his nightly monologues, on February 1942 he told his entourage about "a country girl who had a place in Nuremberg in the household of Herr Hirsch" and had been raped by her employer.[89]

There is more evidence that Hitler suspected his own blood was tainted through his father. This evidence is also not conclusive, but it is interesting. Just two months after taking over Austria in March, 1938, Hitler had a survey made of the lovely little farming village of Döllersheim—the village where his father had been born and his grandmother buried. The purpose of the survey was to ascertain the suitability of the area for an artillery range for the Wehrmacht. General Knittersched, the commanding general of Wehrkreis 17, was given orders directly from Hitler to make the area ready "as soon as possible."[90] The inhabitants were evacuated, the village demolished by artillery fire, and the graves in the cemetery rendered unrecognizable.[91] Why? There are thousands of empty acres in this part of lower Austria; why did Hitler choose this particular village as an artillery range? Was it not because he felt a great compulsion to wipe out—quite literally—the suspicion of his own Jewish blood by obliterating the birthplace of his father and the grave of his grandmother?

It is also curious that in the so-called Gestapo reports on Hitler in the main archives of the Nazi party, there are records of several separate investigations into Hitler's family background.[92] The most thorough of these inquiries was made in 1942—just prior to the onset of the massacres that killed about 6 million Jews. Why these special investigations? Hitler rarely talked about his own family. Why then this remarkable concern about his ancestors unless he was anxiously hoping to prove that he was a pure Aryan—or at least as Aryan as his own racial laws required?

It is reasonable to conclude that we do not know—and it really does not matter very much—whether Adolf Hitler's grandfather was actually a Jew. But it seems certain that Hitler believed that he might have been. The consequences of that belief, along with other psychopathological factors, produced the greatest deliberate mass murder of history. In order to prove to himself that he could not conceivably be Jewish, in order to convince himself that such a direct threat to his psyche and his life work was an utter impossibility, Hitler fanned his already developed hatred of the Jews to beserk fury and screamed that he would annihilate the Jews down to the third generation. Which is to say, the degree of blood relationship he was trying so desperately to prove could not possibly have been his own.

It has been argued here that historians who seek to understand Adolf Hitler should consult psychiatrists, for they can help explain the subterranean processes by which his tortured and sick mind became convinced that the Jewish people were his personal enemy and the mortal foe of Germany. The reason *why* he believed that lies in the murky realms of the unconscious and the irrational. But there was nothing irrational about the conclusion that he reached as a consequence of that conviction. To him the whole thing was perfectly logical and very simple: because the Jew was *the* enemy he must be destroyed. The Jew was responsible for every evil thing, for moral corruption, sexual perversion, incest, and poisoning of the blood. The Jew alone had started the war. He had launched a cunning and vicious attack on the Motherland. But Adolf Hitler would show that he was no weakling to flinch before the adversary. He would show them! He would prove that he was the brutal conqueror who could conquer this most monstrous of all enemies. He would utterly destroy the Jews; he would wipe them from the face of the earth.

NOTES

I have profited enormously from discussing various aspects of this essay with the following people: Dr. Gertrud Kurth of New York, Prof. Erik H. Erikson of Harvard, Drs. Robert Harris and Lawrence Mamlet of the Austen Riggs Center, Stockbridge, Massachusetts, and Dr. Norman Reider of Mt. Zion Hospital, San Francisco.

1. Alan Bullock, "Foreword" to the English edition of Franz Jetzinger, *Hitler's Youth* (London, 1958).

2. Further exploration of the problems of applying psychoanalysis to a study of Hitler will be made in an article to be published in *The Journal of Interdisciplinary History* and in a forthcoming full-length study provisionally entitled, *Adolf Hitler: The Pathological Personality as Political Leader.*

3. Percy E. Schramm, "Introduction," in Henry Picker, *Hitlers Tischgespräche im Führerhauptquartier, 1941–1942* (Stuttgart, 1965), pp. 51–52.

4. *Ibid.*, p. 119.

5. Ernst Deuerlein, "Hitler's Eintritt in die Politik und die Reichswehr," *Vierteljahrshefte für Zeitgeschichte* 7 (1959): 204.

6. Quoted in Max Domarus, ed., *Hitler, Reden und Proklamationen, 1932–1945*, 4 vols. (Munich, 1963), 4:2239.

7. There are conflicting versions of Hitler's death. Trevor-Roper writes that Hitler committed suicide by shooting himself through the roof of his mouth. He bases his version on the testimony of Hitler's secretaries who said that they had heard the story from two men who were subsequently taken prisoner of war by the Russians, Hitler's S.S. adjutant, Otto Günsche, and his S.S. valet, Heinz Linge. (H. R. Trevor-Roper, *The Last Days of Hitler* [New York, 1947], p. 201.) Günsche gave the same account to

Hitler's chauffeur Kempka, the man who actually burned the bodies. (Erich Kempka, *Ich habe Adolf Hitler verbrannt* [Munich, 1950], pp. 107–109.) The story of the shot in the mouth is also recorded by Robert G. L. Waite, *Hitler and Nazi Germany* [New York, 1965], p. 13. I was also incorrect in writing that "[Hitler's] bones have not been found." Evidence recently released by the Soviet Union gives a different cause of death. On May 4, 1945, Russian soldiers found the half-burned and hastily buried bodies of Eva Braun and Adolf Hitler in the courtyard of the Reich chancellory. Positive identification was made by dental examination and a distinguished team of Russian pathologists and specialists in forensic medicine performed autopsies on the bodies on May 8, 1945. The official report of the autopsy shows that splinters of glass from a thin-walled ampule were found in Hitler's mouth and that cyanide compounds were discovered in his internal organs. One of the examining physicians, Professor Krayevski, later reported that the smell of bitter almonds on the bodies was his most striking memory of the autopsy. The Russian doctors unanimously concluded that Hitler's death was caused not by a pistol shot but "by poisoning with cyanide compounds." The official autopsy and the doctors' comments are given in Lev Bezymenski, *The Death of Adolf Hitler: Unknown Documents from Soviet Archives* (New York, 1968). The autopsy also shows that virtually the whole of Hitler's cranium was missing, but that the upper and lower jaws, the mouth cavity, tongue, and parts of the brain were preserved. No visible signs of bullet wounds were reported. It seems unlikely that Hitler shot himself through the roof of his mouth. If he had, there would have been evidence of destruction in the floor of the skull. Further, the blast of a heavy caliber pistol fired directly into the mouth almost certainly would have distintegrated the thin glass walls of the poison ampule. But a pistol shot could have gone through his temple—a part of the cranium that was not preserved. The Soviet historian Bezymenski is anxious to show that Hitler lacked the courage to shoot himself "like a man." He therefore argues that Hitler took poison and had someone else pull the trigger. Mr. Bezymenski suggests that Hitler had ordered either his adjutant Günsche, or his valet, Linge, to deliver this *coup de grâce*. Thus, he writes (p. 75) was the cowardly Fascist dictator "killed like a dog." But Linge, who has recently returned from a Russian prisoner of war camp, has flatly and explicitly denied having shot his dead Führer. (Reuters Dispatch, *The New York Times*, August 4, 1968.) He gives a different version of Hitler's death, and in my judgment his story must be taken seriously for he and Hanfstaengl are two of the most reliable living witnesses on the life of Hitler. Linge says that when he entered Hitler's private room with Martin Bormann after hearing a pistol shot about 3:30 P.M. April 30, 1945, he saw the dead Hitler sitting with his hands folded in his lap at the right end of a sofa. Eva Braun was sitting on the sofa at Hitler's left. Hitler's 7.65 Walther pistol lay unfired on a small table in front of the sofa. Eva Braun's 6.35 Walther lay on the floor between the two bodies. Hitler had been shot through the left temple, his head was inclined to the right, and blood was still dripping from the right temple onto the carpet. Linge concluded that his Führer had shot himself through the left temple. (*Der Spiegel*, Nr. 22, 1965.) Bezymenski tries to ridicule and discredit Linge's testimony by misquoting him and saying that even though Hitler was shot through the head, "not a drop of blood had been drawn." (Bezymenski, *Death of Hitler*, p. 70.) On the contrary, Linge reported that though no blood came from the bullet wound in the *left* temple, "blood still dripped from the right temple . . . and had formed a little pool of blood by the front leg of the sofa." By misusing evidence, the Soviet historian succeeds only in raising doubts about his own version of what happened. Still another version of the shooting is given by a confidant of the Braun family who talked with survivors of the Bunker. According to this story, the pistol that was fired was Hitler's heavier 7.65 Walther, which lay at his feet, while Eva's 6.35 Walther was found unfired on the table. (Nerin Gun, *Eva Braun-Hitler: Leben und Schicksal* [New York, 1968], p. 205.) But this account is less credible than Linge's. Nerin Gun got his information from Frau Traudl Junge, one of Hitler's secretaries. It is true that Frau Junge is normally a reliable witness. But in this case she is relying on hearsay evidence given to her either by Günsche or Linge before they were captured by the Russians. That is to say, in talking recently to Gun she relied on her memory of an event that happened some twenty years previously and one in which she had no first-hand knowledge. For, unlike Linge, Frau Junge did not herself enter the death room; she never saw the position of the pistols or the bodies. Indeed she testifies that as soon as she heard the shot she immediately left the scene and took the Goebbels children away to eat.

My own conclusion is that Hitler did not shoot himself either through the mouth or through the temple. It was Eva Braun who administered the *coup de grâce* after Hitler had taken a lethal dose of cyanide. (The suggestion that Hitler was shot by his wife was first made by Erich Kuby in an article in *Der Spiegel* in 1965.) A number of reasons bring me to this conclusion: (1) There is no doubt that a pistol shot was fired in Hitler's private room at about 3:30 P.M. April 30, 1945. Several reliable witnesses heard the shot and smelled gunpowder. (2) But Linge's conclusion that Hitler shot himself through the left temple cannot be accepted. Hitler was not left-handed. We also know that during the last months of his life his left hand shook so badly—probably from advanced Parkinson's disease—that he had to hold it down with his right hand. (For extreme shaking of Hitler's left hand, see Gerhard Boldt, *Die Letzten Tage der Reichskanzlei* [Hamburg, 1947], p. 15, and Karl Wahl, "*. . . es ist das deutsche Herz*": *Erlebnisse eines ehemaligen Gauleiters* (Augsburg, 1954), p. 391.) The diagnosis of Parkinson's disease is given by Dr. Johann Recktenwald, *Woran hat Adolf Hitler gelitten?* (Munich, 1963), by Dr. Anton Braunmühl "War Hitler Krank?" in *Stimmen der Zeit* (May 1954), and most recently by Prof. Hans Berger-Prinz, a leading German psychiatrist. Dr. Berger-Prinz is probably correct in saying that Hitler suffered from Parkinson's disease. He is manifestly mistaken in insisting that Hitler was never sick in a psychiatric sense. (*The New York Times,* November 21, 1968.) If he suffered from acute paralysis agitans, it is highly improbable that he could have aimed a pistol at his left temple and have pulled the trigger after taking a massive dose of cyanide—a poison that acts almost instantaneously. And it would have been impossible for him to have taken the poison, shot himself, released the pistol from his grip, and folded his hands in his lap in the posture Linge found him. (3) It is, of course, possible that Linge fired the shot. But I see no reason to doubt his recent denial. Furthermore, his testimony rings true when he says that, having heard the shot that afternoon, he did not wish to enter the room alone so he asked Bormann to accompany him. (*Der Spiegel*, Number 22, 1965.) Bormann, the dangerous and forboding guardian of Hitler, was the obvious person Linge would have asked to accompany him into the death room. (4) Eva Braun was the only person Hitler would have entrusted with a task that was now so important to him. It must be emphasized that toward the end, Adolf Hitler was obsessed with the fear that he might be captured alive and exhibited by the Russians "like a circus freak." He needed to make absolutely sure that he would be killed and his body incinerated. But whom could he trust? In the whirling world of his paranoic suspicions, everyone was deserting and betraying him. Even the elite S.S. could no longer be trusted. Their leader, whom Hitler had once called "My faithful Heinrich," was now a traitor who, behind the Führer's back, was suing for a separate peace with the Western Allies. In Hitler's mind, Himmler's whole organization had become honeycombed with spies and traitors who sought to betray their Führer. Thus when Hitler's personal S.S. doctor Stumfegger attempted to reassure him that the cyanide capsule he had prepared would certainly work lethally and immediately, Hitler was suddenly suspicious and asked, "But who will administer the *coup de grâce*?" Who indeed? The obvious candidates—and the ones accused by Bezymenski—were Hitler's personal adjutant Günsche, and Linge, his valet for more than a decade. But both were members of the S.S. By now their very uniform had become anathema to Hitler and their motto, "My honor is loyalty," a mockery. Who then? The only person in the world whom Hitler could really trust was Eva Braun. She had proven her courage and determination by flying into crumbling Berlin to die with him. She was a sportswoman who knew how to handle pistols. She loved him completely. That she was absolutely loyal and obedient she had proven hundreds of times by obeying his most extreme and bizarre sexual requests. She alone could be entrusted to carry out his last order: to shoot him through the head at point-blank range. She alone was in the room with him when the shot was fired. The shot, from her pistol, went through his left temple. Her body was found sitting to the left of Hitler's. I conclude that Hitler, knowing that he would not feel strong enough or steady enough to aim a pistol after having taken cyanide, had asked his wife to perform the deed for him. She did so and then took poison herself as the Russian autopsy shows.

The question of the length of time the bodies were burned is important to the report of the Russian autopsy. Kempka insists that he fulfilled his Führer's orders and completely destroyed the bodies of Hitler and his wife by using some 400 liters of petrol and burning the bodies for more than five and one-half hours. (Kempka, *Hitler verbrannt*, pp. 116–118.) If so, the Russians could scarcely have performed so thorough an autopsy on internal organs as their report reveals. (The smell of cyanide noticed by the Russian doctors could still have been present, however, because cyanide is not volatile. It decomposes only under an extreme heat of 350° centigrade—a degree of heat that could not have been obtained under the methods used.) There are other reasons to doubt Kempka's testimony. Understandably he sought to exaggerate the length of time the bodies were burned in order to show that he had fulfilled his beloved Führer's last command. But other testimony indicates that those charged with destroying the bodies had botched the job. Two police guards named Mansfeld and Karnau insisted that the bodies burned for less than two hours (Trevor-Roper, *Last Days*, pp. 204–205) and one of Hitler's bodyguards testified to the Russian authorities that the bodies burned for only half an hour (Bezymenski, *Death of Hitler*, p. 36). Apart from the evidence of the Russian autopsy, there is another reason for believing that the bodies were not completely consumed. Linge stresses the lack of effective planning and the great confusion surrounding the whole incident. He and his helpers had collected enough petrol to do the job, but they had not thought of where they would burn the bodies. Hence, with Russian artillery shells bursting about them, they hurriedly placed the bodies in a shallow indentation in the sandy soil of the courtyard. This, of course, was a mistake, for the soil rapidly absorbed much of the petrol. The burning, Linge admits, had not destroyed the bodies, so Bormann ordered that they be buried. Again, the job was done hurriedly and ineffectively, for the men suddenly given the task did not have the proper equipment, and with Russian shells zeroing in on the garden of the Reichschancellery they also had little desire to risk their lives for their now dead Führer. Hence they barely covered the bodies with loose earth, broken stones, and rubble. (Testimony of Linge, *Der Spiegel*, Nr. 22, 1965.) This evidence seems consistent with the conditions of the time and with the Russian report that the bodies were quite easily discovered by a search party and were sufficiently intact to permit a rather thorough autopsy.

8. Hans Frank, *Im Angesicht des Galgens* (Munich, 1953), p. 403.

9. Fritz Wiedemann, *Der Mann der Feldherr werden wollte: Erlebnisse und Erfahrungen des Vorgesetzten Hitlers im I. Weltkrieg und seines spätern Persönlichen Adjutanten* (Hanover, 1964), p. 205.

10. Thomas Orr, "Das war Hitler: Das Ende eines Mythos" a series of articles running in *Der Münchener Revue*, writes flatly, "Frau Zakreys was a Polish Jew" (November 1952). I was unable to substantiate the claim in Vienna because the records of the Jewish community there were all destroyed by the Nazis.

11. Michael A. Musmanno, *Ten Days to Die* (Garden City, N. Y., 1950), p. 82. Musmanno was General Mark Clark's naval adjutant and interviewed many of the servants and survivors of the Hitler bunker.

12. His chief patrons were Retschay, Feingold, Altenberg, and a picture-framer named Morgenstern. The list of those who purchased Hitler's paintings during 1909–1913 is preserved in the former Hauptarchiv der NSDAP, folders 26 and 17A. Most of this archival collection, which is now in the Bundesarchiv in Koblenz, has now been microfilmed by the Hoover Institution.

13. Wiedemann, *Der Mann der Feldherr*, pp. 25–26. Wiedemann had been Hitler's commanding officer during World War I.

14. See, among others, Eva Reichman, *Hostages of Civilization: The Social Sources of National Socialist Anti-Semitism* (Boston, 1951); Paul W. Massing, *Rehearsal for Destruction: A Study of Political Anti-Semitism in Imperial Germany* (New York, 1949); and Peter J. Pulzer, *The Rise of Political Anti-Semitism in Germany and Austria* (New York, 1964). For

the continuity of racist thought in Germany, see George L. Mosse, *The Crisis of German Ideology* (New York, 1964).

15. See especially Paul Hilberg, *The Destruction of the European Jews* (Chicago, 1961), and Gerald Reitlinger, *The Final Solution* (London, 1953).

16. In addition to Reichman, *Hostages*, see the valuable work of a social psychologist, Zevedei Barbu, *Democracy and Dictatorship: Their Psychology and Patterns of Life* (New York, 1956).

17. Karl Dietrich Bracher, "Stufen der Machtergreifung," part 2 of *Nationalsozialistische Machtergreifung* (Cologne, 1960).

18. Gordon W. Allport, "The Use of Personal Documents in Psychological Science," *Social Science Research Council Bulletin* no. 49 (1942), 46. For an excellent discussion of this problem, see "Introduction," in Bruce Mazlish, ed., *Psychoanalysis and History* (Englewood Cliffs, N.J., 1963).

19. Quoted by H. G. Adler, *Die Juden in Deutschland von der Aufklärung bis zum Nationalsozialismus* (Munich, 1960), p. 128.

20. Adolf Hitler, *Mein Kampf* (New York, 1939), p. 73.

21. Wilfried Daim, *Der Mann, der Hitler die Ideen gab* (Munich, 1958), pp. 21–22. Daim has annoyed many students of Hitler by the inflated title of his book and his insistance on the exclusive influence of Liebenfels. He is nevertheless correct that Liebenfels was of very great importance to Hitler's intellectual development.

22. One should be cautious, however, in reaching conclusions about Hitler's intellectual interests by relying too heavily on an examination of the contents of his library. Most of the books were not chosen by Hitler himself, but were given to him as gifts. On the other hand, the fact that he accepted and kept in his library so many books on racism and the occult would seem to indicate that he was interested in their themes. It should also be noted that the present collection of some 1,500 volumes is only a small part of the original library. Of those books extant, as Arnold Jacobius has pointed out, books on racism and anti-Semitism comprise "the most conspicuous characteristic of the collection." (See his article in *Information Bulletin, The Library of Congress*, April 27, 1953, and an unpublished manuscript, "The Books Hitler Owned." For an excellent general account of the contents of the library see Reginald H. Phelps, "Die Hitler-Blbliothek," *Deutsche Rundschau* 80 (1954): 923–931.)

23. Hermann Rauschning, *The Voice of Destruction* (New York, 1940), p. 229. Italics are mine.

24. Guido von List, *Die Rita der Ario-Germanen* (1908) (Vienna, 1920), pp. 117–182.

25. I disagree with George Mosse when he writes in his excellent book on the growth of racist ideas in Germany that Dietrich Eckart "played the key role in crystalizing Hitler's political attitudes." Mosse, *Crisis of German Ideology*, p. 296.

26. Hitler, *Mein Kampf*, p. 162.

27. The characteristics of the anti-Semitic personality given here are drawn from the following studies: the indispensible work of Nathan W. Ackerman and Marie Jahoda, *Anti-Semitism and Emotional Disorder: A Psychoanalytic Interpretation* (New York, 1950); the great cooperative work

edited by T. W. Adorno, Else Frankel-Brunswik, et al., *The Authoritarian Personality* (New York, 1950); Martin Wangh, "National Socialism and the Genocide of Jews: A Psychoanalytic Study of a Historical Event," *International Journal of Psycho-Analysis* 45 (1964): 386–395; and Ernst Simmel, ed., *Anti-Semitism a Social Disease* (New York, 1946), especially the following essays: Ernst Simmel, "Anti-Semitsm and Mass Psychopathology," Else Frankel-Brunswik, "The Anti-Semitic Personality: A Research Report," and Otto Fenichel, "Elements of a Psychoanalytic Theory of Anti-Semitism."

28. Erik H. Erikson, *Identity, Youth and Crisis* (New York, 1968).

29. The memoirs of Heinz Linge, "Kronzeuge Linge," a series of articles in the *Revue* (Munich, 1955–1956), Nr. 9 (March 3, 1956).

30. Speech in Munich of March 14, 1936, quoted in Domarus, ed., *Reden*, I:18. He told an admirer, "Like Christ, I have a duty to my people . . ." (Georg Schott, *Das Volksbuch von Hitler* [Munich, 1941], p. 74.) He announced his infallibility in political matters to Nazi editors and journalists in a meeting in Munich in June 1930, saying, "I hope that the world will grow as accustomed to that claim as it has to the claim of the Holy Father." (Albert Krebs, *Tendenzen und Gestalten der NSDAP Erinnerunger an die Frühzeit der Partei* [Stuttgart, 1959], p. 123.)

31. Jetzinger has made a great and not unsuccessful effort to show that Alois Hitler was a better man than Hitler painted him (Franz Jetzinger, *Hitler's Youth*, trans. by Laurence Wilson [London, 1958] pp. 43–53). But the important point here is not what kind of person Alois was "in fact"; it is rather what Adolf believed him to be. Clearly Adolf thought him a drunken brute. See the description of his father which he gave to his lawyer (Frank, *Im Angesicht*, p. 321). In public, however, he always spoke well of his father.

32. *Mein Kampf*, 42–43. I am indebted to Dr. Gertrud Kurth for calling this passage to my attention and suggesting the interpretation given here.

33. August Kubizek, *The Young Hitler I knew* (Boston, 1955), p. 188.

34. Good descriptions of Hitler's personal habits and tastes may be found in the memoirs of his private secretary (Albert Zoller, ed., *Hitler Privat: Erlebnisbericht seiner Geheimsekretärin* [Düsseldorf, 1949]), in the memoirs of his valet, Linge ("Kronzeuge Linge"), and Karl Wilhelm Krause, *Zehn Jahre Kammerdiener bei Hitler* (Hamburg, n.d.).

35. Personal interview with Ernst Hanfstaengl, Munich, June 1967.

36. Kubizek, *The Young Hitler*, p. 54, and Jetzinger, pp. 153–154; 177–178.

37. Hitler was born in 1889. Geli Raubal was born in 1908; Eva Braun, in 1912; Maria "Mimi" Reiter, who had a strange and intimate relation with him sporadically from 1926 to 1931, was born in 1909; Unity Mitford was born in 1914.

38. He told his secretaries, "I like Eva [Braun] very much but I really loved only Geli. I'll never marry Eva. The only woman I could ever have married was Geli." Zoller, ed. *Hitler Privat*, p. 92.

39. Mimi Reiter almost succeeded in hanging herself in 1926; Geli Raubal's suicide took place in 1931; Eva Braun's self-inflicted wound of 1932 came within a quarter of an inch of her heart; Renée Mueller shot herself through the head in the late 1930's; Unity Mitford tried unsuccess-

fully on September 3, 1939 to kill herself in the same way. Miss Mitford's attempted suicide seems clearly to have been a consequence of the despair she felt at having failed in her life mission of bringing England and Nazi Germany together as allies.

40. Hitler employed every one of the major defenses that Anna Freud catalogues in her classic work, *The Ego and the Mechanisms of Defence*, Cecil Baines, trans. (New York, 1964). He used denial to get rid of unwelcome facts by declaring that they did not exist: he denied that Russian tank production was as great as statistics showed. He "restricted the ego" by carefully choosing "outside stimuli": he chose, for example, a chauffeur who was shorter than he was, he chose associates he could dominate; when he could not succeed as an artist, he chose to become a politician; when he failed in that, he told Speer that he had always wanted to be an artist. He used "denial by fantasy": as a youth he lived in a dream world; at the end he conducted imaginary armies and plotted their progress on a road map as it disintegrated in his sweaty hands. He "identified with the aggressor": he feared the Jews and therefore adopted what he thought were their own methods: the use of cunning, deceit, cruelty. Hence the importance to him of the bogus "Protocols of the Elders of Zion" which proved to him that his fantasies of a "Jewish peril" were justified. He "reverted" to childhood by remaining infantile in his tastes, his political beliefs, and in his temper tantrums. On the ego and its defenses, in addition to Miss Freud, see also Heinz Hartmann, "Comments on the Psychoanalytic Theory of the Ego," *Psychoanalytic Study of the Child*, X (1950), 74–96, and Norbert Bromberg, "Totalitarian Ideology as a Defense Technique," *Psychoanalytic Study of Society*, I (1960), 26–38.

41. Gordon W. Allport, *The Nature of Prejudice* (Boston, 1954), p. 389.

42. These passages from Hitler's speeches and writings were collected by the psychiatrists and psychologists who drew up a valuable report on Hitler's personality for the Office of Strategic Services during the war. This study also stresses the burden of guilt and self-hatred Hitler felt and the need for projecting it onto the Jews. The report was written by Dr. Walter C. Langer with the collaboration of Prof. Henry A. Murray and Drs. Ernst Kris and Bertram D. Lewin, "A Psychological Analysis of Adolph [sic] Hitler" (typescript, declassified historical O.S.S. records, National Archives, Washington, D.C., n.d.) Italics are mine.

43. Gertrud Kurth, "The Jew and Adolf Hitler," *Psychoanalytic Quarterly* XVI (1947), 11–32.

44. Hitler, *Mein Kampf*, p. 78.

45. Letter to Jetzinger, May 6, 1949, Oberösterreichisches Landesarchiv, Linz, Austria, Hitler Atken, Folder 64.

46. Hitler, *Mein Kampf*, pp. 448–449.

47. *Ibid.*, p. 906.

48. Kubizek, Oberösterreichisches Landesarchiv, Folder 63.

49. Bernhard Lösener, "Das Reichsministerium des Innern und die Judengesetzgebung," *Vierteljahrshefte für Zeitgeschichte* IX (1961), 273. Lösener had been the legal expert for "racial law" in the ministry of interior.

50. The full text is given in the *Völkischer Beobachter*, September 16, 1935.

51. Quoted in *Der Spiegel* Number 31, p. 47.

52. Hitler, *Mein Kampf*, p. 160. Italics are mine.

53. A photostatic copy of the dispensation is in Hauptarchiv, folder 17A. As far as the church records were concerned, Klara was the second cousin of Alois. She always called him "uncle," however.

54. Gustav died at the age of two, Ida died at the age of two, Otto lived three days, Edmund died at the age of six. Dr. Bloch testified to members of the O.S.S. that Adolf Hitler had an older sister who was always kept hidden when he came to visit and that the younger sister Paula was "a little on the stupid side, perhaps a high-grade moron." (Langer et al., "Psychological Analysis.") Aunt Johanna's mental condition is described by Dr. Edward Kriechbaum, an old family doctor, in a report dated 1952, now in the provincial archives in Linz (Oberösterreichisches Landesarchiv, Folder 143.

55. Quoted in Domarus, ed., *Reden*, 1:745.

56. Dr. Bloch, *Collier's*, March 15, 1941, p. 36.

57. There is a dispute between Kubizek and Jetzinger over whether Hitler returned to Linz to nurse his mother. Kubizek's picture of the solicitous and devoted son (*The Young Hitler*, pp. 122–124) is denied by Jetzinger (p. 103) who bases his case on the second-hand information of a postmaster's widow who lived in the same building on the Blütengasse and purportedly said that Hitler returned only for his mother's funeral. But in 1938 this same widow told a reporter for a racist newspaper that Adolf had indeed returned from Vienna and had nursed his mother with the solicitude reported by Kubizek. (See Hauptarchiv, Folder 17A.) Inasmuch as her testimony was given to a newspaper that was anxious to put Hitler in a favorable light it is of course suspect. On balance, I am pursuaded to support Kubizek's version of the loving and solicitous son largely because it is completely consistent with Hitler's remarkable devotion to his mother and because his story is endorsed by Dr. Bloch who, as a Jew writing in exile in America, had no apparent reason for inventing the degree of devotion Hitler showed for his mother. In his otherwise careful and impressive study of Hitler's youth, Bradford Smith writes that "an unnamed postmaster's widow . . . does not mention Adolf as present at his mother's death. Inasmuch as the article was tailored for a Nazi audience, this ommission strengthens Jetzinger's conclusion that Adolf did not arrive in time" (*Adolf Hitler: His Family, Childhood and Youth* (Stanford, Calif., 1967), p. 110). On the contrary, this postmaster's widow, whose name was Frau Presenmayer, makes a point of stressing that when Hitler learned of the serious illness of Klara "he interrupted his studies and hurried to the sickbed of his mother" (Adolf Hitler in Urfahr," Hauptarchiv, Folder 17A).

58. Krause, *Zehn Jahre Kammerdiener*, p. 52. His testimony is supported by Hanfstaengl, personal interview, June 1967, and Musmanno, *Ten Days to Die*.

59. Kurth, "The Jew and Hitler," pp. 21–22. Adolf felt very close to Angela. He may have voluntarily surrendered his orphan's pension to her—though Jetzinger disputes the point. Certainly he later set her up as his housekeeper and hostess both at the Obersalzberg and in his apartment on the Prinzregentenstrasse in Munich.

60. Testimony of Ernst Hanfstaengl to O.S.S. officials, (typescript, de-

classified historical O.S.S. records, National Archives, Washington, D.C., n.d.), 3: 915. (Hereafter cited as Hitler Source book.)

61. Rauschning, p. 237.

62. Hans Bernd Gisevius, *Adolf Hitler: Versuch einer Deutung* (Munich, 1963), pp. 383–384. (Italics are mine.) Gisevius saw the photographs.

63. Evidence regarding Hitler's sexual habits is conflicting and I have made the above statement only after great hesitation. Reliable witnesses who knew him well over a long period of time are emphatic that to their knowledge Hitler was sexually normal. These people include his boyhood intimate, Kubizek, his valets, Krause and Linge, both of whom served him for ten years, and his private secretaries. It may be presumed, however, that none of them ever had an opportunity to observe him indulging in aberrrant sexual activity. Their testimony to the contrary, I have concluded that Hitler had the perversion mentioned here. The five distinguished American psychiatrists and clinical psychologists who collaborated on the O.S.S. report on Hitler and described his perversion were all convinced that the evidence for it was completely reliable. (Langer *et al.*, "Psychological Analysis," p. 138.) Their chief source was Otto Strasser, with Ernst (Putzi") Hanfstaengl and several "other informants" giving supporting testimony. (See Testimony in Hitler Source Book 3: 902–915, 917–919, 921–923.) Historians may well raise questions about accepting the testimony of such people as Strasser and Hanfstaengl; yet in a case like this, it is precisely because of their character that they could become privy to such information. Moreover, Hanfstaengl holds a doctorate in history and prides himself on historical accuracy. In many hours of conversation with him, I found him to be remarkably accurate in his statements and generally a reliable witness. His testimony given to me in June and July 1967 was completely consistent with the testimony he gave O.S.S. officers in 1943. I am also persuaded by other evidence that is consistent with a perversion encompassing masochism and a fetish about feces and urine. Let us consider seven points. (1) Hitler enjoyed talking about sexual abnormalities. In a private letter, Kubizek reports that his friend chattered "by the hour" about "depraved [sexual] customs." (Kubizek to Jetzinger, May 6, 1949 Oberösterreichisches Landesarchiv, Folder 64.) (2) Hanfstaengl told me that he always suspected Hitler of sexual perversion and that one of Hitler's maids informed him that "very strange and unspeakable things" went on in the relations between Hitler and his niece. Hanfstaengl suspected that Hitler whipped Geli—which would be completely consistent with sadomasochism. (3) Both in public speech and private conversation, Hitler showed a pathological concern with filth, dirt, feces, and urine, saying, for example, that lipstick was manufactured from "Parisian urine." (Zoller, ed., *Hitler Privat*, p. 231.) Hitler used the defense of "reaction formation" against this preoccupation and insisted on punctilious personal cleanlinesss: he often changed his underwear and bathed twice a day; he felt uneasy if he could not wash his hands after greeting a stranger; he was terribly concerned about flatulation and took Dr. Gösterschen's antigas pills daily for this condition. He became a vegetarian in part because he thought that the eating of meat increased his body odors. The water in which his vegetables were boiled had to be specially cleaned by distillation. (4) The perversion is consistent with

his general conduct with women, which was marked by elements of sadomasochism. He was much given to bowing and clicking heels in a social situation and "almost knelt in his zeal to please, beaming in his servile attitude." (Bella From, *Blood and Banquets* [New York, 1942], p. 97.) On one occasion while visiting his photographer, Hoffman, he asked Hoffman's fifteen-year-old daughter for a goodnight kiss. When the girl demurred, Hitler beat his hand viciously with the dog whip he habitually carried. His whip—a traditional symbol of sadomasochism—figures largely in other scenes involving women. In 1926, apparently in order to impress Maria ("Minni") Reiter, a sixteen-year-old girl with whom he had intimate relations, Hitler whipped his dog so savagely that Fräulein Reiter was overwhelmed by his brutality. (See her memoirs, edited by Günter Peis, "Die unbekannte Geliebte," *Stern* Nr. 24 (1959, p. 30.) And there was a curious episode that took place in June 1923 in Berchtesgaden where he was staying in the Pension Moritz. Frau Büchner, the wife of the proprietor, was a striking six-foot, buxom, blonde, Brünhilde who towered over Hitler and inflamed him sexually. He tried desperately to attract her attention by striding up and down in front of her as he swung his whip and beat himself against his thigh. The more she ignored him, the wilder he became. Almost beside himself, he spoke loudly about an experience he had had in Berlin which showed the decadence and moral depravity of the Jews. As he lashed about with his whip he screamed, "I nearly imagined myself to be Jesus Christ when he came to his Father's Temple and found it taken over by the money-changers. I can well imagine how He felt when He seized a whip and scourged them out." This story was told by Dietrich Eckhart, a close friend and admirer of Hitler. (See the manuscript "Adolf Hitler," a special report compiled, presumably, by the O.S.S., marked "personal-confidential" and given to President Roosevelt. Franklin Delano Roosevelt Library, Hyde Park, New York, typescript, 1942, pp. 35–36). The German movie actress, Renée Mueller reported that when she was invited to spend the night with Hitler in the chancellory he first described in detail and at great length medieval and Gestapo techniques of torture. Then, after they were undressed, Hitler "lay on the floor . . . condemned himself as unworthy, heaped all kinds of accusations on his own head and just grovelled around in an agonizing manner. The scene became intolerable to her and she finally acceded to his wishes to kick him. This excited him greatly and he begged for more and more . . . As she continued to kick him, he became more and more excited." Shortly after this experience, she committed suicide. (See the testimony of A. Zeissler, the cinema director, O.S.S. Hitler Source Book, II, 222.) (5) I have made the statement because Hitler's personality fits what we know about the psychopathology of sexual perverts. In the chapter on perversion in his standard work on psychoanalysis, Otto Fenichel notes that such patients tend to be infantile, that they have acute Oedipus complexes and pronounced castration anxiety. Indeed he concludes that "*castration anxiety* (and guilt feelings, which are derivatives of castration anxiety) must be the decisive factor." *Psychoanalytic Theory of Neurosis* [New York, 1945], p. 326. Italics are in the original.) Castration anxiety manifests itself in many ways, but most notably patients dwell on the theme of heads and decapitation and may show a fascination with the Medusa legend. (See especially Sigmund Freud,

"Medusa's Head," *International Journal of Psycho-Analysis* 12 [1941].) Hitler was fascinated with heads, and decapitation. He promised that when he came to power, "heads will roll in the sand." When he flipped a coin to determine whether he would go on a picnic, heads did not win. Heads invariably lost. His elite S.S. wore the death's head as their insignia. When asked what he would do on first landing in England he replied without hesitation that he wanted most to see the place where Henry VIII chopped off the heads of his wives. Both as a boy and man his favorite doodling was to draw human heads (Testimony of a boyhood acquaintance, Wilhelm Hagmüller who had been a boarder in the Hitler household on Humboldstrasse, Linz (Oberösterreichisches Landarchiv, Folder 56). Baldur von Schirach recalls that after meals the Führer would sit "drawing on one of the little cards he always had with him—mostly heads of men and women." ("Ich glaubte an Hitler," serialized memoirs in *Stern* Nr. 30 [July 23, 1967].) Several drawings of the heads have been preserved in the Library of Congress, manuscript division.) When Hitler designed a sort of promissory note for the Party during the mid-1920's, he showed an idealized German warrior holding in his right hand a sword dripping blood, while in his left, he held the severed head of a woman suspended by her blonde hair. Under the picture in heavy gothic type is printed, "Warrior of the Truth, Behead the Lie." It is to be noted that the warrior is enjoined not to fight, not to pierce, but to decapitate the young lady. (A photostat of the promissory note may be found in the Library of Congress, Prints and Photographs Division, Folder 568.) Hitler was infatuated with the Medusa. He once expressed great enthusiasm for the mosaic Medusa head in the rotunda of the University of Munich; one of his favorite paintings was by Franz von Stuck, a sinister, flashing-eyed Medusa. When Hitler first saw the painting in a book in Hanfstaengl's home he exclaimed, "Those eyes are the eyes of my mother!" (Hanfstaengl interview.) When he designed his gigantic desk for the new chancellory in Berlin, three heads adorned the great front panels. One of them was the head of Medusa complete with the writhing snakes emerging from her hair. (A picture of the desk may be seen in *Die Kunst im Dritten Reich* [1939], III, 413.) On at least two occasions when talking to foreign dignitaries he made a special point of insisting that the so-called Polish atrocities included the *castration* of Germans. (See the memoirs of the Swiss historian who served as the League of Nations' high commissioner for Danzig, Carl J. Burckhardt, *Meine Danziger Mission, 1937–1939* [Munich, 1960], p. 345), and of the French ambassador to Germany, Robert Coulondre, *Von Moskau nach Berlin, Errinnerungen des französischen Botschafters* [Bonn, 1950], p. 422.) Fears of castration and anxieties about masculinity were certainly not diminished by the knowledge that he lacked one testicle. The official autopsy reads, "In the scrotum, which is singed but preserved, only the right testicle was found. The left testicle could not be found in the inguinal canal." (Full report of autopsy is given in Bezymenski, *Death of Hitler*. (If, as Fenichel says, castration anxiety is the mark of perversion, Hitler had the symptoms. Perverts also often show a background of an overly meticulous mother who was stringent about toilet training. Klara Hitler had a reputation in Leonding and Linz, her former neighbors tell us, of having had "the cleanest house in town" and keeping her children "absolutely spotless." In one case of perversion the patient showed identification with his mother and in his sexual relations displayed a desire "to have his sweetheart urinate in his presence while he encouraged her in a friendly way. He was playing the role of his mother who used to put him on the chamber pot when he was a baby." (Fenichel, *Psychoanalytic Theory*, p. 332.) (6) I believe that Hitler had a perversion of the dimensions here described because such a perversion helps to explain the degree of self-loathing and the intensity of its projection onto the Jews. (7) I have accepted this interpretation because of the professional reputation enjoyed by the men who have endorsed it. Drs. Walter C. Langer, Henry A. Murray, Ernst Kris, Bertram Lewin, and De Saussure are among the most respected American psychiatrists and clinical psychologists.

64. Hitler, *Mein Kampf*, p. 14.

65. The actual operation was performed by a Doctor Urban in The Sisters of Mercy Hospital in Linz, but Dr. Bloch, at Frau Hitler's request, was present and stood at the operating table.

66. Hauptarchiv, Folder 17. (Italics are mine.) Werner Maser argues that Hitler was already an anti-Semite while living in Linz. (*Die Frühgeschichte der NDSAP, Hitlers Weg bis 1924* [Frankfurt-am-Main, 1965], pp. 96–99.) But he relies heavily on the testimony of the editor of an anti-Semitic newspaper who told party officials in 1938 that the Führer had read his paper as a boy in Linz. It is completely understandable that the editor would seek to ingratiate himself with Nazi officials by showing his contribution to Hitler's development. The only anti-Semitic journals Hitler himself mentions are those he read in Vienna. Mosse dates the real genesis of Hitler's racist thinking from the Munich period just after the war (*Crisis of German Ideology*, pp. 295–297). My position is that Eckhart and others of the Thulegesellschaft did indeed influence Hitler but their function was not to initiate racist ideas, rather it was to reinforce those ideas he had already picked up in Vienna. Hitler himself in a revealing passage in *Mein Kampf* gives further support for this position. He says that when he was handed a racist pamphlet in Munich in 1919 he was immediately reminded of a similar event that took place years before in Vienna. "Involuntarily I saw thus my own development come to life again before my eyes" (p. 296). It is true that August Kubizek remembers his boyhood friend as expressing anti-Semitic sentiments as early as 1904 (*Young Hitler*, p. 79). But, as we have seen, Hitler did not work out his political program of anti-Semitism until his Vienna period. Kubizek himself in an unpublished memoir gives the precise date of Hitler's real interest in anti-Semitism: "One day in 1908," he writes, Hitler came home to their room and announced, "Hey! Today I became a member of the Anti-Semitic Bund and I enrolled you too." (August Kubizek, "Erinnerungen an die mit dem Führer gemeinsam verlebte Jünglingsjahre 1904–1908 in Linz and Wien," Oberösterreichisches Landesarchiv, Folder 63.)

67. Hitler, *Mein Kampf*, pp. 83–84.

68. The analysis given here draws heavily on Kurth's brilliant "The Jew and Hitler." I am also indebted to Norman Reider, whom I have consulted on this interpretation. Though still endorsing this view, Kurth now feels that Hitler was far sicker than her earlier thinking indicated. She now considers him to have been a paranoid schizophrenic. Personal interview, January 21, 1968.)

69. The Gestapo seized the cards from Dr. Bloch in 1938. A record of them may be found in Hauptarchiv, "*Gestapoberichte*", Folder 17A.

70. Kurth, "The Jew and Hitler," p. 30. Kurth had interviewed Dr. Bloch.

71. Hitler once told Hanfstaengl, for example, that he could not marry because, "My bride is my Motherland." (Hitler Sourcebook, II, 903.)

72. Schramm, "Introduction to Picker's *Tischgespräche*", pp. 35–37.

73. Personal interview with Hanfstaengl, Munich, June 1967.

74. "Hitler über die Justiz: Das Tischgespräch vom 20 August 1942," *Viertelsjahrshefte für Zeitgeschichte* XII (1964), 94.

75. Svend Ranulf, *Hitler's Kampf gegen die Objectivität* (Copenhagen, 1964), p. 32.

76. F. W. Deakin, *The Brutal Friendship* (London, 1962).

77. Hitler, *Mein Kampf*, p. 282.

78. Speech of November 8, 1940, Munich. Quoted in Domarus, ed., *Reden*, III, 1603.

79. "Wissenshaft gegen Willkür: Bonhoeffer und Planck im Dritten Reich" (typescript of radio script for program R.I.A.S., Berlin, November 24, 1966).

80. Frontispiece to a collection of speeches, *Adolf Hitler an seine Jugend* (Munich, 1938).

81. Langer et al., "Psychological Analysis of Hitler." There is no date given, but internal evidence suggests it was written during 1942 or early 1943.

82. *The Psychology of Dictatorship, Based on an Examination of the Leaders of Nazi Germany* (New York, 1950).

83. See, for example, Jetzinger *Hitler's Youth*, who argues that the grandfather might have been Jewish; Gisevius, *Adolf Hitler: Versuch einer Deutung*, who says that the question of the Jewish grandfather is immaterial because Hitler would not have cared, and a forthcoming biography by Werner Maser who will insist that Hitler's grandfather was not a Jew. Germany's leading news magazine, *Der Spiegel* has devoted at least two long and detailed articles (June 1, 1957 and July 24, 1967) to the problem of ascertaining whether or not there was a Jewish grandfather. In his recent book on Hitler's early years, Bradley Smith feels it important to provide an appendix in which he argues that Hitler's grandfather was not a Jew.

84. I am indebted to my colleague, Benjamin W. Labaree, for this information.

85. Letter of Father Franz Ledl who examined the birth certificate and baptismal record of Hitler's father. (Oberösterreichisches Landesarchiv, Folder 3.)

86. Frank, *Im Angesicht*, pp. 320–321. The research of Nikolaus Preradovic of the University of Graz does not support Frank's conclusions. In the books of the Jewish *Kultusgemeinde* in Graz there is a record neither of the name Frankenberger nor of Frankenreiter, the name mentioned by Hitler's nephew. True, the books of the Jewish congregation only go back as far as 1856 and Alois Hitler was born in 1837, but during all that time there was in Graz "not one single Jew" because the Jews had been drummed out of the Steiermark in 1496 and were allowed to return only after 1856. Preradovic did find the name Leopold Frankenreither listed as living in Graz in

1837. But he was the son of a Catholic cobbler and his son—the probable grandfather of Hitler (according to Jetzinger)—was ten years old in the year 1837, when the forty-one-year-old servant gave birth to a child. As Preradovic points out, "A remarkably precocious boy!" (quoted in *Der Spiegel* 11 no. 24 (June 12, 1957). Simon Wiesenthal, who knows as much about investigating family backgrounds as anyone, writes that he has searched through all the archives of Graz and could not find any trace of a Jew named Frankenberger having lived there. (Letter to the editor, *Der Spiegel* 21 no. 23 (August 7, 1967).

87. Zoller, ed., *Hitler Privat*, p. 232.

88. *Hitlers Zweites Buch* (Stuttgart, 1961), p. 104. (Italics are mine.) As the editor, Gerhard L. Weinberg, points out, the rumor about Erzberger had no basis in fact. The interesting point, however, is that Hitler repeated the story in writing.

89. *Secret Conversations*, p. 269.

90. Knittersched's statement may be found in Oberösterreichisches Landesarchiv, Folder 161.

91. The village still lies in ruins. I was unable to visit it in the summer of 1967 because it remains off limits to civilians.

92. Hauptarchiv, "Gestapoberichte," Folder 17A. Actually it is not clear who was responsible for the file marked "Gestapo Reports" but it seems highly unlikely that Himmler and the Gestapo would have dared to investigate so sensitive a subject as Hitler's own ancestry without his explicit approval. One important group of documents on Hitler's early life and family background in the file was collected in 1938 by Dr. Bleibtreu, who was simply a party archivist, but these documents and others collected in 1938 by the Linz branch of the Gestapo were taken over by Himmler who gave orders on August 4, 1942 "to give the documents personally and directly to Reichsführer SS Himmler." Evidence of other Gestapo inquiries into Hitler's family background may be found in Oberösterreichisches Landesarchiv, Hitler Akten, Folder 3, which shows that the Gestapo made an investigation in 1941 and in the archives of the Institut für Zeitgeschichte, Munich, which gives the negative results of a Gestapo Investigation of Hitler's family conducted as late as December 1943–January 1944 (Hitler Dokumente, pp. 1141–1153). Another investigation is dated March 3, 1935 (Hauptarchiv, Folder 17A).

INDEX

absurdity, sense of, 42–44
"action painting," 40
Adler, Alfred, 125
Adventures of Augie March, The (Bellow), 38
Afro-Asian states, and Suez campaign (1956), 11, 12
aggression, pathological, 109
Akhenaton, 7, 26, 82
Akiba, Rabbi, 107
Albania, 143
Albright, William Foxwell, 7; quoted, 7
Alexander the Great, 101, 158
Algerian rebels (1950's), 10
Alkalai of Semlin, 151
Allport, Gordon, 203
Altneuland (Herzl), 158, 174
Alvarado, Fernando de, 19
Amba, Achmed, 141–142
Ambivalent feelings, of protean man, 46–49
Anatomy of Criticism (Frye), 55
Ancient Mariner (Coleridge), 55
anti-Semitism, 94, 155, 160, 166, 167, 170, 202; clinical syndromes of, 199, 200–201, 202; Hitler's, 192–216 *passim*; identity crisis in, 199; projection in, 202, 203–204, 206, 207, 209, 211, 228; and sadomasochism, 201; *see also* Herzl, Theodor; Hitler, Adolf; Israel; Jews; Nazism; Zionism
"Antithetical Sense of Primal Words, The" (Freud), 56
Antonescu, Ion, 195
anxiety: as force in history, 21, 22; in protean man, 46
Aquinas, St. Thomas, 100
Archetypal Patterns in Poetry (Bodkin), 55
archetypes, Jung's, 54–56, 63
Arendt, Hannah, 94
Ares, 96, 98, 101
Aron, R., 101
art: Baudouin on, 57, 58, 59; Freud on, 51–54, 55, 58; Jung on, 55, 56; kinetic, 40; new psychological approach to, 70; pop, 43; Sartre on, 67, 68; work of, 55, 56–57, 63, 67–75 *passim*
asceticism, 158
Athens, ancient, 105
Augustine, St., 100
Austria, 9, 18, 93, 131, 160, 181, 214, 215
Austrian Revolution (1918), 22–24
autonomy vs. nurturance (Lifton), 45–46
Autopsie du Stalinisme (Rossi), 147

Babylon, destruction of, 91
Bachelard, Gaston, 63–66, 76; on language, 66
Balfour Declaration (1917), 30, 179
Balzac, Honoré de, 51
Basseches, N., 146
Batory, Stefan, 92
Baudelaire, Charles, 51, 54
Baudouin, Charles, 57–59
Beard, C. A., 101
Beethoven, Ludwig van, 134
behavior, history as study of, 87–89
Bein, Alex, 186
Bell, Daniel, 42
belligerence, human, 89–91, 99
Bellow, Saul, 38
Benedict, Ruth Fulton, 33
Berger-Prinz, Hans, 218
Bergson, Henri, 51
Berkeley free speech movement, 44

Bezymenski, Lev, 217, 218, 219, 220, 227
Bismarck, Otto, 163
black humor, 44
Black Power, 10, 44
Bloch, Edmund, 208, 209, 228
Blomberg, General, 206
Bodkin, Maud, 55
Bolshevism, 115, 116, 120, 124, 131, 137; *see also* Marxism; Russian Revolution; Soviet Union; Stalin, Joseph V.
Bonaparte, Marie, 54, 60
Bormann, Martin, 195, 217, 219, 220
brainwashing, 34, 139
Braun, Eva, 202, 217, 218, 219
Brecht, Bertolt, 17
Brothers Karamazov, The (Dostoyevsky), 140
Bruno, Giordano, 107
Buber, Martin, 186
Bukharin, Nikolai, 134
Bullock, Alan, 192; quoted, 192–193
Burckhardt, Carl J., 227
Burckhardt, Jacob, 12
Butterfield, H., 101
Bychowski, Gustav, 115–147

Caesar, Julius, 8–9, 93
Cage, John, 41
Calvin, John, 95, 100
Camus, Albert, 43
Canaan, 24, 27, 82
carbon-dating, 5, 6
Carthage, 90
Cassirer, Ernst, 33
castration anxiety, 226, 227; as force in history, 24
Catholic Church, 92
Central Zionist Archives, 186, 187
Champollion, Jean François, 82
charisma: depth dynamics of, 159; study in, 150–186 *passim*
China, 94, 139
"chosen people," Hebrew idea of, 27
Christ, 107
Christians: martyrdom of, 107; religious wars of, 92
Civil War, American, 92
class struggle, Marxian theory of, 105, 116
Cohen, M. R., quoted, 85, 88–89, 100
Cold War, 142
Coleridge, Samuel Taylor, 55
collective ego ideal, in Soviet Union, 138
collective unconscious, 55
Commonwealth of Nations, British, 21, 22
communism, 140; *see also* Bolshevism; Marxism; socialism; Soviet Union
Communist Manifesto, 117
condensation, and work of art, 58, 59
consciousness, expanded, 48
cooperation, origins of, 101–104
Cortez, Hernando, 19
Coulondre, Robert, 227
Cowen, Joseph, quoted, 165–166
Croce, Benedetto, 80, 87, 88
cross-cultural studies, 33–37
Crusades, 93
Cuba, and John F. Kennedy, 9, 15
Cyrus, King, 25
Czechoslovakia, 93, 94

death, fear of, 98–100
death instinct (Thanatos), 95–98
debunkers, in history, 11, 12
Defense of Terrorism (Trotsky), 116
de Gaulle, Charles, 13
Delle Grazie, Maria E., 159; quoted, 159
democracy: lack of basis for, 28, 29; Lenin's concept of, 116; success of, in United States, 27–28, 29
destrudo, 97, 109
Deuerlein, Ernst, 194
dialectical materialism, 100, 109
Diaries (Herzl), 150, 154–158 *passim*, 162, 170, 171, 186
Dictators and Their Disciples (Bychowski), 115*n*.
dictatorship of proletariat, 116, 117, 118, 121, 122, 137

Dilthey, W., 86
dislocation, historical (Lifton), 36
displacement, and work of art, 58
"Dizzy with Success" (Stalin), 145
Djilas, Milovan, 142, 143, 145; quoted, 143
Donleavy, J. P., 40
Dorn, Robert M., 190
Dostoyevsky, Feodor, 51, 139–141
dreams, 56, 57, 58, 64
Dreyfus case, 151, 162
Dühring, Eugen Karl, 178

Eckhart, Dietrich, 195, 198, 226, 228
ego: and external authority, 17; and mutuality in human interaction, 107
ego ideal, collective, in Soviet Union, 138
Egypt, ancient, 7, 25, 26, 27, 82
Eichmann, Adolf, 94
Einstein, Albert, 96, 194
Eisenhower, Dwight D., 12
Eissler, K. R., 30
Elias, Norbert, 6
Eliot, T. S., 55
Elizabeth II, 20
emotional-symbolic substrate (Lifton), 49
Engels, Friedrich, 120; quoted, 119, 120
England, *see* Great Britain
Erikson, Erik, 33, 37, 199
Eros, 95, 96, 98, 101
Erzberger, Matthias, 214, 230
European Romantic Movement, 50, 51
existential psychoanalysis (Sartre), 66, 68
expanded consciousness, 48
experiential transcendence (Lifton), 48

families, types of, 103
fantasy, 180–181; defined, 180; initial trigger for, 180
Feder, Gottfried, 210
federalism, 29; in United States, 27, 29
Federn, Paul, 18, 23
Fenichel, Otto, 226, 227, 228
Filthy Speech Movement, 44
Fourier, Charles, 99
France: attempts of, to restore prestige, 13; colons in, 47; and Suez campaign (1956), 11, 12
Franchet d'Esperey, Louis, 23
Francis Joseph, Emperor, 9
Frank, Hans, 213, 229
French Revolution, 10, 115; Reign of Terror in, 91, 128
Freud, Anna, quoted, 109, 171
Freud, Sigmund, 13, 16, 17, 20, 38, 56, 61, 63, 67, 81, 82, 83, 89, 106, 123, 183, 194; on art, 51–54, 55, 58; on death instinct, 95–96, 97–98; on Dostoyevsky, 140, 141; and Einstein, 96; on Eros, 95; on Moses, 13, 25, 26; quoted, 29, 52, 95, 96, 104, 119, 140, 141, 163; and Sartre, 66; on Wilson, 29
Frye, Northrop, 55

Gambetta, Léon, 163
gambling, psychoanalytical meaning of, 156, 157
Germany, 20, 21, 28, 29, 92–95 *passim*, 195, 201, 212; Hitler's dictatorship in, 28; Nuremberg racial laws promulgated in (1935), 197, 204, 214; Romanticism in, 51; *see also* Hitler, Adolf; Nazism
Gilbert, G. M., 212
Ginger Man, The (Donleavy), 40
Goering, Hermann, 17
Goethe, Johann Wolfgang von, 13
Goldberg, Alfred, 190
Gorky, Maxim, 144; quoted, 117
Grass, Günter, 40
Great Britain: monarchy in, revival of popularity of, 20–22; and Suez campaign (1956), 11, 12
Greek Orthodox Church, 92, 125
Gregory, Dick, 44
Grimsley, Ronald, 50–76
group psychology, applied to history, 16–19
Grozny, Ivan, 130
guilt, 123, 124, 184; and projections

guilt (*Cont'd*)
in anti-Semitism, 203; in protean man, 39, 40, 46
Gun, Nerin, 218
Günsche, Otto, 216, 217, 218, 219
Gutmann, Hugo, 195

Hagmüller, Wilhelm, 227
Haines, G., quoted, 85–86
Hamlet, 53–54
Hanfstaengl, Ernst, 217, 225, 227, 229
Hartmann, Eduard von, 50, 51
Hegel, Georg, 51, 80, 87, 88, 100, 109
Hegelianism, 50, 100
Heine, Heinrich, 165
Herzl (Naschauer), Julie, 157, 159, 175
Herzl, Theodor, 150–186; boyhood of, 151, 152; as charismatic leader, 159, 162, 163, 182, 185–186; *Diaries by*, 150, 154–158 *passim*, 162, 170, 171, 186; ego strength of, 184; and father figures, relation to, 176–177; as gambler, 156, 157; homosexuality of, latent, 182; honor code of, 170, 171; id impulses of, 184; infatuations of, early, 153–154; marriage of, 158, 159, 177; melancholy moods of, alternating with elation, 154–155; and metamorphosis of Jewish people, 169–171; and mother figures, 183–184; narcissism of, 158, 162, 182, 185; parents idealized by, 157; quoted, 151–152, 154, 160, 161, 164, 165, 168, 173, 176–177, 178; and stereotypes of Jews, 171; theater brought into politics by, 166, 167; validation of historical vision of, 186; value of fantasy for, 181, 185; venereal disease contracted by, 152, 153; writings of, as self-revelation, 172–176; *see also* anti-Semitism; Israel; Jews; Zionism
Heymann, Michael, 186
Himmler, Heinrich, 195, 200, 219, 230
Hiroshima, survivors of, 45
Hirsch, Baron de, 165, 170
historical dislocation (Lifton), 36
historical method, 5, 81–82
historical truth, 82–83, 85
historiosophy (science of history), 79–80, 83, 84
history (historiography): anxiety as force in, 21, 22; as behavioral study, 87–89; bias in, 86; debunkers in, 11, 12; empirical data in, 81, 83; group psychology applied to, 16–19; hurt pride (castration complex) as force in, 23, 24; idiophenomena in, 80; and image of man, 8–10; made by people of world, 109; methodological problems in, 5, 81–82; and mixed motivations, 10–12; myth formation in, 13–16, 25, 26; and psychoanalysis, 3–32 *passim*, 192–216 *passim;* and reconstruction of past, 84–85; as science, 79–80, 83, 84; sense and nonsense in, 79–109; theory formation in, 80, 83–84; three tasks of, 4–8; and wars, 90–91, 92–93, 99, 108
Hitler, Adolf, 28, 87, 93, 95, 102, 129, 131, 144, 146, 158; anti-Semitism of, 192–216 *passim*, 228; compensatory mechanisms of, 209–211; and decapitation, fascination with, 227; Gestapo reports on, 215, 230; guilt feelings of, 203, 204, 206, 207, 211; and incest, preoccupation with, 204, 205–206, 207, 209, 214; infantile personality of, 201; Jewish ancestors of, question of, 211–216, 229–230; and *Lohengrin*, 200; masochistic perversion of, 201, 207, 225, 226; and Medusa legend, 227; Oedipus complex of, displaced, 207–209; parents of, 199–200, 205, 206, 207, 208, 209; and Parkinson's disease, 218; quoted, 196, 203–204; self-doubt of, 209–211; self-hatred of, 203, 207, 228; suicide of, 194, 216–220; and women, relations with, 201–202,

205, 226; in World War I, 195; *see also* anti-Semitism; Germany; Nazism
Hitler, Alois, 199, 205, 206, 213, 222, 229
Hitler, Klara, 199, 200, 205, 206, 207, 208, 227
Holy Roman Empire, 93
Hong Kong, 34
Huch, Ricarda, 13
Hugo, Victor, 58
Hull, Clark, 83
humor, black, 44
Hundred Years War, 93
Hungary, 23
Huss, John, 92

identity diffusion (Erikson), 37
ideology: end of (Bell), 42; revolutionary, 124, 135, 136
idiophenomena, 80
illuminism, 51
imagination, 64, 65, 66; materializing, 64
immortality, symbolic, 47, 48
incest, Hitler's preoccupation with, 204, 205–206, 207, 209, 214
instrumentalism, in human interaction, 104–105
interaction, human, patterns of, 104–107
intragroup fights, 91–92
Introductory Lectures on Psychoanalysis (Freud), 52
introjection, in anti-Semitism, 202
Irish Republicans, 10
Isaacs, Susan, 60
Israel, 24, 27, 30, 106; and France, 13; and Suez campaign (1956), 11; *see also* anti-Semitism; Herzl, Theodor; Jews; Zionism
Israelites, in ancient Egypt, 7

James, Henry, 172
Japan, 19, 35, 47, 136; democracy in, 35; self-process of young in, 35–36
Jerusalem, 91, 168, 169, 174
Jetzinger, Franz, 222, 224, 225, 229, 230
Jewish Colonial Trust, 179
Jews: ethos of, Herzl's view of, 169; as Hitler's scapegoats, 198; metamorphosis of, in response to aggression, 169; *see also* anti-Semitism; Herzl, Theodor; Hitler, Adolf; Israel; Nazism; Zionism
Johnson, Lyndon B., 14, 15, 16
Jones, Ernest, 53
Journal of Soviet Psychiatry and Neurology, 135
Joyce, James, 51
Judaism, 24
Judenstaat, Der (Herzl), 165, 177
Jung, Carl: archetypes of, 54–56, 63; on art, 55, 56; quoted, 55
Junge, Traudl, Frau, 218

Kafka, Franz, 51
Kamenev, Leo B., 128
Kana, Heinrich, 152, 153, 177
Kant, Immanuel, 50, 132
Karolyi, Michael, 23
Kautsky, Karl, 117
Kellner, Leon, 186
Kempka, Erich, 217, 219
Kennan, George F., 143, 145, 146; quoted, 144
Kennedy, John F., 15; assassination of, 14, 15, 16; and Cuba, 9, 15; myth of, 14, 15, 16; quoted, 14; and Vietnam, 15
Kerensky, Alexander, 115
Kerouac, Jack, 40
Khrushchev, Nikita, 14, 147
kiddush hashem, 107
Kierkegaard, Søren, 50
kinetic art, 40
King Kong, 201
Klein, Melanie, 60
Kratky Kurs, 132
Kravchenko, Victor, 129
Kris, Ernst, 3, 13, 32
Kropotkin, Peter, 91
Krylenko, Nikolai, quoted, 134
Kubizek, August, 199, 204, 225, 228
Kuby, Erich, 218
Kurth, Gertrud, 204, 228

Laforgue, René, 54

Lamprecht, Karl, 85
Langer, Susanne, 33
Langer, Walter C., 211; quoted, 211
Langer, William L., vii-x
Latin America, 28
Lawrence, D. H., 51
League of Nations, 29, 30
Ledl, Franz, 229
Lenin, Vladimir I., 92, 115–120 *passim*, 122, 123, 131, 134; quoted, 118, 122
"Lenkbare Luftschiff, Das" (Herzl), 173
Lesseps, Ferdinand de, 168
Lewis, R. W. B., 44
Lewy, Ernst, 187
liberal utopianism, 29–30
libido, 103, 182, 183; cathexis of, 103; and destrudo, 97
Lichtenstein, Alois, 160, 170
Liebenfels, Lanz von, 196, 197, 208
Lifton, Robert Jay, 33–49
Linge, Heinz, 216, 217, 218, 219, 220, 225
List, Guido von, 196, 197, 198, 208
literary criticism, and psychoanalysis, 50–78 *passim*
literature, 71, 72, 73, 172; Baudouin on, 57; Freud on, 51, 54; Mauron on, 59–62; of mockery, 44; and readers, 73–75; "rich ambiguity" of (Trilling), 70
Locarno Treaty (1925), 87
Loewenberg, Peter, 150–186
Lohengrin, 200
Lombroso, Cesare, 164
Lorenz, K. Z., quoted, 90
Los Angeles Interdisciplinary Psychoanalytic Study Group, 186
love: as protection of life, 103; unselfish, 107
Lovejoy, A. O., 101
Lueger, Karl, 160, 166, 167, 170, 196
Luther, Martin, 93, 100, 195

Mackinder, Halford, 13
magic, escape into, 100–101
Maimonides, 100
Mallarmé, Stéphane, 60, 62
Mann, Thomas, 51
Marie Antoinette, 212
marriage, 106
martyrdom, Christian, 107
Marx Karl, 80, 87, 88, 99, 100, 105, 109, 116, 118; quoted, 118
Marxism, 34, 35, 72, 105, 120, 126; *see also* Bolshevism; communism; Russian Revolution; Soviet Union; Stalin, Joseph V.
Maser, Werner, 228, 229
masochism, 95; Hitler's, 201, 207, 225, 226
Massenpsychologie (Freud), 17
Mastroianni, Marcello, 40, 41; quoted, 40–41
masturbation, 157
materialism, dialectical, 100, 109
materializing imagination, 64
matriarchal family, 103
matter, psychoanalysis of, 64
Mauron, Charles, 59–62
Mead, Margaret, 33
meaning: problem of, 70–73; theories of, 57
Measure, The (Brecht), 17
Medusa legend, 226, 227
Mein Kampf (Hitler), 200, 205
melancholia, 123, 155, 159
minorities, 95; radical, domination by, 10
mixed motivations, 10–12
mockery, literature of, 44
Mohammed, 100
Molière, 62
Moltke, Helmuth von, 163
Mommsen, Theodor, 8, 85
monotheism, Freud's explanation of, 20, 27
Montezuma, 19
moon, landing on, 87
Moses, 24, 25, 26, 152, 163
"Moses and Monotheism" (Freud), 13, 30
motivations, mixed, 10–12
Moussorgsky, M. P., 134
Mueller, Renée, 226
Mussolini, Benito, 210
mutuality, in human interaction, 105–107

myth, personal (Mauron), 61, 62
myth formation, 13–16, 25, 26

Namier, Lewis, 4
Napoleon Bonaparte, 93, 163
narcissism, Herzl's, 158, 162, 182, 185
Naschauer (Herzl), Julie, 157, 159, 175
nation, childhood of, 24, 25, 27, 30
Nazism, 10, 26, 44, 94, 122, 144, 169, 195, 215; *see also* anti-Semitism; Germany; Hitler, Adolf
Nerval, Gérard de, 62
Neue Freie Presse, 158, 140
neurosis, regression as core of, 108
New Ghetto, The (Herzl), 161, 162, 170
Nietzsche, Friedrich, 50, 116, 121
N.K.V.D., 129, 130
Nordau, Max, 80, 164, 166
Nuremberg trials, 212
nurturance vs. autonomy (Lifton), 45–46

occasionalism (Toynbee), 101
occultism, 51
Oedipus complex, 226; in anti-Semites, 201; and *Hamlet*, 54; Hitler's displaced, 207–209
On the Interpretation of Dreams (Freud), 56
On the Road (Kerouac), 40
oneiric temperament (Bachelard), 65
Ostara pamphlets (Liebenfels), 197

"painting, action," 40
Palestine, 30, 151, 159, 168, 171, 174, 175
paranoid projections, in revolutions, 124
patriarchal family, 103
Pauling, Linus, 15
Pavlov, Ivan, 83
"persecuted persecutor," 146
personal myth (Mauron), 61, 62
phenomenology, 64
Philo, 100
Picker, Henry, 193
Planck, Max, 210
Plato, 100
Plechanov, Georgi, 117
Plutarch, 8
Poe, Edgar Allan, 54
poetry, 51, 55, 57, 59, 60, 62, 64, 65, 66, 172
Poincaré, Henri, 83
polyandry, 103
polygamy, 103
polymorphous perversity, 38
pop culture, 43
Posidonius, 25
Possessed, The (Dostoyevsky), 140
Pravda, 132, 133
Preradovic, Nikolaus, 229
prereflective *cogito* (Sartre), 67
primary-process thinking, and assassination of John F. Kennedy, 16
primitive societies, 123, 124, 139
projection: in anti-Semitism, 202, 203–204, 206, 207, 209, 211, 228; paranoid, in revolutions, 124
protean man (Lifton), 33–49; and absurdity, sense of, 42–44; affinity of, for young, 48; ambivalent feelings of, 46–49; guilt in, 39, 40, 46; and nurturance vs. autonomy, 45–46; style of, 37–41; and technology, 45
psychoanalysis: application of, to history and historiography, 3–32 *passim*, 192–216 *passim;* existential (Sartre), 66, 68; and literary criticism, 50–78 *passim;* of matter, 64
psychocriticism (Mauron), 59–62
psychohistorical dislocation (Lifton), 36
"Psychopathology of Everyday Life, The" (Freud), 56

Racine, Jean Baptiste, 62
Rameses II, 7
Randall, J. H., quoted, 85–86
Ranke, Leopold von, 4, 85, 193, 212
rape, 103, 106
rationalism, Lockean, 27
Raubal, Geli, 201–202, 206, 225
Rauschning, Hermann, 197
reason, rejection of, 50–51

regression, as core of neurosis, 108
Reider, Norman, 228
Reiter, Maria, 226
"Relation of the Poet to Day-Dreaming, The" (Freud), 52
reverie, 64, 65, 66
Riesman, David, 33, 41
Rimbaud, Arthur, 51
Robespierre, Maximilien, 91, 128, 135
Róheim, Geza, 123
Röhm, Ernst, 199
Romantic Movement, European, 50, 51
Rome, ancient, 90, 92, 105, 106
Roosevelt, Franklin D., 194, 226
Rosetta stone, 82
Rothschild, Baron, 165
Rousseau, Jean-Jacques, 50
Rudolph of Habsburg, 13
Russia, *see* Soviet Union
Russian Revolution, 10, 82, 92, 115, 121, 122; *see also* Bolshevism; Marxism; Soviet Union; Stalin, Joseph V.
Rycroft, Charles, 57

sadism, 95, 103, 201
sadomasochism, 201, 225, 226
Sargon, King, 25
Sartre, Jean-Paul, 38, 39, 66–68, 76; quoted, 39
scapegoating: in Nazi Germany, 198; in Soviet Union, 120, 145
Schelling, Friedrich, 51
Schicklgruber, Maria Anna, 213, 214
Schirach, Baldur von, 227
schizophrenia, 97
Schnitzler, Arthur, 161
Schönerer, George von, 160, 170
Schopenhauer, Arthur, 50, 51, 155
Schramm, Ernst, 193, 210
science, 79, 80, 83–84; of history, 79–80, 83, 84; and protean man, 45, 46
scientific method, 80, 82
Seignobos, Charles, 85
self-process (Lifton), 33, 34, 35, 36, 37; constriction of, 41–42
sexuality: and mutuality in human interaction, 105–106; and origins of cooperation, 102–103
Shakespeare, William, 54
Shaw, George Bernard, 9
slavery, 104, 105
Smith, Bradley, 229
Smith, Elliot, 7
Solotaroff, Theodore, 39
Sorel, Georges, quoted, 116
socialism, 115, 116, 117, 118, 137, 140
Souvarine, B., quoted, 128
Soviet Union, 15, 44, 121; bureaucracy in, 121; collective ego ideal in, 138; Communist party in, 105; concentration camps in, 130; contempt in, for individuality, 136; enslavement of masses in, 122, 137; ideological purity in, 135, 136; mass deportations in, 122, 136; public opinion molded in, 135; secret police in, 129, 130, 146; and Suez campaign (1956), 11, 12; unconscious identifications in, 138–139; in World War II, 21, 102; *see also* Bolshevism; communism; Marxism; Russian Revolution; Stalin, Joseph V.
Sparta, 102
Spengler, Oswald, 80, 87, 109
Stalin, Joseph V., 95, 102, 121, 122; and Amba, 141–142; childhood of, 125–126; and Djilas, 142, 143, 145; identification of, with enemies, 129; organic inferiority of, 125; paranoid personality of, 146, 147; as professional revolutionary, 126–127; purges by, 129, 139, 142, 144, 145; quoted, 121; reprisals by, policy of, 134–137; ruthlessness of, 127, 128, 129, 130, 131, 137; in struggle for succession, 123–125; suspiciousness of, 126, 142; thirst of, for flattery, 132–134; violence of, 143–145; *see also* Bolshevism; communism; Marxism; Russian Revolution; Soviet Union
Stendhal, 51

Strasser, Otto, 225
Streicher, Julius, 206
Stürmer, Der, 206
Suez Canal, 168; and crisis (1956), 11, 12
Sullivan, Harry Stack, 83
superego, 39, 107; appeal to, by radical minorities, 10; collective, Stalinist disruption of, 139; and external authority, 17
Supreme Court, U.S., 9
Sykes-Picot agreement (1915), 82
Symbolist movement, 51
symbolization, and work of art, 58

Tanner, Tony, 38
Tarle, E., 128
Tarn, W. W., 158
technology, 108; and protean man, 45
Ten Commandments, 101, 106
territorial wars, 91, 92
Thanatos (death instinct), 95–98
"Theme of the Three Caskets, The" (Freud), 54
Themistocles, 105
theory, scientific, defined, 83–84
Thirty Years War, 93
Thoreau, Henry David, 172
Thornton, A. P., 14
Tiberius, Emperor, 95
time, historical, 82
Time magazine, 40
Tin Drum, The (Grass), 40
Tinguely, Jean, 40
Tischgespräche (Picker), 193
Tito, Marshal, 142
Tolstoy, Alexey, 133
Torquemada, Tomás de, 95
Totem and Taboo (Freud), 106
Toynbee, Arnold, 80, 87, 100, 101
transcendence, experiential (Lifton), 48
transference, and work of art, 58, 59
transformation, mode of (Lifton), 47
Treitschke, Heinrich, 195
Trevor-Roper, H. R., 159
Trilling, Lionel, 70
Trotsky, Leon, 83, 116, 128, 129, 146
Truth and Fiction (Goethe), 13
Tukhachevsky, Mikhail, 129

unconscious, 63, 64, 67, 68, 69, 70, 71, 75, 83; collective, 55; philosophy of, 51
United Nations, 12, 29
United States: democratic doctrine in, 27–28; federalism in, 27, 29; formative period of, 27–28, 30; revolution in, irrationality of, 108; and status quo in Berlin, 15; and Suez crisis (1956), 11, 12; in World War I, 20; in World War II, 21
U.S.S.R., *see* Soviet Union
utopianism, liberal, 29–30

Valéry, Paul Ambroise, 62
vectorialism, in human interaction, 107
Versailles Treaty (1919), 198, 214
Vico, Giovanni Battista, 80, 87
Vietcong, 10
Vietnam, 10, 15, 29, 44, 87, 93
Village Voice, 41
violence: Bolshevist justification of, 116, 117, 121; Stalin's, 143–145
Voltaire, 192

Waelder, Robert, 3–30
Wagner, Richard, 155, 165, 200
Waite, Robert G. L., 192–216
Wannsee Conference (1942), 210
war, 90–91, 92–93, 99, 108; intragroup, 91, 92; religious, 92; territorial, 91, 92
Waste Land (Eliot), 55
Waza, Zygmunt, 92
Weber, Max, 19, 158, 159
Weinberg, Gerhard L., 230
Welt, Die, 179
Wiesenthal, Simon, 230
Wilder, Thornton, 9
Wilhelm II, Kaiser, 176, 181
Wilson, Woodrow, 29, 30
Windelband, Wilhelm, 80

Wolffsohn, David, 165, 177
Wolman, Benjamin B., 79–109
World War I, 9, 18, 20, 22, 28, 95, 195, 198
World War II, 11, 21, 87, 133
World Zionist Organization, 179

xenophobia, 97

Yezhov, N. T., 145
youth movements, 48
Yugoslavia, 143

Zangwill, Israel, 159
Zetkin, K., quoted, 119
Zionism, 30, 150, 151, 152, 161, 167, 169, 170, 177, 178; *see also* anti-Semitism; Herzl, Theodor; Israel; Jews
Zionist Congress, First, 165, 166

73 74 75 12 11 10 9 8 7 6 5 4 3 2 1